JERUSALEM

GUIDE

BE A TRAVELER - NOT A TOURIST!

OPEN ROAD TRAVEL GUIDES SHOW YOU
HOW TO BE A TRAVELER – NOT A TOURIST!

Whether you're going abroad or planning a trip in the United States, take Open Road along on your journey. Our books have been praised by Travel & Leisure, The Los Angeles Times, Newsday, Booklist, US News & World Report, Endless Vacation, American Bookseller, Coast to Coast, and many other magazines and newspapers!

Don't just see the world – experience it with Open Road!

ABOUT THE AUTHOR

Stephanie Gold is a writer who has traveled around the world, lived in Israel, and written Open Road's *Israel Guide* and *San Francisco Guide*. She now lives in San Francisco, is a Travel Editor for Amazon.com, and writes freelance articles for a variety of magazines.

ACKNOWLEDGMENTS

I'm deeply indebted to a lot of people. In Israel, folks were extremely generous with their time and their opinions. People put up with endless lists of questions, took me by the hand to my destinations, shared recipes, political insights, conversation, humor, and generally made me feel welcome. But I'm especially grateful to Vered Shai and her invaluable help.

JERUSALEM

GUIDE

BE A TRAVELER - NOT A TOURIST!

Stephanie Gold

OPEN ROAD PUBLISHING

For mom and dad.

1st Edition

Text Copyright ©1999 by Stephanie Gold
Maps Copyright ©1999 by Open Road Publishing
- All Rights Reserved -

Library of Congress Catalog Card No. 97-66337
ISBN 1-883323-88-6

TABLE OF CONTENTS

MAPS

SIDEBARS

JERUSALEM

GUIDE

1. INTRODUCTION

Jerusalem evokes a swirl of glory, religious splendor, historic battles, and political conflict, and that's before you even set foot in the city. *Yerushalayim* in Hebrew and *Bayt al-Muqaddas* in Arabic, the city is holy to Jews, Christians, and Muslims. It's beautiful and hilly, with cool, clean air, strategically located along an important trade route passing through the Judean Hills. For this reason, Jerusalem has been desired and fought over for a long time. It's a city that takes traditions seriously; conflict is one of them, and religion is another, though the two often go hand in hand.

For Jews, Jerusalem has been at the core of their religion for 3,000 years, since David set up the holy Ark of the Covenant there and Solomon built the First Temple. Christians revere the city as the place where Jesus taught and was crucified. And Muslims count Jerusalem as their third most holy site (after Mecca and Medina) because Mohammed is believed to have ascended to heaven from the Temple Mount. Out of a total of roughly 550,000 inhabitants, Jews now make up about 72 percent of the Jerusalem population and Arabs about 26 percent, while the Christian minority continues to dwindle. Both Hebrew and Arabic are spoken, and English is known about as well as elsewhere in the country, which is to say it depends on whom you talk to.

Jerusalem is a magnet that draws people from all over the world and for a wide array of reasons. Religious pilgrims of many denominations have been coming here for centuries to see and worship at the holy sites, students of archaeology come for the excavations and museums, and fans of political history come to see what happens when so many different groups want to honor and possess the same place. The main thing to bear in mind, whether this is your first or your tenth visit, whether you're staying for a day or a month, is that *there is no way you'll see and do it all.*

Don't try, and don't berate yourself for what you didn't get to; that's the rule for a good visit to Jerusalem. Figure out your interests and priorities, and whether you'd get more from a few sights seen in depth or many seen less thoroughly (or some combination thereof), and take it from there.

It's a resplendent and special place, with some of the best dining, cafes, and nightlife in Israel to supplement the religious, cultural, and historic points that shout from every corner. Not surprisingly, Jerusalem is the place where many immigrants come to establish a new life, and tourism is the city's primary pot of gold. Take a deep breath and enjoy the city on your terms and at your pace.

I've also included excursions to the Dead Sea region and the territories under jurisdiction of the Palestinian Authority, to add some more possibilities to your plate. Whatever you choose, we hope you have a great trip.

2. OVERVIEW

Jerusalem has so many different ways to enjoy a vacation it can become overwhelming, even daunting. Despite its tiny size, no matter whether you have a week, a month, or a year, you're not going to be able to do it all and the sooner you make peace with that, the better. Travel isn't a competition sport, but it's so easy to get sucked into the game. You meet another traveler in a Jerusalem cafe. You drink coffee and you talk.

Then it begins. Did you go to the Dead Sea? Of course I went to the Dead Sea, what do you take me for, an oaf? Did you *do* Masada? Oh yes, we *did* Masada and walked up the snake path. But did you walk up the snake path before dawn to see the sunrise over Masada? Silence. Time to pay for that coffee and get going, because you just lost.

And so you will always do, because there's so much on offer in Jerusalem, and what's one traveler's thrill will make another cringe with boredom. So, set your priorities, choose what will make you happy, and don't worry overmuch about the excavation not seen or the dive not taken.

RELIGIONS

Religious Jerusalem is a trip and a half just by itself.

Many come to the Holy Land as pilgrims, and if that's your motivation your course will be fairly well mapped out in advance. Christians will be kept busy seeing the many sacred Jesus-related sites and churches, from Bethlehem's **Grotto of the Nativity** to Jerusalem's **Via Dolorosa**.

Muslims come to Jerusalem as well to pray at the **Dome of the Rock**, the third Muslim pilgrimage site after Mecca and Medina. Believed to be where Abraham bound Ismael for sacrifice (Muslims believe it was Ismael rather than Isaac who was involved) and the site Mohammed took off from on his journey to heaven, the **Temple Mount** is holy to both Jews and Muslims alike (hence the continued tug-of-war over Jerusalem).

The Temple Mount is the site of the **Western Wall** (the only remaining vestige of Israel's Second Temple, the focal point of Judaism

before the Romans destroyed it in 70 CE), and thus is the most important Jewish religious site.

And **Hebron** is crucial to everyone, but is so tense and volatile it's not considered safe for now.

ARCHAEOLOGICAL SITES

Some of the other attractions in Israel, though affiliated with one religion or another (or a number heaped together) are archaeological in nature and require some interest in excavation digs to appreciate the finds. Given all the powers that have held sway over this little plot of land, Israel is a rocky treasure chest of preserved remnants of ancient civilizations. The best finds from all over Israel are conveniently gathered under one roof in East Jerusalem's **Rockefeller Museum**. The excavations, substantiating Biblical references, uncover layers of civilizations from the Bronze Age (from around 2,000 BCE) on up, with remnants of the Canaanites, Hyksos, Israelites, Assyrians, Babylonians, Persians, Greeks, Seleucids, Hasmonaeans (Maccabees), Romans, Byzantines, Arabs, Crusaders, Mamluks and Turks.

Jerusalem itself is full of excavations. There's **David's City, Hezekiah's Tunnel** (engineered to help withstand an Assyrian siege), and the **Cardo** (main street in Roman Jerusalem), for starters. And to the south along the Dead Sea, there's **Qumran**, where the Dead Sea Scrolls were discovered, and **Masada** (the Zealots' mountain stronghold against the Romans), which needs a few hours worth of exploration to take in Herod's palaces and the adaptations made by the Zealots as they attempted to weather the siege.

BACK TO NATURE

Tourists are often drawn by Jerusalem's religious and historical magnets, but its nearby natural bounties are equally impressive.

There are stalagmite and stalactites caves to see in **Avshalom**, a **Biblical Landscape Reserve** with 625 acres recreating the terrain of ancient Israel, and the **Ein Gedi Nature Reserve** near the Dead Sea, with tended trails and clean facilities.

But the **Judean desert** to the south is especially lovely, in its own way, and you don't have to be a geologist to appreciate its rugged charms. There are day or week-long treks that guide you into the hills and *wadis* (dry desert river beds), using various means of transportation (feet, bicycle, jeep, or camel) to explore the country up close and physical. This sort of activity not only gives you the leisure to appreciate the appeal of the land, you also gain insights into the history and culture in a more visceral, less academic way. Sure it's athletic and healthy to tromp through the Judean Hills, but climbing up the parched paths to the Judean desert caves where Bar Kokhba and his men hid lets you appreciate that segment of history more keenly than by viewing the cave finds in the air-conditioned haven of the **Israel Museum Shrine of the Book.**

WATER FUN

The **Dead Sea** offers a unique bathing experience, buoyed up to an extreme by the mineral dense waters, and there are fresh, cool springs to rejuvinate you in the **Ein Gedi Nature Reserve.** The **Attraction Water Park** near Qumran is another alternative, and popular with kids.

MUSEUMS & MEMORIALS

Then there are the museums and memorials. Between those showcasing archaeological finds, those honoring national triumphs, and those commemorating the dead, there are more museums and memorials than you could shake a stick at, and more importantly, more than you could possibly see in one, two, or three Jerusalem visits. Yet they are all of interest to one taste or another, and it's up to you to decide which sort and how many to take in.

Yad Vashem, a memorial to the victims of the Holocaust, is a special place, sad and moving and unique. **Israel Museum** is a storehouse of national treasures, and an amazing place to spend a day (or a week). The Israel Museum and East Jerusalem's **Rockefeller Museum** with its archaeological riches house the best that's found throughout Israel, and it's a remarkable collection. And then there are some 20 or so smaller museums, from the **Islamic Museum** near the Dome of the Rock to the **Burnt House** in the Jewish Quarter, all located in Jerusalem. There are also tombs galore. Kidron Valley has been a prime burial site for centuries, featuring **Absolom's Tomb,** the **Tomb of Jehoshaphat,** and many more.

KIBBUTZIM

Visiting a kibbutz lets you in on another side of Israel. **Kibbutz Ramat Rachel,** in the Talpiot neighborhood of Jerusalem, has a guest house, a museum, and guided tours. Spending some time on a kibbutz, relaxing, and talking a bit to the people who live there, gives a different view of Israel.

CULTURE

While religion, archaeology, museums, and the great outdoors are all important and rewarding, the living, breathing culture of Jerusalem today shouldn't be ignored. There is a wealth of traditions, customs, and foods brought by the many cultures who've settled here, just as vital to understanding Jerusalem as what you'll find in the display cases after you've paid your entrance fee.

The research necessary to understanding it entails hanging out at cafés, following your nose down alleys to small restaurants, and hobnobbing with the locals at a variety of night spots. Jerusalem offers extraordinary Arabic cuisine, traditional Jewish foods, and Hungarian, Kurdish, and Tunisian as well. And if superior Jewish Italian food is to your liking, Jerusalem has that as well. Jerusalem also has a very active café scene, and you could easily spend hours pursuing sedentary cultural research over some cappuccino and Mozart Cake while reading *The Jerusalem Post* and making conversation with the locals. There's a stimulating nightlife as well, with jazz pubs, historic bars, wee-hour discos, chamber music and organ recitals.

3. LAND & PEOPLE

LAND

Jerusalem is located some 2,440 feet up in the Judean Hills, 59 kilometers southeast of Tel Aviv. Thanks to its lofty elevation, the winters are colder and the summers less glaringly hot than other spots in Israel. The air feels clean, dry, and cool, which is refreshing in summer but less so in winter, when dryness isn't a salient characteristic.

It's a very hilly city, thanks to the Jordan River which has eroded the narrow ridges of **Mount Scopus** (2,684 feet) and **Mount of Olives** (2,652 feet) over the years. Built on light-colored limestone (Jerusalem Stone), the mounts are bissected by the **Tyropoeon Valley** and the valleys of **Bet Seita**, **Kidon**, and **Hinnom**.

As in Tel Aviv, street numbers include several buildings. Jerusalem is divided into three sections: the **Old City** to the southeast, with its Muslim, Jewish, Christian, and Armenian quarters, **West Jerusalem** (the New City), and **East Jerusalem**.

Most of Jerusalem's religious landmarks are located within the Old City walls: the **Western Wall** (or **Wailing Wall** as it's often known – a remnant of the supporting wall of the Second Temple), the gold-topped **Dome of the Rock** and silver-domed **al-Aqsa** mosques, the **Via Dolorosa** (believed to be the site of the original Stations of the Cross), and the **Church of the Holy Sepulcher**.

BE CAREFUL IN EAST JERUSALEM!

East Jerusalem is considered safe to visit, as are Jericho and Bethlehem, but it's best not to be out on the streets there after dark. It's also a good idea to check the State Department's US Travel Advisory for their latest update.

David Street is one of the main streets of the Old City, running eastward through the Christian quarter from Jaffa Gate through the shuk toward the Temple Mount. **El Wad** and **Khan ez-Zeit** are other major thoroughfares (in Old City terms this means crowded narrow alleys) running southward through the Muslim quarter from Damascus Gate, and also full of food stalls and souvenir stands. And in the Jewish quarter, **Jewish Quarter Road** (running north-south) is a main street. Jaffa is the most frequented gate, connecting the Old City to Jaffa Road in West Jerusalem, and Damascus Gate comes next, connecting the Old City to Nablus Road in East Jerusalem.

West Jerusalem, built mostly by Jews, has expanded since the 19th century. This section was under Israeli control during the partition and has all the government buildings and Jewish museums. **Derekh Jaffa** (also called Yafo) is the central downtown street, with the central bus station on the western end and the tourist information office to the east near the Old City. **King George V** cuts north-south, has hostels, hotels, and the Great Synagogue, and turns into Keren Hayesod towards the southern end.

King David runs north from Plummer Square (the intersection with Keren Hayesod) to Agron, but its continuation, **Shlomzion**, goes on till Jaffa. On King David you'll find some major landmarks like the **King David Hotel** and the **YMCA**, as well as most of the car rental offices in town. Off King George and Jaffa is the **Pedestrian Mall** section comprising Ben Yehuda as well as a few smaller streets like Luntz. Agrippas runs north of King George, and has the wonderful **Mahane Yehudah** market and lots of good restaurants. Yoel Salomon off Zion Square is another pedestrian mall, south of Jaffa, cluttered with restaurants and cafes. North of Jaffa is the Horkanos/Heleni HaMalka bunch of cafes, restaurants, and music bars.

East Jerusalem, located just north of the Old City, is the primarily residential modern Arab section, although Jews have outnumbered Arabs there since 1993. It is also the site of the **Rockefeller Museum**, with its fine archaeological collection. **Sultan Suleiman** runs east-west between the Old City and East Jerusalem. And **Nablus Road** is one of the main north-south thoroughfares, site of many hotels and one of the Arab bus stations. To the east, **Salah ed-Din** runs parallel to Nablus and also has restaurants and hotels, and to the west is **HaNevi'im**, Prophets' Road, which connects East to West Jerusalem.

CLIMATE

Generally speaking, the summers are long, hot, and dry, while the winters resemble San Francisco weather, raw and wet with rejuvenating sunny, warm days mixed in. There are many different terrains, however, and you don't have to travel very far to find yourself in a totally different weather zone. You can rely on the coastal areas to be warmer and more humid (i.e. hot and steamy in summer), the hilly regions to be cooler and drier, and the desert zones, not surprisingly, to be more arid, with hot days and chilly nights.

The **rainy season** (with occasional snow on the mountains) is November to April with the heaviest rains falling in December-February. You can get over 1000 millimeters a year on Mount Hermon in the north, 550 millimeters in Jerusalem, and less than 100 millimeters in Eilat in the south.

The hottest areas are those below sea level, such as the Jordan Valley, the Dead Sea, and the Arava Valley. There are also occasional *hamsin*, strong easterly winds that blast hot air during spring and fall. The coolest breezes come from the hilltops, but the desert also gets rather chilly at night.

PEOPLE
THE RELIGIONS OF ISRAEL

Israel has proven a fertile land for religions and, while some like Baalism exist now only in archaeological finds and Biblical references, there are plenty still thriving in the Holy Land.

Freedom of religion is guaranteed by law, and all holy places are to be protected. The national religion of Israel however, is Judaism, and at present and due to current politics, rigid Orthodoxy is the only form of Judaism officially recognized in Israel (in solemnizing marriages, for example), despite the large portion of the population who are secular (a whopping 85% are not orthodox).

For the **Jewish** population, supreme religious authority is vested in the Chief Rabbinate, made up of a chief rabbi from the Ashkenazim and one from the Sephardim, along with the Supreme Rabbinical Council. Small Jewish minorities that reject the rabbinic tradition and law include the Karaites (near Tel Aviv) and the Samaritans (in Holon and Nablus). Israel's Arab minority is 76 percent **Muslim** and 14 percent **Christian**. Also followers of Islam are the **Circassians**, a small group brought to the region in the 19th century from the Caucasus and now concentrated in Galilee. The **Druzes** broke away from Islam in the 11th century and practice their own religion, and Israel is also a center of the **Baha'i** faith.

Canaanite Religion (Baalism)

Baal, the storm god and Lord of the Universe, had a strong following for a long time, way after Joshua led the Israelites into Canaan. Various deities were revered by common folk in the open country at high places on hilltops, beneath sacred trees and at natural springs. According to legend, Baal was killed by monsters but restored to life, and his death and resurrection were celebrated annually as a part of Canaanite fertility rituals.

The cult of Baal (and particularly the human sacrifice and temple prostitution associated with it) was frequently denounced by Old Testament prophets. Another popular deity was Astarte, goddess of fertility, sexual love, and war. Crops, newborn animals, and firstborn children were sacrificed to her to assure fertility (her Babylonian and Greek counterparts were Ishtar and Aphrodite). The Bible refers to Astarte as Ashtoreth, and she was worshipped by the Philistines and, at times, the Israelites.

The Big Three

Judaism, the oldest living religion in the Western world, is practiced (in some manner or other) by over 17 million Jews throughout the world, and is the national religion of Israel. A springboard for both Christianity (with a following of around one billion) and Islam (with around 950 million adherents and growing at a rate of about 25 million a year), the three together claim half the world's population.

Judaism

Judaism is a religion, a culture, and a people. True, much of Judaism is based on religious beliefs and practices, but there's a Jewish culture as well, made up of food and humor, legend and lore, perspectives and values, and a sense of community shared by Jews around the world. Generalizations are tricky, verging on the stereotypical as they do, yet some overall flavor of the Jewish people, in all their various ethnicities and forms, holds true.

"Hear O Israel, the Lord our God, the Lord is One," the opening words of the Shema and recited daily, sums up the monotheistic basis of Judaism. According to Genesis (17:5) in the Hebrew Testament, God made a pact with Abraham, the First Patriarch of the Jews, saying "You shall be the ancestor of a multitude of nations," and the religion was on. The covenant signature is the circumcision, called "the seal of God."

A WORD ON HISTORICAL DATES

In this book, I've used the Jewish system of **BCE** *– Before the Common Era – and* **CE** *– Common Era – rather than the usual BC and AD. BCE corresponds exactly to BC, and CE is the same as AD.*

Known as *brithmilah*, it's performed on eight-day-old sons, and the ritual remains a way that Jews (male ones) continue their covenant with God as prescribed by Genesis (17:10). At the age of 13, a boy is deemed responsible for performing the commandments (**bar mitzvah**). To mark his new status, the bar mitzvah boy takes part in the Bible readings during a synagogue service. (The synagogue service is sometimes popularly referred to as the bar mitzvah.) A similar ceremony for 12-year-old girls (**bat mitzvah**) is a recent innovation. Somewhat older than the bat mitzvah is the confirmation ceremony for both sexes introduced by Reform Judaism; it is usually a class observance on or near Shavuoth.

The Hebrew Testament is full of tales of how Judaism was passed along, tested and established, doubted and renewed. **Isaac**, the Second Patriarch, was Abraham's son, born at long last to the First Matriarch, **Sarah**. According to Jewish tradition, Isaac was nearly sacrificed as part of God's test of Abraham's obedience and faith, but spared at the last moment (the Muslims believe it was Ismael, Abraham's son by concubine Haagar, who was spared the knife). Only his deceit made him heir to his father's birthright, instead of his twin **Esau**, the favored, hirsute hunter.

But get it he did, and he passed along both his faith and his favoritism to **Jacob**, the Third Patriarch. His son **Joseph**, with his many-colored robe, was sold into slavery in Egypt by his jealous brothers, and this was the start of the story of Exodus, how eventually the Jews all moved to Egypt to escape the hardship of famine, how they were pressed into bondage, and how **Moses** led them out of Egypt, through the Sinai, and to the Promised Land.

The **Tanakh** (the Hebrew Bible, also called the Old Testament by Christians) is an acronym for the three categories of books that make it up: *Torah, Neve'im (Prophets), and Ketuvim (Writings)*. It is the primary Jewish religious text. The first five books of Moses (also called the Pentateuch, or *khamesh* in Hebrew, meaning five) comprise the **Torah** (Hebrew for 'teaching') and are regarded as Judaism's central document, just as the concept of teaching is central to Judaism, relating to study of the Torah, the whole Tanakh, Judaism in general, and education even more generally. According to religious belief, even God studies torah in heaven, where it's written in black fire upon white fire, and He used it as a blueprint for Creation. The Torah (the Written Law), made up of stories and commandments, is believed to have been dictated to Moses by God around 1220 BCE, shortly after the Exodus from Egypt.

While the final version of the Tanakh was canonized in 90 CE, the religion kept on growing. Not all Jewish sects have agreed through the ages on all facets of Jewish theology, and during the first century CE, the Sadducees differed with the Pharisees on the topic of **Oral Law**. The Pharisees believed that along with the written Torah, God also taught

Moses the oral traditions of Judaism, explaining how the commandments were to be carried out, and by which he (and later, other judges and rabbis) could interpret the laws and adapt them to the issues and concerns of the time. The Sadducees (and today's Karaites as well, see *Sects*) rejected the Oral Law, and interpreted quite literally such injunctions as "an eye for an eye."

The Sadducee sect died out, however, and the importance of the Oral Torah continued. Originally viewed as something to be memorized and passed on but not written down, around 200 CE (after the deaths of many of Jewish sages in the Great Revolt and Bar Kokhba rebellion), Judah HaNassi from Kursi decided to start writing them in a volume called the **Mishna**, expounding on such topics as Shabbat, blessings, marriage, divorce, and so on. In the centuries after HaNassi put together the Mishna, Palestinian rabbis studied and discussed it, commented on and notated it, and around 400 CE they compiled a volume of all this commentary called the Palestinian Talmud.

A century or so later Babylonian rabbis compiled another, more extensive edition of the discussions on the Mishna, and the Babylonian Talmud is now the most authoritative compilation of the Oral Law. The Mishna and the rabbinic discussions (the *Gemara*) make up the **Talmud**, though the terms *Gemara* and Talmud are usually used interchangeably.

Asked by a would-be convert to explain the essence of the Torah while standing on one leg (to ensure brevity), the revered rabbi Hillel answered "What is hateful to you do not do to your fellow. The rest is commentary. Now go and study." Though Hebrew Bible stories such as Job ask such basic questions as why a God who is good allows so much evil in the world, much of Judaism focuses more on this world and the rules and regulations by which to lead a virtuous life rather than beliefs dealing with the afterlife – though faith in the eventual coming of the Messiah has often flavored Jewish life during hard times, such as the Messianic fervor in the first century, and again in the Middle Ages. The system of law known as **Halakhah** regulates civil and criminal justice, family relationships, personal ethics and manners, social duties, worship and other religious observances.

Along with Shabbat, festivals are observed both in the home and in the **synagogue** (an institution for prayer and instruction that became the model for the church in Christianity and for the mosque in Islam, called *shul* in Yiddish and *beit knesset* in Hebrew). Traditionally observant Jews wear **tefillin** (Hebrew for 'prayer objects' or Aramaic for 'ornaments'). Called phylacteries in English (meaning 'amulets'), the two black leather boxes containing four biblical passages are attached with leather straps, one to the left arm and the other on the forehead, during morning prayers.

SHABBAT

Shabbat (the Jewish Sabbath) is observed by many as a holy day, as per the commandment to remember your Sabbath. Shabbat, from sunset Friday to sunset Saturday, is observed by refraining from work and by attending a synagogue service, and during this time much of Israel, including offices, most stores, and buses, is shut for business. The religious follow a number of rituals as part of the holy day, often starting the day before. On Thursday afternoons the streets are full of women lugging home groceries and flowers. The mother lights two candles Friday evening (having prepared the meal in advance, since no cooking is allowed once the sun sets), and the men go to pray in the synagogue and welcome the Shabbat bride with much dance and song.

After service is Shabbat dinner. The family sings songs, kiddush (a ceremonial blessing affirming the sanctity of the day) is said over a cup of wine, between the hand-washing prayer and the bread-breaking prayer no talking is allowed, and then the meal of traditional foods (and the traditions differ by Ashkenazi and Sephardi background) begins. The end of the Sabbath is marked by parallel ceremonies called havdalah. Similar home ceremonies occur on the festivals.

The religious rationale for observing Shabbat could fill a chapter all on its own, and the individual rationales another, but for here suffice it to say it's an important day for cultural, religious, political, and individual reasons. Some travelers feel inconvenienced by the restrictions, but it offers a good way to experience the country and the people differently than when everything's on. It's a time when family, friends, and strangers are welcomed, and it's easy to get invited to a home to share a Shabbat meal in Jerusalem or Tsfat.

In accordance with biblical law, men wear a fringed shawl (**tallith**) during prayer, and it's important for both men and women to cover their heads. Jews also affix to their doorposts a **mezuzah** (a favorite souvenir from Israel), a little box containing a parchment scroll inscribed with passages from the Torah that emphasize the unity of God, his providence, and the resulting duty of serving him.

The **kosher** (meaning" fit" in Hebrew) dietary laws or *kashrut* started with the Genesis (9:4) law forbidding animal blood to all the seed of Noah, and for over 2,000 years rabbis have been developing and refining an elaborate code of rules to govern slaughtering, preparing, and eating. The only animals that can be eaten are those with cloven hooves that chew their cud (thus ruling out pigs). But to be considered kosher, even these approved beasts have to be slaughtered ritually by a *shokhet* with one quick cut across its throat. If the stroke is delayed, thus needlessly prolonging death, the animal is unkosher and forbidden to Jews.

As for fish, only those with fins and scales are kosher, nixing all shellfish (Leviticus 11:9-12 and Deuteronomy 14:9-10). Sturgeon and swordfish are subjects of controversy, because consensus hasn't been reached (between Orthodox and the more lenient Conservatives) as to whether their scales qualify. And among poultry, birds of prey are not acceptable, but chicken, duck, and turkey are.

And then there's the milk issue. The Torah states "You shall not seethe a kid in its mother's milk" and rabbis spent a lot of time debating the intended meaning. The final ruling was that milk and meat aren't supposed to be cooked in the same pots or eaten off the same dishes, let alone blended in the same meal. Homes that observe *kashrut*, therefore, have two sets of dishes, cutlery, and pots: one for meat (called *fleishig* in Yiddish) and the other for milk (or *milchig*).

The neither-here-nor-there foods (fish, fruit, vegetables, etc.) are called *pareve*, and can be eaten with either. Jewish law rules that you need to wait for one category of food to digest before adding the other to your stomach, but just how many hours this takes depends on the accepted wisdom of your community. Dutch Jews thought one hour would do it, the German Jews waited three hours, while in Eastern Europe they felt it took six hours for the meal to properly digest.

Some Jews today observe kashrut in all its minutiae, others keep kosher in a more limited form (maybe they won't eat pork or shellfish, but don't bother with the meat and dairy rules), and some don't keep kosher at all and eat **treif** – the opposite of kosher.

Modern Judaic Divisions

Orthodox Judaism, an umbrella term describing traditionalists who rejected the reforms of the 18th century, distinguishes Jews from the more modernist Conservative and Reform Jews. The Orthodox, however, can be further divided into the Modern Orthodox (who wear modern clothes and pursue secular education while preserving a strong commitment to halakhic norms) and the Ultra-Orthodox (who reject modern values, wear clothes that were in vogue a few centuries ago, and speak the language (Yiddish) from those days as well.

Hasidim are an Ultra-Orthodox group whose traditions (and clothing styles) hark back to 18th century Poland. While "Hasid" is often used as a synonym for Ultra-Orthodox, the religious movement actually started as a revolutionary and liberal reaction to the Mitnagdim, the status quo Orthodox of the time. One of the best known Hasidic families is the Lubavitchers, many of whom live in Brooklyn, New York, and whose leader Rabbi Schneerson died a couple years ago. In addition to Brooklyn, there are strong Hasidic communities in **Mea She'arim** in Jerusalem, Bnei Brak in Tel Aviv, and in Tsfat as well.

The men generally wear long black frock coats and black hats (sometimes trimmed with fur), based on the styles of the 18th century Polish aristocracy, and sport beards and long uncut side curls called *peyot.*, while the boys wear shorts and skull caps (*kipah* in Hebrew, *yarmulke* in Yiddish). The women don't dress in 18th century clothes, but they take care to keep their heads covered (sometimes with scarves and sometimes with hats), and most of their body covered as well with long dresses or skirts with modest shirts. And after marriage, Orthodox women shave their heads and wear wigs.

If you go walking in one of these Ultra-Orthodox neighborhoods, you'd do well to keep yourself covered up as well, and respect their traditions by not imposing proximity or conversation on members of the opposite sex. Orthodox Judaism is a patriarchal religion, and religious practices are very gender-conscious. Synagogues are divided into the men's section and a much smaller women's one (prayer is a duty for men, but not for women), the Western Wall is similarly divided, and rights and duties are prescribed according to gender as well. In addition, contraception is frowned on, and large families are the norm.

THE LEADERS OF THE MITNAGDIM & THE HASIDIM

*The **Mitnagdim** were quite proud of their leader, the **Vilna Gaon** (a name that has become synonymous with genius in the same way Einstein has), for the advanced Talmud discourse he delivered while just seven years old, and because he studied 18 hours a day. The Hasidim's leader was **Israel Ba'al Shem Tov** (meaning Master of the Good Name), and he rose from a very poor background to redirect the religion. He veered from the traditional yeshiva (a Talmudic college that focuses on halakhah), focused far more on an individual's personal relationship with God and his fellow man than on the intricacies of Jewish law, and defied the ascetic Mitnagdim by teaching that pleasure and joy were worthy expressions of God's glory.*

*The **Hasidim**, in turn, subdivided still more into various family dynasties, all led by revered Tsaddikim (religious sages).*

Conservative Jews adhere to the halakhah, but believe it should be adapted to the requirements of modern life, a trend also known as Traditional or Mesorati Judaism.

Reform Jews are even more lenient in the application of halakhah, and emphasize the ethical aspects and universals that can be gleaned from the texts.

And then there are the **secular** Jews, who don't attend synagogue or pray, but are strong in their Jewish identity and culture.

Jewish Culture

The Jewish culture, often expressed through humor and food, and a warm, rich amalgam, with old traditions influenced by host countries during the Diaspora when Jewish communities existed mainly in Europe and North Africa. While the food will be attended to in the Food & Drink chapter, some sample anecdotes here can give a taste of Jewish story-telling.

Many jokes celebrate the simpleton or fool (known as the *shlemiel*). One story begins in a little inn in a Russian town, crowded to capacity. The *yeshiva* student who remained overnight was put in the same room with a visiting rabbi. The student had to catch an early morning train, so he asked the clerk to wake him on time. While getting dressed in the dark the student by mistake put on the rabbi's long alpaca coat. At the railroad station he passed a mirror and, seeing himself in such unusual garb, muttered angrily: "What a dunce that clerk is! I asked him to wake me up but instead he woke up the Rabbi!"

There are also plenty of jokes about the *moyel*, the man who performs the *brit milah*, or circumcision. In one story, a man is walking down a street and sees an enormous watch hanging over a store window. He brings in his watch to be repaired, but the proprietor tells him he doesn't repair watches, he is a *moyel*. "Why then are you hanging a watch in the window?" asks the man. "What do you suggest, mister, I put in the window?" the *moyel* replies. And there are a zillion more.

Offshoots

A couple of other Jewish offshoots, the Samaritans and the Falashas, also have small communities in Israel. The term **Samaritans**, which originally referred to the inhabitants of Samaria, is now generally restricted to a sectarian Jewish community that lived in the area. In Jewish tradition the Samaritans are viewed as colonists introduced after the Assyrian conquest of the region (722 BCE) who adopted a distorted form of Judaism, though the Samaritans themselves claimed descent from the tribes of Ephraim and Manasseh and believed that they had preserved the way and will of Yahweh.

The Samaritans held to the Pentateuch as their Scripture and honored Moses as the only prophet. The Jews refused to let them participate in building the Second Temple in Jerusalem because of all the intermarriage with non-Jews that had gone on during the Babylonian Exile. A small civil war was fought between the two until the walls of Jerusalem were built back up (leading to the parable of the Good Samaritan, Luke 10:25-37, in which Jesus rebuked the Jews for their hostility toward the Samaritans). Small communities of Samaritans still exist today in the north of Israel. The Samaritans believe Mount Gerizim in Nablus is the place where Abraham bound Isaac in sacrificial preparations and also where the original 10 Commandment tablets are buried. Every Passover the Nablus Samaritans sacrifice a lamb up top the mount in honor of Isaac.

JEWISH CALENDAR & HOLIDAYS

*The **Hebrew calendar** in use today begins at the Creation, which is calculated to have occurred 3,760 years before the Christian era. The week has seven days (reckoned from sunset to sunset), ending with the Sabbath, and the year consists of 12 lunar months that start around September: Tishri, Heshvan, Kislev, Tevet, Shevat, Adar, Nisan, Iyar, Sivan, Tammuz, Av, and Elul. Since these lunar months add up to 354 days a year, six times in a 19-year cycle a 13th month (Adar II) is added to keep the festivals on solar track.*

*The holidays prescribed in the Torah are the two "days of awe," **Rosh Hashanah** (New Year, ushered in by a blast on the shofar, the ram's horn) and **Yom Kippur** (Day of Atonement, the holiest of holy days, when the devout pray, request forgiveness and fast for 25 hours), and three joyous festivals, **Passover** (or Pesakh, celebrating the Exodus from Egypt with special seder meals during which you recite the story and sing songs), **Shavuoth** (Feast of Weeks), and **Sukkot**, the Feast of Tabernacles, a harvest celebration during which people are meant to move to a simple shack called a sukkah in which to eat, sleep, and remember their ancestors.*

*Later additions are the festive occasions of **Hanukah** (Festival of Lights, celebrating the Maccabee triumph with menorah lightings, games, and songs), and **Purim** (a holiday commemorating Queen Esther's success over evil Hamman with Halloween-like costumes and parties and games), and the fast of **Tisha B'Av** (the Ninth of Av), commemorating the destruction of the Temple. Other holidays are **Simkhat Torah** (the rejoicing of the torah, when the annual reading of the torah is concluded and scrolls are paraded about before starting again with Genesis), and **Lag B'Omer**, the 33rd day of Omer, which is the anniversary of the second century death of kabbalistic sage Simeon Bar Yochai. It's celebrated with a pilgrimage to his tomb near Tsfat, and is a popular time for weddings.*

The **Falashas** are a group of Ethiopians who claim Jewish origin as descendants of Menelik, the alleged son of King Solomon and the Queen of Sheba, though others believe they stem from a group of converts. Numbering about 30,000, until recently they lived a segregated life in villages north of Lake Tana. The Falashas observe the traditions of Judaism. They obey the biblical laws of purity and circumcision, observe the Sabbath and biblical holidays, recite traditional prayers, and follow biblical dietary customs. In their synagogues they read the Bible in the Geez (an Ethiopian dialect) translation (it includes the Tanakh and some Apocrypha), but they do not know the Talmud.

They call themselves Beta Israel ("House of Israel"); the name Falasha (Amharic for "stranger") was given to them by other Ethiopians. When they lived in Ethiopia they also followed some old Jewish traditions no longer observed by other Jews, such as setting *niddah* (ritually unclean menstruating women) aside in special housing during their periods, but this was dropped upon immigrating to Israel.

The Falashas suffered great hardship in the civil wars and famines that afflicted Ethiopia in the 1970s and 1980s, and many sought refuge in Sudan. In 1984, 1985, and 1991, almost all of them were airlifted to Israel in a rescue operation sponsored by the Israeli government, and their integration into modern Israel's ways has not been an easy one.

Christianity

Christianity, based on the person and teachings of Jesus Christ, was born with **Jesus of Nazareth** nearly 2,000 years ago. To Christians, Jesus was and is the Messiah or Christ promised by God in the prophecies of the Old Testament (the Hebrew Bible). By his life, death, and resurrection he freed those who believe in him from their sinful state and made them recipients of God's saving Grace. Many also await the Second Coming Of Christ, which they believe will complete God's plan of salvation. The Christian Bible (Holy Scripture) includes the Old Testament and also the New Testament, a collection of early Christian writings proclaiming Jesus as lord and savior. Arising in the Jewish milieu of first-century Palestine, Christianity quickly spread through the Mediterranean world, and in the fourth century became the official religion of the Roman Empire.

Christians have tended to separate into rival groups, but the main body of the Christian Church was united under the Roman emperors. During the Middle Ages when all of Europe became Christianized, this main church was divided into a **Latin** (Western European) and a **Greek** (**Byzantine** or **Orthodox**) branch. The Western church was in turn divided by the **Reformation** of the 16th century into the **Roman Catholic** church and a large number of smaller **Protestant** churches: Lutheran, Reformed (Calvinist), Anglican, and sectarian. These divisions have continued and multiplied, but in the 20th century many Christians joined in the Ecumenical Movement to work for church unity. A stroll through Jerusalem's Old City will illustrate the handiwork of all the various church branches.

Christians are monotheists (believers in one God). The early church, however, developed the characteristic Christian doctrine of the **Trinity** in which God is thought of as Creator (Father), Redeemer (Son), and Sustainer (Holy Spirit), but one God in essence. Certain basic doctrines drawn from Scripture (especially from the Gospels and the letters of Saint Paul), have been accepted by all three of the major traditions. According to this body of teaching, the original human beings rebelled against God, and from that time until the coming of Christ the world was ruled by sin.

The hope of a final reconciliation was kept alive by God's Covenant with the Jews, the chosen people from whom the savior sprang. This savior, Jesus Christ, partly vanquished sin and Satan. Jesus, born of the **Virgin Mary** by the power of the Holy Spirit, preached the coming of God's Kingdom, and was betrayed by Judas, who delivered him to the Romans to be crucified. On the third day after his death God raised him up again. He appeared to his disciples, commanding them to spread the good news of salvation from sin and death to all people. This, according to Christian belief, is the mission of Christ's church.

Although Christians today tend to emphasize what unites them rather than what divides them, substantial differences in faith exist among the various churches. Those in the Protestant tradition insist on Scripture as the sole source of God's Revelation. The Roman Catholics and Orthodox give greater importance to the tradition of the church in defining the content of faith, believing it to be divinely guided in its understanding of scriptural revelation, and in Roman Catholicism the pope is regarded as the final authority in matters of belief.

Christians also vary widely in worship. Early Christian worship centered on two principal rites or Sacraments: **Baptism**, a ceremonial washing that initiated converts into the church, and the **Eucharist**, a sacred meal preceded by prayers, chants, and Scripture readings, in which the participants were mysteriously united with Christ. As time went on, the Eucharist, or Mass, became surrounded by an increasingly elaborate ritual in the Latin, the Greek, and other Eastern churches, and in the Middle Ages Christians came to venerate saints (especially the Virgin Mary) and holy images.

Early Christian History

The early Christian years extend from Jesus' birth through the fall of the western half of the Roman Empire in the fifth century. After Jesus was crucified, his followers, strengthened by the conviction that he had risen

CHRISTIAN HOLIDAYS

*In most Christian churches **Sunday**, the day of Christ's resurrection, is observed as a time of rest and worship. **Lent** is a 40-day penitential period of prayer and fasting that precedes Easter. Observed since the fourth century, in the Western church, Lent begins six and a half weeks prior to Easter (Sundays not included), starting on **Ash Wednesday** right after the hoopla of **Mardigras** (Fat Tuesday), while in the Eastern church the period lasts over seven weeks because both Saturdays and Sundays are excluded. Formerly a severe fast was prescribed where only one full meal a day was allowed, and meat, fish, eggs, and milk products were forbidden.*

*Today, however, prayer and works of charity are emphasized, along with a token denial. Good Friday remembers Christ's crucifixion, while his resurrection is commemorated at **Easter**, a festival in the early spring that has its roots in a pagan spring festival and in the Jewish holiday of Passover. Another major Christian festival is **Christmas**, December 25th, which celebrates Jesus' birth.*

from the dead and that they were filled with the power of the Holy Spirit, formed the first Christian community in Jerusalem. By the middle of the first century, missionaries were spreading the new religion among the peoples of Egypt, Syria, Anatolia, Greece, and Italy.

Chief among these was **Saint Paul**, who laid the foundations of Christian theology and played a key role in the transformation of Christianity from a Jewish sect to a world religion. The original Christians, being Jews, observed the dietary and ritualistic laws of the Torah and required non-Jewish converts to do the same. Paul and others favored eliminating this obligation, thus making Christianity more attractive to Gentiles. The separation from Judaism was completed by the destruction of the temple of Jerusalem by the Romans during the Jewish Revolt of 66-70 CE.

After that Christianity took on a predominantly Gentile character and began to develop in a number of different forms. At first the Christian community looked forward to the imminent return of Christ and the establishment of the Kingdom. This hope carried on in the second century by **Montanism**, an ascetic movement emphasizing the action of the Holy Spirit. **Gnosticism**, which rose to prominence about the same time, also stressed the Spirit, but it disparaged the Old Testament and interpreted the crucifixion and resurrection of Jesus in a spiritual sense. The main body of the church condemned these movements as heretical, and when the Second Coming failed to occur, organized itself as a permanent institution under the leadership of its bishops.

Following the recognition of Christianity by **Emperor Constantine I** in the early fourth century, lengthy controversy about the person of Christ wrestled with the problem of Christian monotheism and the charge that the church also worshipped Christ as Lord and the Holy Spirit of God promised by Christ. In one solution, Monarchianism, God the creator was supreme but shared his power with Christ, the Logos or Word. Another (Modalism) held that the three persons of the Trinity were aspects of the same God. These doctrines were rejected, and the Council of Ephesus (431 CE) condemned **Nestorianism**, which denied that Mary was the mother of God, and the Council of Chalcedon (451 CE) repudiated **Monophysitism**, which emphasized the divinity of Christ over his humanity. The condemnation of Monophysitism alienated the churches of Egypt, Syria, Mesopotamia, and Armenia, creating dissension in the Eastern Roman (Byzantine) Empire and diminishing its ability to withstand the Islamic invasion in the seventh century.

The **Coptic church** and the **Syrian Orthodox** (also known as Jacobites) are Monophysite branches of Christianity which go back to the fifth century controversies over the identity of Christ. The Coptic church is the major Christian community in Egypt, numbering between six and seven million. The name Coptic is derived from the Greek word for "Egyptian" and reflects the national character of this ancient church. Most Egyptian Christians sided with the Monophysite party, which held that Christ has one nature, a doctrine condemned at the Council of Chalcedon. Coptic is sometimes used improperly to refer to the Ethiopian church because of its unity in faith and close affinity with Christian Egypt. The Ethiopian church, however, declared itself independent of the Coptic patriarch in 1959.

The Copts have had a strong community in Jerusalem since 1236, as evidenced by their churches, their monastery at the back of the Church of the Holy Sepulchre, and their distinctive black garb, and the Syrians have had a bishop there since 1140. The head of the Jacobite church bears the title of Patriarch of Antioch and resides in Homs, Syria, while the Coptic church is headed by the "patriarch and pope of Alexandria, Pentapolis and Ethiopia," who is elected by the entire community of clergy and laity and resides in Cairo. Long discriminated against by the Egyptian government, the Copts have more recently been the target of attacks by Muslim fundamentalists.

The **Armenian church**, also known as the Armenian Apostolic or Gregorian church, is an independent Christian church of about 1,600,000 embracing the majority of the Armenian people. At the end of the third century, the king of Armenia, Tiridates III, was converted to Christianity by Saint Gregory the Illuminator, and since the fifth century the Armenian church, like the Copts and Syrians, has embraced the Monophysite doctrine stating that Christ has a single human and divine nature. Adherence to Monophysitism has kept the Armenian church separated from other Christian groups, but in other respects, most practices of the Armenian church resemble those of the Orthodox Church. The head of the church is called the supreme catholicos, and his permanent residence is at Echmiadzin in the Republic of Armenia. They have a waning population in Jerusalem, with an Armenian quarter in the Old City, and much of Mount Zion, owned by the Armenians since the 10th century, is graced by their monasteries and churches.

Islam

The **Prophet Mohammed** was born in Mecca in 570 CE. He was orphaned at an early age, raised by his uncle, and had his first revelation from the Angel Gabriel in the month of Ramadan, 610 CE. From those beginnings, Islam has become a major world religion, and dominates in Middle Eastern and North African countries. **Muslims** (sometimes spelled Moslems) are those who believe in Islam, and should not be confused with Arabs, which is a regional rather than a religious designation.

The Arabic word *al-islam* means the act of committing oneself unreservedly to God, and a Muslim is a person who makes this commitment. Widely used translations such as "resignation," "surrender" and "submission" fail to do justice to the positive aspects of the total commitment for which *al-islam* stands, a commitment in faith, obedience, and trust to the one and only God (**Allah**). All of these elements are implied in the name of this religion, which is described in the **Koran** (*Qur'an* in Arabic, the sacred book of Islam) as "the religion of Abraham."

In the Koran, **Abraham** is the patriarch who turned away from idolatry, who "came to his Lord with an undivided heart" (37:84), who responded to God in total obedience when challenged to sacrifice his son (37:102-105), and who served God uncompromisingly. For Muslims, therefore, the proper name of their religion expresses the Koranic insistence that no one but God is to be worshipped. Hence, many Muslims, while recognizing the significance of the Prophet Mohammed, have objected to the terms Muhammedanism and Muhammedans (designations used widely in the West until recently) since they smack of a worship of Mohammed parallel to the worship of Jesus Christ by Christians.

While many Muslims vehemently oppose the assertion that the Prophet Mohammed is the "founder" of Islam (an expression they interpret as an implicit denial of God's initiative and involvement in the history of Islam's origins) none would challenge that Islam dates back to the lifetime (570-632 CE) of the Prophet and the years in which he received the divine revelations recorded in the Koran. Most of them would stress, however, that it is only in a sense that Islam dates back to the seventh century, since they regard their religion not as a seventh-century innovation, but as the restoration of the original religion of Abraham. They further believe that Islam is a timeless religion, not just because of the "eternal truth" that it proclaims but also because it is "every person's religion," the natural religion in which every person is born.

While Islam is a religion, its precepts apply more fully to all aspects of life than in some other religions. Islam encompasses personal faith and piety, the creed and worship of the community of believers, a way of life, a code of ethics, a culture, a system of laws, an understanding of the function of the state. The revelations Mohammed set down in the Koran provide guidelines and rules for life in all its aspects and dimensions. While Muslims differ on how fixed or adaptable the *Sharia* (the "way," denoting the sacred law governing the life of individuals as well as the structures of society) is, the basic notion of Islam's comprehensive character is so intrinsic to Muslim thought and feeling that neither the past history of the Muslim world nor its present situation can be understood without taking this characteristic into consideration.

Mohammed was born in **Mecca**, a trading center in western Arabia. After he received the first of a series of revelations that convinced him that he had been chosen as God's messenger, he began to preach the message entrusted to him, that there is but one God to whom all humankind must commit themselves. The polytheistic Meccans resented Mohammed's attacks on their gods and finally he emigrated with a few followers to **Medina**, an agricultural oasis town. This migration (called the *Hegira* or *Hijrah*) took place in 622 and Muslims adopted the beginning of that year as the first year of their lunar calendar (Anno Hegirae, or AH).

At Medina, Mohammed was accepted as a religious and military leader. Within a few years he'd gained control of the surrounding region, and in 630 he finally conquered Mecca. There, the **Kaaba**, a shrine that had for some time housed the idols of the pagan Meccans, was rededicated to the worship of Allah, and became the object of pilgrimage for all Muslims. Before he died in 632, most of the Arab tribes nearby had converted to Islam, and Mohammed had put in place the foundation for a community (*umma*) ruled by the laws of God. The Koran records that Mohammed was the Seal of the Prophets, the last of a line of God's messengers that began with Adam and included Abraham, Noah, Moses, and Jesus.

Islamic doctrines are taught under six headings: God, angels, Scriptures, messengers, the Last Day, and predestination. The Muslims' notion of God (**Allah**) is, in a sense, interrelated with all of these points. There are lots of **angels**, and some play a particularly important role in the daily life of many Muslims. There are the guardian angels, the recording angels (those who write down a person's deeds, for which he or she will have to account on Judgment Day), the angel of death, and the angels who question a person in the tomb. One of those mentioned by name in the Koran is **Jibril** (Gabriel), who transmitted God's revelation to the Prophet.

The promise and threat of the **Last Day**, which occupies an important place in the Koran, continues to play a major role in Muslim thought and piety. On the Last Day (and only God knows the hour) every soul will stand alone and will have to account for its deeds. The last of the six articles, **Predestination**, is also a big issue. Because the divine initiative is all ("had God not guided us, we had surely never been guided," 7:43), some concluded that God is not only responsible for guiding some, but also for not guiding others and allowing them to go astray or even leading them astray. Those opposed to the concept of predestination were concerned less with upholding the notion of human freedom and human dignity than with defending the honor of God, and it's been as fertile a field for Muslim debate as it was for Christians.

Many other theological debates have raged over the unity of Allah and whether the Koran was created, and on some level they boil down to the division between the Shi'ites and the Sunnites. The term **Sunnites** refers to the great majority of the world's Muslims, distinguishing them as the *ahl al-sunna wal-jamaa* ("the people of the sunna and the community") from the Shi'ites. Sunnites are, by this definition, Muslims who strictly follow the sunna (practices) of the Prophet Mohammed and preserve the unity and integrity of the community. Anyone who stands within the mainstream of the Islamic tradition and acts in accordance with generally accepted practices of the community is, therefore, a Sunni.

The **Shi'ites** were those who maintained that only "members of the family" (Hashimites, or, in the more restricted sense, descendants of the Prophet via his daughter, Fatima and her husband Ali) had a right to the **caliphate** (successors to Mohammed). This power struggle, born of a succession dispute around 660 CE, continues unresolved today. Another group, the **Kharijites** (literally "those who seceded"), broke away from Ali (who was murdered by one of their members) and from the Umayyads. They developed the doctrine that confession, or faith, alone did not make a person a believer and that anyone committing grave sins was a non-believer destined to hell. They applied this argument to the leaders of the community, holding that caliphs who were grave sinners could not claim the allegiance of the faithful.

While the mainstream of Muslims accepted the principle that faith and works must go together, they rejected the Kharijite ideal of establish-

ISLAMIC CALENDAR & HOLIDAYS

Muslims begin their calendar at the day and year (July 16, 622 by the Gregorian calendar) when Mohammed fled from Mecca to Medina. The 12 lunar months (alternating 30 and 29 days) make the year only 354 days long, so the months move backward through all the seasons and complete a cycle every 32.5 years. The months are Muharram, Safar, Rabi I, Rabi II, Jumada I, Jumada II, Rajab, Shaban, Ramadan, Shawwal, Zulkadah, and Zulhijjah.

*During **Ramadan** (held holy since it's the month when the Koran was revealed to Mohammed), Muslims must fast during the day (a prohibition which includes food, water, smoking, and sex) but are permitted to partake in any or all of the above between dusk and dawn. This month-long obligation is taxing enough during the winter, but due to the nature of the Islamic calendar, Ramadan sometimes falls during summer months when days are longer and the water restriction is more of a challenge.*

***Id al-Fitr** is the festival that breaks the fast at the end of Ramadan. **Eid al-Adhah**, the festival of the sacrifice in memory of Abraham's willingness to sacrifice his son, is the occasion of the hajj. The festival of the sacrifice, observed on the 10th day of the month of pilgrimage, is celebrated not only by the participants in the pilgrimage, but also simultaneously by those who've stayed at home. And **Ras as-Sana** (the Islamic New Year) is celebrated on the first of Muharram.*

ing on Earth a pure community of believers, insisting that the ultimate decision on whether a person is a believer or an unbeliever must be left to God. Suspension of the answer until Judgment Day enabled them to recognize anyone accepting the "five pillars" (see below) as a member of the community of believers, and to recognize those Muslims who had political authority over them, even if they objected to some of their practices.

The basic duties of any Muslim, the "**five pillars**" of Islam, are *shahada* (the profession of faith in God and the apostleship of Mohammed), *salat* (the ritual prayer, performed five times a day facing Mecca), *zakat* (almsgiving), *sawm* (abstaining from food and drink during the daylight hours of the month of Ramadan), and *hajj* (the pilgrimage to Mecca, incumbent on every believer who is financially and physically able to undertake it). Muslim worship and devotion, however, are not limited to the precisely prescribed words and gestures of the *salat*. Also important are personal prayers, gathering in the central mosque on Fridays, and celebrating the two main festivals.

The interpretations of *jihad* (literally "striving" in the way of God), sometimes added as an additional duty, vary from sacred war to striving to fulfill the ethical norms and principles expounded in the Koran. The fundamentalist Muslims have been growing in power in recent years, affecting the governments of Egypt and Israel, among others. Hamas, a Palestinian extremist group, is against any peace talks with Israel, wants to replace the Jewish state with an Islamic fundamentalist one, and has taken the credit for a series of terrorist attacks against Israelis.

The Druze

The **Druze**, monotheists with a difference, are an offshoot of the Ismailis, and the religion began in the reign of Fatimid caliph al-Hakim (996-1021). In 1017 there was a public proclamation to the effect that **Hakim** was the final manifestation of God, and this remains the central and distinguishing tenet of their belief. Their name comes from al-Darazi, al-Hakim's first missionary. The sect was founded in Egypt, but they fled to Palestine to avoid persecution. The Druze, all 400,000-500,000 of them, live mostly in Syria or Lebanon, but some communities still exist in Israel and Jordan.

Their faith centers on the belief in Hakim as the ultimate *maqam* (location or incarnation) of God. They further believe in the five cosmic emanations: Universal Intelligence, Universal Soul, the Word, the Right Wing, and the Left Wing, as embodied by their five highest ranking disciples. Their community is divided into the *uqqual*, those initiated into the teachings of the *hima*, the religious doctrine, and the *juhhal*, the vast majority who aren't familiar with the religious tenets. They follow seven basic duties, among which truthfulness and mutual support figure strongly. They allow no conversion or intermarriage, and believe community is of great importance.

Baha'i

Baha'i, a religious movement founded in the 19th century by the Persian **Baha Ullah**, claims members in practically every country of the world. Objecting to polygamy, slavery of any kind, religious prejudices, and politicized religion, Baha'is call for world peace and harmony, the ideals of a world federalist government, and a new world language. Recognition of the common ground of all religions is seen as fostering this move toward global unity, so Krishna, Buddha, Moses, Zarathustra, Jesus, and Mohammed are all recognized as divine manifestations, a series of prophets culminating in Bahaullah. Nonresistance, respect for persons, and legal recognition of the equal rights of both sexes constitute additional aspects of Baha'i teaching.

The **Bab** (Siyyid Ali-Muhammad) was the Martyr-Herald of the Baha'i religion. He broke away from Islam in Persia in 1844 declaring his religious mission, was publicly executed in Tabriz in 1850 at the age of 31, and his bones were transferred to Haifa in 1909 to be buried in the gold-domed mausoleum, the Shrine of the Bab. Baha Ullah, the founder of the religion, was exiled to Akko in 1868 by the Sultan of Turkey after spending some time in Turkish prisons (following the Shah of Iran's banishment). He then spent some more time in prison in Akko till he died there in 1892. His son Abbas Effendi founded a world palace of justice in Haifa, designed the beautiful gardens, and built the Bab mausoleum and archive temple in 1909.

By the time of Baha Ullah's death in 1892, the Baha'i faith had won adherents throughout the Middle East. Under his son Abbas Effendi (or Abdul Baha, 1844-1921), who succeeded him as the movement's leader, it spread to Europe and the United States. Divided into more than 130 national assemblies and more than 26,000 local assemblies, they are estimated to number about two million worldwide. Since the establishment of the Islamic Republic of Iran in 1979, the discrimination to which Baha'is have always been subjected in Iran has escalated into persecution.

THE ISRAELI PEOPLE

The people who live in Israel are, for the most part, so identified with their religions that their cultures in some ways are part and parcel of those religions, not separate, distinct entities. But even within the religions, people have come from so many countries and cultures (this is especially true of the Jews), that their previous nationalities bear some discussion.

Israel was established in 1948 as a homeland for Jews, and the Jewish population now forms 82 percent of the total population. Immigrants (*olim*) come from many different national backgrounds, including the urbanized societies of Europe and North America and the predominantly Islamic areas of Asia and North Africa, and they are divided into the **Ashkenazim** (those Jews hailing from Europe) and the **Sephardim** (Jews from Middle Eastern, North African, and Mediterranean countries). While the Ashkenazi Jews from Germany and Eastern Europe came speaking Yiddish (a Hebrew-German mix) and eating borsht and chopped liver, the Sephardi Jews often arrive speaking Arabic, French or Ladino (an ancient Spanish language derived from the Spanish of 15th century Spain), and eating couscous and mellawach. Some Ashkenazim emigrated to North and South America and to South Africa as well, and some Israel's Ashkenazi population has come via those countries.

The Sephardim, descendants of those Jews expelled from Spain in 1492, have come to Israel after centuries spent in Morocco, Algeria, and

Tunisia, as well as Yemen and Iraq, and the Kurds come from Kurdistan, which is in northern Iraq.

The early Zionist pioneers and government leaders were Ashkenazim, while more than 50% of Israel's Jewish population is Sephardim, contributing to a rift between the two groups and a feeling of discrimination in Sephardi communities. This situation is much less sensitive than it once was, however, and the younger generation claims it's a non-issue. The radio stations now devote air time to Sephardi melodies (unheard of some 10 years ago), and people seem able to blend ethnic pride (be it Yemenite, Polish, Iraqi, Kurdish, or German) with the predominant Israeli identity.

Some groups that have immigrated lately have attracted controversy. The **Black Hebrews** started coming to Israel in 1969 from the midwestern United States. Now living in Dimona in the Negev, they claim that their slave ancestors were descended from Israelites who were forced to migrate to Western Africa when the Romans closed Jerusalem down in 70 CE. The Israeli government rejected their claims and refused them citizenship unless they converted to Judaism, which they refused to do since they said they were already Jews. But they've reached an agreement, and in 1996 the vegetarian community of some 1,200 members became Israeli citizens.

From 1985-1991, the Ethiopian **Falashas** were airlifted in from their famine-struck country. They've had some rough times adjusting to Israeli society, and there was a bit of a debate over whether their version of Judaism qualified them as Jews, but that situation has been replaced by the more recent mass immigration (starting in 1989) of **Russians**. Amid complaints about their attitude (too entitled, just out for themselves, etc.), what is clear is that this is the largest wave of *olim* in Israeli history (200,000 arrived in 1990 alone) and they are becoming the largest ethnic group in the country. Along with the proliferation of Russian restaurants, some neighborhoods feature signs in Russian as well.

The non-Jewish population of Israel consists mainly of **Arabs**, who make up 13 percent of the total population, and **Druzes**, who account for less than two percent, both of whom are concentrated more in the Galilee. In the lands occupied since 1967 (which are in the process of being transferred to the Palestinian Authority), Arabs constitute by far the majority, although thousands of Jews have settled in the West Bank since 1979.

Language

Modern **Hebrew**, Israel's national language, was created from biblical Hebrew by Eliezer Ben Yehuda in the 1920s. It became the language of choice among Zionists, replacing languages such as Yiddish or Ladino which were viewed by many as relics of oppressed times.

Following Hebrew is **Arabic**, which is a required language in all schools, and can be seen on most road signs. Lots of people speak **English** as well, and it, too, is taught in schools. Most of the people in the tourism (and hotel and restaurant) business speak it fairly well, and people on the street have varying levels of competency. Other languages that are spoken a bit (and that help getting around) are **French** (brought by Tunisian and Algerian *olim*) and **Russian**.

4. A SHORT HISTORY

The area that we today call the Middle East has an enormously complex history. The political boundaries and ruling governments have changed so many times that historians tend to chronicle civilizations and eras rather than countries.

The following condensed history will focus on the area that is now Israel, while noting important events in other parts of the Middle East. The development of the major religions will be recounted in more detail in the Religion section of Chapter 3, *Land & People*.

Notation of years: the more ancient the history is, the more approximate the dates given. Dates get branded "circa" to indicate approximately, but it all means that the experts just aren't sure about exact dates way back when. And even when dates are known, there are different calendars and various ways of representing the years.

The **Hebrew calendar** follows lunar months and begins at the Creation, calculated at 5759 years ago. The **Muslim calendar** also follows lunar months and started 1379 years ago, when Mohammed moved from Mecca to Medina. The **Gregorian calendar**, commonly accepted in the Western world, is based on the suggestion of a monk (Dionysus Exiguus) to count years in reference to the birth of Christ, with BC for Before Christ and AD for Anno Domini ("the year of the Lord").

The dating system commonly accepted by Jewish historians, with **BCE** for Before Common Era and **CE** for Common Era (corresponding to BC and AD) is used in this book.

PREHISTORY

Prehistory – the years before written records began to document history – is generally divvied up into eras based on the materials people used for their tools and weapons. Four such ages are Stone (itself subdivided into Paleolithic, Mesolithic, and Neolithic or Old, Middle, and New), Copper, Bronze, and Iron. One problem with these categories, however, is that while one group may be evolving into the Iron Age, another civilization in another setting may still be using stone, so assigning years to these eras depends on the location of the groups being studied.

The approximate years that follow are for civilizations in the Middle East.

THE STONE AGES - PALEOLITHIC AGE

(Old Stone Age): *3,500,000-10,000 BCE*

The earliest known human settlements outside of Africa lived in the Galilee (Tel Ubeidiya is where the artifacts were found) some 600,000-800,000 years old, on the shores of a prehistoric lake. During this time people were hunters and gatherers, and tools were made of stone, especially flint. **Mesolithic Age (Middle Stone Age)** and **Neolithic Age (New Stone Age)**: 10,000-4,000 BCE. Stone and bone were used, goats, sheep, and cattle were domesticated, and agriculture begun.

COPPER AGE

(Chalcolithic Age): *4,000-3,000 BCE*

Copper and brass tools and weapons appeared on the scene, and communities thrived around Israel. Remains of communities from this time can be seen at Tel Megiddo, Beit She'an, and Ein Gedi.

BRONZE AGES

Early Bronze: *3,000-2,000 BCE, Middle Bronze: 2000-1600 BCE, and Late Bronze: 1600-1200 BCE - also known as the Canaanite period.*

During these years, bronze (an alloy of copper and tin) was developed for improved tools and weapons, and the camel was domesticated. Also around 3000-1200 BCE, the **Canaanite** civilization ruled in what is now Israel, Syria, Lebanon, and Jordan, establishing city-states at places like Hazor, Megiddo, Jericho and Jerusalem. When archaeological sites such as Megiddo report Canaanite findings, they are talking about Bronze Age artifacts from this time.

When the Israelites, Philistines, and Aramaeans invaded around 1200 BCE, the Canaanites were for the most part absorbed into the new peoples and cultures (with the exception of a group that lasted another few centuries in Phoenicia on the Mediterranean), but some of their religious and cultural advancements contributed significantly to the new civilizations. For one, the Canaanite's Semitic language grew into Hebrew (and Phoenician).

Perhaps more importantly, by 1500 BCE they had developed the alphabet as their system of writing. The Phoenicians, who were great travelers and merchants, brought their alphabet to the Greeks, and it ultimately became the basis for modern Western alphabets. The legacy of Canaanite religion also played a part in the development of the new culture. Icons and shrines dedicated to Baal, the storm god, and Astarte, the fertility goddess, have been found at many archaeological digs. The development of Judaism is intricately woven with the clash of belief systems between the old Canaanite gods and the Israelites' one god. As late as circa 850 BCE, Elijah was trying to discredit the formidable belief in Baal.

This period of time was important in **Egyptian** history as well. In roughly 2665-2180 BCE the Egyptian Old Kingdom was busy building **pyramids** and developing **papyrus** and writing techniques. In 2000-1700 BCE was the migration into Egypt of the **Hibiru**, a tribe some scholars believe were the ancestors of the Hebrews.

It is postulated that the **Patriarch Abraham** lived somewhere around 1800-1700 BCE, and that the descent of Israel into Egypt, as told in the **Book of Exodus**, took place around 1700-1600 BCE. From 1500-1100 BCE Egypt ruled over parts of Canaan, and it's thought that **Joseph** might have lived under the Hyksos rulers in Egypt in 1400-1370 BCE. Around that time there was a **famine** in Egypt, perhaps the one that moved Joseph's family in Exodus. The **Moses-led Exodus** from Egypt is thought to have happened in 1280 BCE, and their **conquest of Canaan** under Joshua is dated at 1250-1200 BCE.

IRON AGE

1200-586 BCE - also known as the Israelite Age

In these years iron was hardened (alloyed) by the addition of carbon, so that it took the place of bronze for tools and weapons. A lot happened in the 600+ years of the Iron Age. From the 1100s-1000 BCE, the **Philistines** ruled much of Palestine. These are also the years of the five **Judges** (Deborah, Gideon, Samson, Eli, and Samuel) who ruled in succession. **King Saul** reigned from 1020-1004 BCE, followed by the United Empire of **King David** and the origins of **Jerusalem.** Five thousand years ago, present-day Jerusalem was a **Canaanite** stronghold, and after that the **Jebusites** (a tribe co-existing with the Canaanites in pre-Israelite days) built a citadel here, so for a time this place was called Jebus as well as Jerusalem. The city's Jewish history begins around 1,000 BCE when David, who had been anointed king over all Israel in 1004 BCE and ruled till 961 BCE, conquered the city, sending his man Joab into the water system shaft to get inside the fortress walls. David built up his city and made it the capital of his kingdom, but it was vain **Solomon** who taxed his people to the hilt and built the magnificent first Temple to house the Ark of the Covenant, and glorify God (and Solomon). **King Solomon's** rule lasted from 961-922 BCE, and the great **Temple** he had built in Jerusalem was consecrated in 955 BCE. After Solomon's death in 922, the **United Kingdom of Israel** was united no more, and in the aftermath of civil war, Jerusalem was the capital of the southern **Kingdom of Judah**, governed by Rehoboam (Solomon's son), who ruled over the tribes of Benjamin and Judah, the only two who had remained faithful. The northern **Kingdom of Israel** had its capital in **Shekhem**.

The next few centuries were complicated and eventful, and none of it was good for the Jews. **Jezebel** (the infamous Jezebel) became queen to King **Ahab** (876-855 BCE), and brought her devotion to the Phoenician (old Canaanite) gods Baal (called Melkart in Phoenicia) and Astarte. She wanted temples raised to her gods, and to convert the Jews to her religion. Mosaic priests were persecuted by her, especially the **prophet Elijah** of Tishbi. Later, Pharaoh Shishak from Egypt stormed Judah (at the invite of Jeroboam up in the northern Kingdom of Israel), thoroughly looted Solomon's palaces and the Temple, and imposed a fairly heavy annual tribute as well. Judah was an independent kingdom no longer, but existed as a vassal of one dominant force or another for years to come, first to Israel in the north, then to Assyria, and then Damascus.

From 780-740 BCE there was peace in Judah. Uzziah ruled and it was known as the **Silver Age**, then feuds, greed, and bad foreign policy returned. Prophets such as Isaiah and Jeremiah rebuked and wagged their fingers and warned, but (as is generally the way with prophets) to no avail. Tiglath-pileser swooped down on Damascus in 734 BCE, and then came Israel. Tiglath-pileser killed the northern king, Pekach, and took the districts of Galilee and Gilead as additional provinces. He also deported lots of Israelites into Assyria, beginning the strange "disappearance" of the Ten Tribes. The remaining northern districts of Israel were taken by the new Assyrian king Sargon in 720 BCE and the kingdom of Israel was renamed **Samaria**.

King Hezekiah of Judah also ran into trouble with the Assyrians (first with Sargon and then Sennacherib). While Jerusalem escaped the drumming the rest of Judah was subject to (46 cities were demolished and 200,000 Judeans were taken captive), fear of a prolonged siege prompted Hezekiah to reinforce the fortifications and build a subterranean tunnel to carry water from the river Gihon to within the city walls. The resulting **Pool of Siloam**, discovered by archaeologists in 1880 and now on display near Dung Gate, was an impressive work of engineering skill, but Hezekiah still failed at his attempted revolt and had to pay the price to Assyrian Sennacherib in humility, humanity, and gold.

Then in 586 BCE Nebuchadnezzar of Babylon stomped in, ending the fun and games, razing Solomon's Temple, and taking the Jews off for 50 years of exile, with their blinded King Zedekiah in tow. **Zedekiah** (597-587

BCE), the last king of Judah, was a weak monarch who ignored the **prophet Jeremiah's** plea to refrain from calamitous rebellions. Zedekiah was taken prisoner, forced to witness the death of his sons, and led off in chains after having his eyes gouged out (2 Kings 24-25). Nebuchadnezzar is known to many for the "hanging gardens of Babylon," terraced roof gardens the Greeks listed as one of the seven wonders of the world, but in Jewish history he is viewed as one of the most evil of villains, responsible for great cruelty, not to mention the destruction of the sacred Temple.

PERSIAN RULE OVER ISRAELITES
538-322 BCE (Achaemenid Dynasty 549-330 BCE)

Cyrus of Persia founded the Achaemenid dynasty in 549 BCE. A relatively benign monarch, Cyrus made Hebrew Bible history by permitting the Jews in 538 BCE to return to **Jerusalem** and rebuild their **Temple**. Though most Jews elected to stay in Babylon, about 40,000 picked up and returned to what was left of Jerusalem. While the skilled and fit Jews had been marched off to Babylon in 587 BCE, the poor, weak, and ill had remained in Samaria. These Jews intermarried and intermingled with the colonizing Assyrians and Babylonians, and became known as the **Samaritans**.

When the exiled Jews returned 50 years later they rejected the Samaritans and their desire to help rebuild the temple. Zerubbabel, the leader of the second wave to return to Jerusalem, told them "Ye have nothing to do with us to build a house for our God." **Ezra the Scribe** is a Jew who had remained in Babylon to study religious texts, and in 458 BCE he was named religious head by King Artaxerxes and sent to Jerusalem to officiate. When he got there he was horrified by the widespread intermarriage between the Samaritans and the returned exiles. Ezra declared all Samaritan intermarriages invalid and forced all Samaritans out of the congregation of Israel. Not surprisingly, these harsh decrees didn't go over very well, and civil war resulted. The Persian king sent **Nehemiah** to Jerusalem to pacify and administrate. Nehemiah set about building walls around Jerusalem, a project which took 52 days. Once the walls were up, the threat from the angry Samaritans in the north died down. Despite delays and conflicts with the Samaritans, the **Second Temple** was completed in 515 BCE.

HELLENISTIC PERIOD
333-63 BCE

Alexander the Great smashed the Persian Empire, became the new overlord of Palestine, and initiated the Greek empire. Shortly after taking the throne, Alexander occupied Syria, Phoenicia, and Turkey, and was accepted by Egypt as pharaoh. Alexander went on to occupy Babylon and Persia before setting his sights on India. Alexander III of Macedonia died in June, 323 BCE.

Many of the new Hellenistic cities welcomed and attracted the Jews in Judea, and large Jewish communities grew in Egypt, Syria, and Asia Minor, and in smaller numbers in places as far off as Spain, Morocco, Bulgaria, and Greece. Not only did the Hellenistic culture incite Jews to travel to distant lands, Hellenism was a strong cultural leveler. Greek language, literature, philosophy, art, manners, and dress became shared throughout the Mediterranean world. Jews assimilated to the Greek culture in all ways but religion, and in fact the Hellenistic years was a period of vast numbers of conversions to the Jewish faith.

The synagogues and mosaics uncovered in Israel dating from these years, however, show the strong impact of Hellenistic culture in the excavated statues, Greek inscriptions, and art. All this Hellenistic assimilation, while happily embraced by the upper class, caused tension and conflict among the majority folk of small town Judea.

SELEUCID EMPIRE
281-164 BCE

In the fighting among Alexander's successors, Babylon fell to Seleucus I in 312 BCE. The **Seleucids** established many Greek settlements in the east, and under them Hellenism mixed with local cultures. By 281 BCE the Seleucids controlled most of the Asian provinces of the Macedonian empire—including most of Anatolia, part of Syria-Phoenicia, Babylon, Assyria, and more.

About 198 BC, the Seleucid king Antiochus III conquered Judea (of which Jerusalem was a part), making it tributary to Syria. After the death (163 BCE) of Antiochus IV, the Romans prevented any resurgence of Seleucid power. During this time ancient practices and traditions clashed with 'modern' styles and innovations, and it all came to a head during the Seleucid rule of **Antiochus Epiphanes IV** (Epiphanes was the Greek title he chose for himself, meaning "god-manifest") circa 215-163 BCE.

The first two books of Maccabees paints Antiochus as the arch villain. On his way back from a misguided attempt to conquer Egypt, he stopped off in Jerusalem to plunder and sack and pillage, after which he issued the decree that the Jews must not only cease their own religious practices, but were "to profane the Sabbath and feasts and pollute the Sanctuary...that they should build altars and temples and shrines for idols; and should sacrifice swine's flesh...and that they should leave their sons uncircumcised." And those who didn't obey, of course, were to be put to death. It was under this oppression that **Hannah** and her seven sons became martyrs. On the 15th day of Kislev, 168 BCE, the Temple was desecrated with a huge statue of Zeus, and lewd bacchanalian revels took place in the courts of prayer. In the ensuing resistance, thousands were killed, and many others took to the hills.

In 167 BCE the resistance grew into a full-scale revolt as the old priest **Mattathias the Hasmonean** from Modi'in (17 miles northeast of Jerusalem) refused to "come forward and do the command of the King." Mattathias killed a weak-willed fellow who started to bow down to the altar of Zeus, saying "Whosoever is zealous for the Law and strives to maintain the covenant, come with me." Mattathias, his five sons, and the other faithful fled to the mountains, and the guerrilla warfare fight was on. When Mattathias neared death, he turned the leadership over to his sons.

Judah Maccabee ("the Hammer") became the military leader, and Simon was put in charge of political affairs. The Maccabeean army was small but impassioned, and led by The Hammer, they prevailed. They took Jerusalem, smashed the statue of Zeus, and chased out the Hellenistic leaders. On the 25th of Kislev (in December, usually), 164 BCE, Judah Maccabee rededicated the Temple in an eight-day festival and lit the lamps of the *menorah*, an event celebrated and remembered in the holiday of **Hanukah**.

MACCABEEAN OR HASMONEAN DYNASTY
164-63 BCE

After Alexander died, Babylon fell to Seleucus I in 312 BCE. In 198 BCE, Antiochus III the Seleucid conquered Judah, and Jerusalem came under Macedonian rule. It was against this regime that the Jews revolted in 167 BCE. Antiochus Epiphanes IV (meaning *God-Manifest the Fourth*) was the Seleucid in power at the time, and he plagued the Jews in Jerusalem, plundering and pillaging (favorite kingly pastimes) as well as outlawing religious practices and insisting the Jews profane their Sabbath, worship at pagan temples, and sacrifice swine. The last straw was when he desecrated the Temple in 168 with a huge statue of Zeus and a lewd party. There was resistance, there were deaths, and the revolt led by Mattathias the Hasmonean was on.

After his death, **Judah Maccabee** (the Hammer) led and prevailed. Their small but angry army took Jerusalem, smashed the statue of Zeus, and flushed out the Hellenistic leaders. On the 25th of Kislev (in December, usually), 164 BCE, Judah Maccabee rededicated the Temple in an eight-day festival and lit the lamps of the *menorah*, an event celebrated and remembered in the holiday of Hanukah. By 142 BCE the Hasmoneans had established autonomy and began to return Judah to its Hebrew roots. By 125, however, the Maccabee morals had slid. King

Hyrcanus forced Idumeans to convert to Judaism. King Yannai partied while causing 800 opponents to watch their families be killed before being put to death themselves. The kingdom weakened, civil war ensued, and the Romans solved the power squabbles of Hyrcanus II and Aristobulus by sending General Pompey to arbitrate, besiege, and eventually occupy Jerusalem in 63 BCE, killing priests and defenders, desecrating the Temple, and making Judah part of the Roman Empire.

ROMAN PERIOD
63 BCE-324 CE
The Herod Dynasty started with **King Herod**, who reigned over Judah from 37-4 BCE. He was put on the throne by the Romans, but his lineage links him to the Maccabeean era. His grandparents were among the people King John Hyrcanus had conquered, brought to Judea, and forced into Judaism. Herod is notorious for his ruthlessness – scholars cite him as perhaps the most vile Jewish king ever. He launched his regime murdering 45 of the Sanhedrin, and followed up with many in his family. He murdered his first wife and their two sons, and later murdered his mother-in-law, brother-in-law, and another son from a new wife. Roman emperor Augustus commented: "It is better to be Herod's pig than his son."

When he wasn't doing in his relations, Herod was quite productive. He beautified and expanded the Second Temple (occupying ten thousand laborers and one thousand priests for nine years), rebuilt the walls around Jerusalem, built up theaters, harbors, and fortresses (including Masada) throughout Judea, and founded the city of **Caesarea**. When he died in 4 BCE, emperor Augustus divided the kingdom among Herod's surviving sons: Archelaus, Herod Antipas, and Philip.

RELIGIOUS & REVOLUTIONARY REACTIONS
While the Herod family governed, killed, and built, the people of the land were going through bad economic times. Citizens were taxed dry to support the ego-and-glory-enriching projects of their rulers, the social and economic class split was accentuated, and assimilation was again an issue. These hard time conditions, as usual, resulted in a variety of extreme reactions.

The **Sadducees** were a priestly sect of Jews who belonged to the aristocratic ruling class. They interpreted the Torah very literally, didn't believe in immortality, collaborated with the Romans, and assimilated to Roman ways. **The Pharisees**, the ancestors of contemporary Jews, disagreed with the strict literal Torah interpretation, believed in the oral traditions of the Torah and in an afterlife, and disapproved of the

Sadducee's self-indulgent, luxurious life styles. To them, "Sadducee" took on a derogatory connotation, meaning "heretic." The Pharisees were depicted in a very negative light in the New Testament, and the term came to connote "hypocrite," a development found offensive to Jews.

Another sect were the **Essenes**, pacifists who were big on purity (immersion in the ritual bath was reputedly one of their most important ceremonies). Described by Rabbi Telushkin as "an ascetic and disciplined group of ancient hippies," they left the corrupt cities, eschewed property and material wealth, and set up communities in the countryside to peacefully await the Messiah who would rescue the pure from their evil times. Among other sects living isolated in the desert was the group now known as the **Dead Sea Sect**. The **Dead Sea Scrolls**, found in a cave in Qumran in 1947, indicates that they were an extremist offshoot of the Essenes.

Unlike the Essenes, the **Zealots** were no pacifists. They were a patriotic, militant group who were angry at the Romans and at their own Jewish oppressors. They drew much of their support from the poor, the same pocket of poverty from which, not long after, Jesus recruited many of his followers. The Zealots didn't want to wait for the Messiah, they wanted revolution, and they were responsible for the revolts that led to Masada and the destruction of the Temple.

The concept of the **Messiah** was important to more than these reactionary groups. Messianism among Jews was at an all-time high during this time. It was a tradition among Jews that the Messiah (*Mashiach* in Hebrew, *Christos* in Greek) would come during a period of great suffering, when the pain was unbearable. The harsh rule of the Herods made supernatural redemption a popular construct.

Their understanding of the term 'Messiah,' however, differed a bit from the highly spiritual figure it denotes today. Then, 'Messiah' referred to the military leader who would free the Jews from foreign (Roman) rule and usher in an age of universal peace. Bar-Kokhba, the Zealot military general who led the revolts in 132 BCE, was referred to as a messiah, though no mention was ever made to spiritual greatness. The crucifixion of Jesus under a 'King of the Jews' sign supports the view that the Romans, at least, saw him as a political threat.

JESUS

Approximately 6 BCE-33 CE

Jesus of Nazareth, a first-century Pharisaic Jewish teacher who was crucified by the Romans, is believed by Christians to be the Christ or Messiah. Most knowledge of Jesus comes from the Gospels in the New Testament. From these and a few other first and second century sources (such as Roman historian Tacitus), a brief history of his life can be constructed.

His life began in Roman-ruled Palestine during the reign of Augustus (27 BCE-14 CE), just two years before the death of Herod the Great (as best as biblical scholars can tell, making it 6 BCE). Jesus was born in Bethlehem but grew up in Nazareth. He was a devout Jew and gathered about him a group of disciples attracted by his interpretations of the Torah, and his abilities to heal the sick and perform exorcisms.

According to Luke, his public preaching began in 29 CE after being baptized by John the Baptist. Some of his preachings focused on how God's rule was about to replace human rule, a view that made some Jewish and Roman leaders feel threatened. In 33 CE (again, according to biblical scholar's estimates, since the New Testament doesn't include a lot of dates), Jesus was arrested in Jerusalem, tried and condemned by **Pontius Pilate** (governor of Judea 26-36 CE), and executed according to the Roman policy that mandated crucifixion for political threats. Jesus' followers then claimed he arose from the dead, and Christianity was born.

The largest section of each of the Gospels is devoted to the final events of the conflict between Jesus and the civil and religious authorities. The last confrontation took place in Jerusalem. Jesus entered the great temple of Jerusalem, denounced the commercial operations that were carried on there, and predicted the destruction of the temple and of Jerusalem. This was to be a sign that God would act in a climactic way to restore and vindicate his true people. Meanwhile, however, they must learn to accept suffering, including Jesus' own suffering and death.

He was betrayed by **Judas Iscariot**, and the others apostles abandoned him when he was seized by the authorities in the **Garden of Gethsemene**. A handful of faithful women remained with him when he died at **Calvary**. The women returned to his tomb on the third day after his death and found it empty, whereafter an angel told them that Jesus was alive.

This day of Jesus' **Resurrection** is celebrated by Christians on Easter Sunday. The Roman emperors Claudius and Nero took actions to suppress Christianity in the middle of the first century, and by the end of the century, Jewish authorities in Palestine had adopted policies aimed at sharply differentiating Christians from Jews.

ROMAN PERSECUTION & JEWISH REVOLTS
19-70 CE

Roman rule had a number of practices that stuck in the collective craw of the Judeans. From early in the Common Era, Judea was ruled by Roman procurators, and their main job was to collect and deliver annual taxes for the empire. Whatever they took in above the required amount was theirs for the keeping, so a lot of taxing went on. In addition, Rome handled the Jewish High Priest appointments. This meant, in effect, that they were chosen from the ranks of the Jews who collaborated with Rome (usually the Sadducees), and it further incited hostility among the other groups. **Tiberius**, Emperor Augustus' successor, ruled from 14-37 CE. In 19 CE Tiberius expelled all Jews from Rome and began to impose other repressive measures, such as tampering with the powers of the Sanhedrin. Anti-Roman feelings were further exacerbated during the reign of emperor **Caligula** from 37-41 CE. Caligula's name was actually a nickname meaning "little baby boots," his sanity was pretty questionable (he named his horse as high magistrate), and his rule was full of grief for Judea. In 39 CE he declared himself a deity and insisted that his statue be put up in every temple in his empire. The Jews refused to defile their Temple with Caligula's image and he threatened to destroy the Temple. While his sudden death resolved the conflict, the incident garnered a lot of support for the Zealots' rebellious movement.

After Caligula's death, the provocations continued under emperor **Nero** (54-68 CE). Roman soldiers exposed themselves in the Temple, a Torah scroll was burned, and the financial indignities added to their general woes. In 66 CE Florus (the last Roman procurator) stole huge amounts of silver from the Temple. The resulting outrage sent masses of Jews, led by the Zealots, rioting in the streets of Jerusalem. They wiped out the small Jerusalem garrison, stood off the larger troop sent in from Syria to quell them, and the **Great Revolt** (66-70 CE) was on.

Their initial success was misleading. With the great wisdom of hindsight it's clear they never had a chance, and the Zealots are held accountable by some Jewish historians for the resulting destruction and loss. The Romans returned in force, and led by General **Vespasian**, Roman troops vanquished the Galilee before embarking on the **Siege of Jerusalem**. When Nero died, Vespasian returned to Rome to be crowned the new emperor and his son **Titus** took over as general of the Roman troops.

There was fierce resistance from the Jews who were fighting, but while the Zealots engaged the Romans in the north, the more moderate Jews of Jerusalem remained detached and did not aid the struggle. There was also suspected treachery on the part of **Flavius Josephus**. Josephus was one of the Jewish generals, but he surrendered to Vespasian, and was appointed by him to record the war's progress. Whether he helped out the Romans with his knowledge of Jerusalem and the rebel movement is debated endlessly, but regardless of whether his calls to the besieged to give up and surrender mark him as a traitor or a loyal Jew, he did write an historical account, *The Jewish Wars*, which have provided the best record of the events of the time. Of course he was living under Roman protection so his accounts are skewed a bit to please his patrons and revile the Zealots.

After the Galilee was taken, the survivors of the struggle escaped to Jerusalem and put to death the moderate leaders of the Jewish government. There was terrible squabbling among the factions within the city walls, and hosts of Roman troops outside. Many leaders opposed the revolt, but there were orders out to kill anyone advocating surrender. There's a famous story of **Rabbi Yochanan ben Zakkai** who had his followers smuggle him out of the city disguised as a corpse. Once safe from him countrymen, he surrendered to Vespasian and was granted the right to establish a Jewish seminary in nearby Yavneh.

Eventually the siege machines won out and Jerusalem was taken. The fighters retreated to their Temple, and on the **Ninth of Av**, 70 CE, the Temple was set on fire and destroyed. What survived was one outer wall from the western side of the Temple's courtyard, and this has remained holy to Jews as the *Kotel ha-Ma'aravi*, the **Western Wall**. Historians believe as many as a million Jews died in the Great Revolt, and many more were

MASADA: 73 CE

Though Jerusalem was destroyed, the Temple razed, and the Sanhedrin dissolved, Jewish life limped on. Rabbi Yochanan ben Zakkai's academy at Yavneh thrived though Zealot survivors viewed him as a traitor. These survivors who had successfully fled Jerusalem took up residence in the fortress of Masada overlooking the Dead Sea. They lasted there for three years while Rome's Tenth Legion proceeded stubbornly with catapults and battering rams.

*When it became clear to their leader **Elazar ben Yair** that the Romans would not go away but would prevail, he proposed mass suicide to avoid capture and enslavement. The only account we have of this episode come from the annals of Flavius Josephus, who witnessed the siege and claimed to have met and interviewed two women and five children who hid during the suicide. From them he recounted Elazer's final speech, in which he said "Let our wives die before they are abused, and our children before they have tasted of slavery, and after we have slain them, let us bestow that glorious benefit upon one another mutually." Though we know of Masada from Josephus, the Talmud omits the story, which highlights its equivocal place in Jewish history.*

While for some, Masada is the greatest symbol of resolution and national defense, others (such as the rabbis compiling the Talmud) viewed the Zealots with resentment for their ill-fated rebellions.

led to Rome as slaves. The Ninth of Av marks for the Jews the end of their Temple, their holy city, and their homeland. Since that time it has been a fast day and a day of mourning during which the Book of Lamentations is read to mark the destruction of the First and Second Temples.

BAR-KOKHBA REBELLION
132-135 CE

In 132 CE, **Simon bar-Kokhba** (*Son of the Star*) led another revolt. Bar-Kokhba was the charismatic military mastermind, but Rabbi Akiva, the leading sage of the age, provided the spiritual encouragement and motivating force by attesting that Bar-Kokhba was the Messiah and the End of Days was near. The specific provocation for this rebellion came from Emperor Hadrian (117-138 CE), who forbade circumcision, forbade *Torah* study, and decided to build a shrine to Jupiter on the old site of the Temple in Jerusalem.

As before, initial victories strengthened the conviction that the rebellion was God's will, and as before, the Pharisees and pacifists argued against the wisdom of engaging Rome in battle. Bar-Kokhba managed to drive the Roman legions out of the country, declared the independence of Judea, and minted commemorative coins for the "Redemption of Zion." Hadrian sent Julius Severus to oppose Bar-Kokhba, and one by one he stormed the fortifications. Fifty fortresses and close to a thousand villages were destroyed, and most of Judea lay wasted; Bar-Kokhba died, Rabbi Akiva was burned at the stake, Jerusalem was renamed Aelia Capitolina (after Aelius Hadrian), and the temple to Jupiter was completed on the site of Solomon's Temple.

As with the Great Revolt, the Bar-Kokhba Rebellion was considered a great catastrophe in Jewish history, and the wisdom of the revolt and and bar-Kokhba have remained controversial.

BYZANTINE PERIOD
324-640 CE

Rome's **Emperor Constantine** joined the new Christian religion, thereby redirecting history. Rome became a Christian empire, and the emperor built a new capital in Byzantium (hence our name for the empire, though they still considered it the Roman Empire). He renamed it **Constantinople** after himself, but it's now better known as Istanbul. Under his rule, the Middle East prospered fairly well, and merchants did well with European, Asian, and African trade. Religious tolerance, however, dwindled (and Rome hadn't been all that tolerant before).

Palestine was perhaps more directly affected by the visit of Constantine's mother, **Saint Helena**. She traipsed about identifying holy sites (where Jesus performed miracles, was resurrected, etc.) and commissioning churches to be built, encouraging pilgrimages to the Holy Land. The excavations around the Sea of Galilee, for example, and Bethlehem, are full of Byzantine church ruins or reconstructions (such as the Holy Sepulcher), some with their glorious mosaics still intact.

EARLY ARAB PERIOD
640-1099 CE

The Byzantine Empire lasted until 1453 when the Ottomans took over, but their reign in the Middle East ended sooner in 640 with the Arab invasion. **Mohammed** was born in Mecca in 570 CE, had his first revelation from the Angel Gabriel in the month of Ramadan, 610 CE, and by his death in 632 had conquered and converted most of the Arab tribes. They dealt with the power vacuum his death created by finding new leaders who led them quite successfully against the Byzantine and Persian empires.

Abu Bakr became *khalifat rasul Allah* ("successor of the messenger of God"), soon shortened to *khalifah*, or caliph in English. His conquests (from North Africa to the borders of China) were amazingly speedy, taking little more than a decade to tackle some of the greatest powers around. Not all the Arab fighters were zealous Muslims engaged in a *jihad* (holy war). Christian Arabs (Arab denoting regional origin rather than religion) were welcome, and the Byzantine theological conflicts aided the Arab cause. Economic hardship also spurred on the conquests, as looting was an age-old solution to financial woes.

In 638, the Arabs under Caliph Umar took Jerusalem, and in 661 Mu'awiyah established his caliphate there. It was he who made succession hereditary and founded the **Umayyad** dynasty, followed by the **Abbasid**, and **Fatimid** dynasties. In 688 Abd al-Malik built the **Dome of the Rock** mosque on the Temple Mount, making Jerusalem a third Muslim pilgrimage site after Mecca and Medina, and sending a message to the Christians that Islam was no flash-in-the-pan. The Fatimids were Shi'ite rather than Sunni Muslims (see Religion section, chapter 4), and despite the great conflict between the two they generally respected the religious freedom of the Christians and Jews they ruled, with the exception of al-Hakim. Caliph al-Hakim (996-1021) persecuted Christians and destroyed their churches. Though his motivations and sanity have been debated, the actions perpetrated against the Christian community are indisputable.

The **Seljuks** were a dynasty in the growing Islamic Turkish civilization. The Seljuk Turks did well for themselves, began to expand their territories, took Jerusalem in 1071, and refused to allow the Christian Pilgrims easy access. It was in reaction to this restriction (in part) that the Pope initiated the Crusades.

CRUSADER PERIOD

1099-1291 CE

Promising relief from ecclesiastical penances as an incentive, **Pope Urban II** invited all Christians in 1095 to join a war to retake the Holy Sepulchre in Jerusalem from "the wicked race," responding in part to the pilgrims' plight (though by '95 that problem had been alleviated by a new ruler), in part to a call for help from the flailing Byzantine Empire, and in part to help solidify the papacy's power (and besides, times were bad and the trade routes over there were pretty lucrative). The term Crusade, derived from the Latin crux ("cross"), refers to the biblical injunction that Christians carry their cross (Matt. 10:38). So, Crusaders wore red cloth crosses sewn on their tunics to show how they were soldiers of Christ.

The Crusades were off and the confrontations between Europe and the Middle East were on. In the First Crusade (1096-99) they took Jerusalem in 1099, slaughtered all the Muslims and most of the Jews, and crowned **Baldwin** King of the Latin Kingdom of Jerusalem. The Second Crusade (1147-49) made it as far as Damascus, but the Third Crusade (1188-92) meant business. By 1187 **Saladin** (Salah al-Din, a brave, shrewd, and magnanimous new caliph) had won the decisive battle at the **Horns of Hittin** and taken back most of Palestine (including Jerusalem); the Crusaders weren't pleased.

Led by **Richard the Lionheart**, they weren't terribly successful at reversing things, though they did manage to take Acre and Jaffa. In the Fourth Crusade (1202-04) the concentration was solely on besieging Constantinople and toppling the Byzantine Empire, which is exactly what they did. Many crusades followed in the 13th century, but little changed in the Muslim-Christian balance of power. Acre was the last Crusader stronghold, and it fell to the Mamluk **Sultan Baybars** in 1291.

The **Mamluks** had an interesting rags-to-riches story. The Muslim dynasties had an age-old tradition of taking Turkish boys (mamluks, or "owned men") as slaves and training them to be soldiers. They rebelled against their Ayyubid masters (Saladin's descendants), killed the new Ayyubid sultan, and established an empire that held sway from the late 13th century up until the Ottoman Empire crashed their party in 1517. During their tenure, not a whole lot of development went on in the Palestinian portion of their kingdom. Baybars (1260-1277) had razed many of the towns he conquered to prevent the fortifications from being used against them, and not much was rebuilt, partly because they were pretty busy defending their regime in Egypt and Syria. Under their rule some Jews began to return from Europe, especially after 1492 when Spain kicked out its Jewish population, and the mystic Kabbalists set up shop in Tsfat.

THE OTTOMAN EMPIRE

1517-1918

The Ottoman Turks under Selim I moved against the Mamluks in 1517, beginning their four century reign over Palestine. Though the Mamluks had gunpowder and used it a tad, the Ottomans really began the gunpowder age in the Middle East. **Suleiman the Magnificent** was the next Sultan and he left his mark by rebuilding the walls around Jerusalem.

The Turks had an enormous empire, and they financed it by tax collection. *Multezim* (tax farmers) were assigned sectors to collect from, and so long as they gave a certain amount to the Empire they could keep the rest. Following the same school of thought, officials were authorized to collect fees (*baksheesh*, which has come to mean bribe or handout in common parlance) for services rendered. Later when the treasury needed more money, clerks had to buy their offices, and they would then bleed the public through taxes to recoup their outlay.

This system oiled the works for the next few centuries, and corruption was developed to great flights of glory. Law and order was neglected, and the Jews and Christians in the Galilee weren't treated very well. Still, more Jews kept coming from Europe to form settlements because European conditions were even worse. To stir things up, **Napoleon Bonaparte** made a cameo appearance. He was sent by France to conquer Egypt (and maybe Syria and Iraq) in 1798. Napoleon occupied Jaffa very briefly in 1799, and then besieged Acre but was thwarted by the British Navy. He went to Haifa and used the Carmelite Monastery as a hospital for his soldiers until the Turks forced his retreat.

Corruption, conflict, and the usual afflictions that plague an old empire began to weaken the Turks, and the world began to notice. Britain had a special interest in the region. They had a number of economic motives (their trade route to India involved Ottoman lands), and they didn't care for the French expansion going on in Egypt and Syria. They opened a British consulate in Jerusalem in 1838, and in 1839 **Sir Moses Montefiore** suggested in London that a Jewish state be established. Britain helped defend Ottoman interests in the Crimean War (1853-1856), and in 1869 the Suez Canal opened, increasing world interest in the area.

In 1908 a revolution led by the **Young Turks** overthrew the Ottoman sultanate. The Young Turk leader (dictator) Enver Pasha entered into World War I (siding with Germany and Austria-Hungary), and put the nails in his empire's coffin. Their defeat led to the breakup and foreign occupation of the Ottoman Empire, and Palestine entered a new era.

BRITISH OCCUPATION & THE BRITISH MANDATE

1919-1948

Toward the end of World War I, British troops led by **General Sir Edmund Allenby** invaded Palestine and took Jerusalem in December 1917, ending 400 years of Ottoman sovereignty, but the Mandate period was not a happy time. In 1916 the British high commissioner in Cairo had signed an accord with the sharif of Mecca, leading the Arabs to believe the British would support an independent Arab state that would include Palestine. Then the waffling began, as one year later in 1917 the British government issued the Balfour Declaration, which promised support for a Zionist nation. In 1922 the League of Nations approved a British mandate over Palestine and neighboring **Transjordan** (which became Jordan in 1946), supposedly to encourage the development of self-governing institutions and, eventually, independence. Arabs rioted against Jews and the British tried to stay out of the middle (while keeping their finger on the oil pulse), thereby mucking it up even more.

After World War I, a pattern began to emerge from the chaos. Jewish immigration increased dramatically (the Third and Fourth Aliyahs spanning 1919-1928 nearly tripled the Jewish population in Palestine), Arab Palestinians reacted with fear and violence, and Jews responded by digging their heels in and increasing immigration – a pattern that has continued in some ways up till today. The international political wheels spun and muddied the waters a bit more, and vague antagonisms became entrenched hostilities. In 1919 (the same year **Dr. Chaim Weizmann** led the Jewish delegation to the Peace Conference in Paris), Damascus demanded independence for a Syrian state that would include Palestine, categorically rejecting the concept of a Jewish national home.

The Third Aliyah began, and anti-Zionist riots broke out among Arab Palestinians in April 1920, followed by even more serious violence in May 1921 after Britain announced that 16,500 Jewish immigrants would be admitted. The **Histradrut** (General Federation of Jewish Labor) and **Haganah** (underground resistance movement) were formed, and the Fourth Aliyah got under way. Haj Amin, Mufti of Jerusalem and Supreme Muslim Council head was probably more responsible for intensifying illwill more than any other one individual. In 1929 there was yet another serious clash at the Western Wall in Jerusalem (instigated by Haj Amin), and that same year the Zionists formed the **Jewish Agency** to help develop quasi-governmental institutions among Palestine's Jews. The Haganah began to retaliate in the absence of British intervention. Also in 1929 the Jewish community of Hebron was slaughtered by Arab extremists, beginning a Hebron tension that hasn't yet begun to heal. **Ze'ev Jabotinsky** and **Menachem Begin** responded by forming the **Irgun Zvai Leumi**, an extreme right-wing underground organization.

The Palestine situation became even more complicated in the 1930s when, in reaction to Nazi persecution of Jews in Europe, Jewish settlement soared (the Jewish population totaled more than 400,000 by 1939, comprising nearly a third of Palestine's inhabitants), triggering the Arab attack reaction. The Mufti was finally arrested, but he escaped and fled to join Hitler in Berlin. Between 1935 and 1939, Britain proposed to stabilize the population with an Arab majority. The only common ground between Arabs and Jews was their displeasure with these plans. During these years, the Zionist struggle was a bit eclipsed by the need to fight WWII, but it wasn't by any means forsaken.

Britain's last serious attempts to reach a compromise were the inconclusive **London Round Table Conference** (1939) and the **White Paper** of that year, which promised the establishment within ten years of an independent Palestine retaining an Arab majority. The White Paper also limited Jewish immigration to 1,500 per month until 1944, when Jews would no longer be admitted to Palestine. Britain's solution to the racial tensions led to the sad spectacle of boatloads of Holocaust survivors being turned away, and the Zionists responded with Aliyah Bet, the illicit smuggling of refugees (the subject of a book and movie called *The Exodus*). Zionists disillusioned by British waffling (and believing that British influence after the war would wane and be replaced by American policy) focused on gaining US support, with some success. In May 1942, the **Biltmore Conference** in New York demanded the formation of an independent Jewish commonwealth, a stance strongly endorsed by US political leaders.

ISRAELI STATEHOOD

By 1947, the British washed their hands of the problem and dumped it in the lap of the United Nations, which voted in November for a split Palestine, of Arab and Jewish states, and an international Jerusalem. The partition (accepted by the Zionists but not by the Arab countries) didn't work out very well. The line was drawn such that houses (and families) were split down the middle, no one was happy, and bloodshet filled the streets of the Old City.

The fighting spread. Arab guerrillas, supported by the Transjordanian Arab Legion under the command of British officers, besieged Jerusalem. By April, the Haganah went on the offensive, scoring victories against the Arab Liberation Army in northern Palestine, Jaffa, and Jerusalem, and British military forces withdrew to Haifa.

The British got out on May 14, 1948 (months before the UN plan was to supervise the plan), and **David Ben Gurion** (Israel's first prime minister) declared the Independent state of Israel. Their armed forces were geared for war, and not just defensive action. Based on intelligence reports and Arab incendiary boasts about pushing the Jews out of Palestine and into the sea, they readied to fight tooth and nail. Palestinian Arabs, joined by neighboring Arab allies (though not in anywhere near the numbers promised and expected) engaged in the first in a series of **Arab-Israeli Wars**, Israel's **War of Independence**.

In May of 1949, a UN cease-fire was declared and Israel emerged from the fray with a hard-won victory, new territories, and statehood. More than 700,000 Arab Palestinian refugees left, Israel confiscated the property they vacated (one of the items now sticking in the throats of Palestinians trying to make the peace work), and Palestine ceased to exist as a political entity. Accounts differ, however, over why the Arabs left. The Jews say they just up and vanished, prompted by their higher-ups to set the stage for wiping the Jews out. Arabs, however, say they were forced out by Jewish terrorism. Most of the territory west of the Jordan River that the United Nations had designated as Arab came under the control of Jordan, including the Old City and East Jerusalem, and the Gaza Strip was occupied by Egypt.

Israel's development boomed, as did immigration. In 1950, the Knesset (Parliament) passed the **Law of Return** granting citizenship to any Jew requesting it, and the 1952 Nationality Law allowed non-Jews to claim citizenship. Kibbutzim and moshavim (collective and co-op farms) sprang up all over the place, and a nation took shape. Aliyah rates remained high, with Tunisians and Moroccans flooding in around 1955 and Hungarians in 1956.

THE SINAI (SUEZ) WAR OF 1956

Border conflicts between Israel and the Arabs continued despite provisions in the 1949 armistice agreements for peace negotiations. Hundreds of thousands of Palestinian Arabs who had left Israeli-held territory during the first war concentrated in refugee camps along Israel's frontiers and became a major source of friction when they infiltrated back to their homes or attacked Israeli border settlements. A major tension point was the Egyptian-controlled Gaza Strip, from which Arab guerrillas raided southern Israel. Egypt's blockade of Israeli shipping in the Suez Canal and Gulf of Aqaba intensified the hostilities.

These escalating tensions coincided with Egyptian president **Gamal Nasser's** nationalization of the Suez Canal and ensuing Suez Crisis. Great Britain and France strenuously objected to Nasser's policies, and a joint military campaign was planned against Egypt with the understanding that Israel would take the initiative by seizing the Sinai Peninsula. The war began on Oct. 29, 1956, and Israel's Operation Kadesh, commanded by

Moshe Dayan, lasted less than a week; its forces reached the eastern bank of the Suez Canal in about 100 hours, seizing the Gaza Strip and nearly all the Sinai Peninsula. The war was halted by a UN cease-fire calling for withdrawal of all occupying forces from Egyptian territory.

No one won and everyone was condemned for this or that infraction. The facts show that Israel, allied with British, French, and American forces, reacted to Egypt's decision to close the Suez Canal by attacking and occupying Gaza Strip and the Sinai, and after some world pressure Israel gave up that occupation. The debates go on as to who provoked the trouble.

THE SIX DAY WAR OF 1967

After some relatively calm years followed by a couple years of increased terrorism and "push them to the sea" rhetoric, Egypt blockaded the Tiran Straits as they had done in '56, massed their forces in the Sinai, and ordered the UN peace-keepers out. At the end of May, Egypt and Jordan signed a new defense pact placing Jordan's armed forces under Egyptian command.

Led by Minister of Defense Moshe Dayan, and Army Chief of Staff **Yitzhak Rabin**, the Israeli air force struck first and blasted Egyptian, Syrian, Jordanian, and Iraqi airfields on June 5, 1967. Jordan attacked from the east and Syria from the north, engaging the Israelis on all sides. Six days later after the dust had settled, Israel occupied the Golan Heights, the Sinai Desert, and the West Bank (including Gaza Strip and Jerusalem, Old and East). As with the Sinai War, who planned what, provoked what, and manipulated what is still debated. Raging debates aside, Israeli confidence and developments soared following the brief war. The Jewish quarter of Jerusalem (destroyed in Mandate days) was rebuilt, Tiberias and the Sea of Galilee area were developed for tourism, and all the holy sites in and around Jerusalem became accessible.

After the six days, nearly 500,000 Arabs again departed Israel, and those remaining did so under Israeli military occupation, but the addition of more than 1,500,000 Palestinian Arabs to areas under Israeli control threatened internal security.

THE WAR OF ATTRITION (1969-70)
& THE YOM KIPPUR WAR OF 1973

The next war began two years later. Starting in the spring of '69 and going 16 months, Egypt kept up a steady shelling barrage across the Suez Canal border. Jordan made a few forays, terrorism was up, and so it went until the UN and the US brokered a new cease-fire. A tense quiet lasted a few years. Israel knew it wouldn't last and also knew Egypt was gearing up for a major offensive (supplied by the Soviet Union), still the onslaught in '73 took them by surprise.

Egypt refers to it with pride as the October 6th War (bridges and such are named after it) and Israel calls it the Yom Kippur War (since it was launched on that holiday), but by any name it was a military success for Egypt, and nearly the end of Israel. Egypt and Syria (financed by Saudi Arabia's King **Faisal**) launched a joint offensive on Israel's holiest day of the year, while most of the reserves were in synagogue praying. By the third day, however, Israel's IDF had recovered enough to start its own offensive, and on October 24th, after 18 days of fighting, the UN again called for a cease-fire.

Israel lost lives, lost face, lost the heady confidence engendered by the Six Day War and about $7 million, and ultimately lost Golda Meir as prime minister. Egypt gained a strip of land along the Suez and Syria got a small area in the Golan Heights.

FIRST PEACE

The pursuit for peace became more serious. US Secretary of State **Henry Kissinger** did the diplomatic shuttle all over the Middle East. At the Middle East Peace Conference in Geneva Israel and Egypt reached an agreement, and in May '74 he negotiated a peace between Israel and Syria. In June of 1977 Prime Minister **Menachem Begin** made a call for peace and invited Jordan, Syria, and Egypt to find a solution. The West Bank and Golan settlements that are sticking points still were impediments then as well, and of the three countries, only Egypt took Israel up on the challenge.

Egypt's President **Anwar Sadat** braved the disapproval of the Arab community, actually visiting Israel in November of '77, negotiating a peace, and acknowledging Israel's right to exist. After 16 months of negotiations, the Camp David Egypt-Israel Peace Treaty was signed in March of '79, under which agreement Israel returned the Sinai peninsula to Egypt. Hopes for an expansion of the peace process to include other Arab nations waned, however, when Egypt and Israel were subsequently unable to agree on a formula for Palestinian self-rule in the West Bank and Gaza Strip.

In the 1980s, tensions were increased by conflicts between Israeli authorities and Palestinians in the occupied territories, by PLO guerrilla attacks on Israeli settlements in Galilee, and by Israeli retaliatory raids into Lebanon. Israel and Egypt have not become best of friends, but the peace has held.

Egypt's President Sadat was assassinated by extremists, at least in part for his Treaty signing, and now Mubarak, his successor, has the difficult job of maintaining the peace while dealing with an ever stronger and more dangerous fundamentalist faction.

WAR WITH LEBANON

On June 6, 1982, Israel launched a full-scale invasion of Lebanon to destroy its PLO bases. Israeli commanders pushed northward, reaching the outskirts of Beirut within a week and also tangling a bit with Syrian forces. By the end of June, Israel had captured most of southern Lebanon and besieged PLO and Syrian forces in West Beirut. US mediation ended the fighting in August, when Israel agreed to leave Beirut so long as Syrian and PLO forces also withdrew.

What followed was a mess. On September 15 Lebanese president-elect Bashir Gemayel was assassinated, Israel reoccupied Beirut, and authorized Gemayel's Phalangist militia to "cleanse" Palestinian refugee camps of any remaining PLO fighters. The Phalange massacred hundreds of Palestinians, sparking Israeli antiwar protests. Israel signed an agreement with Lebanon ending the state of war in May 1983, but Lebanon renounced the pact under Syrian pressure in March 1984. Public pressures in Israel led to the withdrawal of Israeli troops by June 1994, leaving 1,000 "security personnel" to assist its Lebanese allies.

Sparring continues. In April '96 the Iranian-backed *Hezbollah* guerrillas upped their Katysha rocket attacks on Israel's northern settlements. Peres retaliated, southern Lebanese residents fled their homes, and northern Israelis slept in bomb shelters. Then on April 19, Israeli missiles hit a UN refugee camp, killing over 100 Lebanese civilians. American Secretary of State Warren Christopher shuttled between Damascus, Beirut, and Jerusalem, and eventually on April 26 brokered a "document of understanding" between Israel, Syria, and Lebanon. The goal of peace was agreed to, and further talks were indicated, but northern peace relations have yet coalesce.

PALESTINE LIBERATION ORGANIZATION (THE PLO)

The PLO was formed in 1964 to represent Palestinian Arabs in a struggle to "liberate" their homeland from what they felt was an illegitimate Israeli state. In 1974 the UN General Assembly recognized the PLO as "the representative of the Palestinian people."

Yasir Arafat became chairman of the PLO in 1969, and remains its head despite serious challenges from without and within. Expelled from Jordan in 1971, PLO guerrillas established a virtual state-within-a-state in Lebanon from which they launched attacks on Israel. They were driven from their Beirut headquarters by the Israeli army in 1982 and scattered throughout the Arab world.

THE INTIFADA

While Israel's borders remained secure, its internal stability was threatened by continued demands for Palestinian autonomy and by an Intifada (uprising) in the occupied territories. It began in the Gaza Strip in December 1987 and spread rapidly to the West Bank and East Jerusalem.

The revolt, which involved commercial strikes, business boycotts, and throwing stones at Israeli soldiers, took both the Israeli government and the PLO by surprise. The Intifada raised the costs of occupation and forced the government to take Palestinian nationalism more seriously. The intifada also contributed to Jordan's 1988 decision to sever its link with the West Bank ,and pushed the PLO to acknowledge Israel's right to exist. Israel's reaction to all this earned international disapproval. Their harsh attempts to suppress the revolt were widely criticized, and their decision in 1980 to name Jerusalem its official capital was bitterly resented by the Arabs and protested by innumerable terrorist acts.

HAMAS

The **Muslim Brotherhood** is a religious and political organization founded in Egypt in 1928. **Hamas**, founded in 1987, is the militant Palestinian branch of the Muslim Brotherhood. They do not recognize the state of Israel, are strongly opposed to Arafat's peace treaties and negotiations, and want to replace the Jewish state with an Islamic fundamentalist one.

As the peace process limps along there have been a number of terrorist suicide bombing attacks against Israel, and Hamas has claimed responsibility for most of them, putting the spotlight on Arafat to see how sincere he is about ending terrorism and how successfully he can control Hamas.

RECENT PEACE ACCORDS & THE PLO

The PLO declared a Palestinian state in November 1988 and conditionally accepted a UN resolution recognizing Israel. Arafat, who recognized Israel's right to exist and renounced terrorism in December, was appointed president of the Palestinian state in April 1989. Israel and the PLO signed agreements in 1993 and 1994 granting Palestinian Arabs self-rule in the West Bank and Gaza Strip, and Israel and Jordan formally ended their state of war in 1994, raising hopes for a permanent peace between Israel and its Arab neighbors.

Israel completed their evacuation from the Gaza Strip and Jericho on May 18, 1994, and the two sides began the process of hashing out the details for Palestinian self-rule in the rest of the West Bank (earning a Nobel Peace Prize for Yitzhak Rabin, Shimon Peres and Yasser Arafat).

In September 1995, Rabin and Arafat signed the 300-page **Interim Agreement** (also known as **Oslo II**) on the West Bank and Gaza Strip, which set forth guidelines on everything from Palestinian elections and Israeli redeployment to security, water allocation, and prisoner release. Much of what was agreed upon has taken place: In January of '96 Palestinian Council elections were held and Yasser Arafat was elected *Ra'ees* (head) of the Authority, the IDF (Israeli Defense Force) evacuated most West Bank cities (with Hebron the notable exception), in April '96, the Palestinian National Charter was amended to remove the articles that called for the destruction of Israel, and in May Israel and the PA began permanent status negotiatons, touching on the touchy subjects of Jerusalem, settlements, and refugees.

YITZHAK RABIN'S DEATH & AFTERMATH

But between the signing of the Interim Agreement and the implementations above, a major setback and national tragedy occurred: On November 4, 1995, 25-year-old Yigal Amir assassinated Israel's Prime Minister Yitzhak Rabin at a peace rally in Tel Aviv before 100,000 Israelis. Over one million Israelis (both Arabs and Jews) paid respects to Rabin's coffin, and nearly 80 world leaders (including representatives from six Arab states) attended the Jerusalem funeral. Just two months after the Interim Agreement was signed, the Jewish right-wing university student shot Rabin in an effort to derail the peace talks, and while they clearly haven't completely come to a standstill, Rabin's death has had a profound effect on Israeli policy and psychology.

SOME NOTABLE TERRORIST ATTACKS

February 25, 1996 - In a suicide bombing of bus No. 18 near the Central Bus Station in Jerusalem, 26 were killed (17 civilians and 9 soldiers).

March 3, 1996 - In a suicide bombing of bus No. 19 on Jaffa Road in Jerusalem, 18 were killed (16 civilians and 3 soldiers).

March 4, 1996 - Outside Dizengoff Center in Tel Aviv, a suicide bomber detonated a 20-kilogram nail bomb, killing 13 (12 civilians and 1 soldier).

July 30, 1997 - 16 people were killed and 178 wounded in two consecutive suicide bombings in the Mahane Yehuda market in Jerusalem.

September 4, 1997 - Five people were killed and 181 wounded in three suicide bombings on the Ben-Yehuda pedestrian mall in Jerusalem.

Benjamin Netanyahu, the Likud party candidate, defeated Shimon Peres by a razor-thin majority of 50.4%. Netanyahu vowed to continue the peace process, but he's had anything but a light touch. Netanyahu appointed one of the most right-wing governments in Israel's history, and his tough-guy stance has elevated the tensions between Israelis and Palestinians, resulting in anger, clashes, and deaths. One of the most explosive incidents took place shortly after he took office. In September 1996, Netanyahu decided to open an archaeological tunnel near Jerusalem's Al Aqsa Mosque (one of Islam's holiest sites), in the dead of night under heavy military security, thereby stepping on a lot of Palestinian toes. Palestinian forces and rock-hurling Arab youth clashed with Israeli troops in the worst street fighting since the *intifada*, and Israeli tanks were called in for the first time since the 1967 war.

Since then, the Palestinians have continued to be angered by Israel's Agreement infractions: continued emphasis on new and expanded settlements, feet-dragging on troop withdrawal, humiliations imposed on Palestinians, and border-closings that keep workers from their jobs. On Israel's side, they've accused the Palestinian Authority of not doing their part to control Hamas and their terrorist activities.

The recriminations go on and on, with little progress. In January 1997, Netanyahu and Arafat agreed to a partial Israeli military pull-back from Hebron, but shortly thereafter Netanyahu came up with a plan to double the number of homes in Jewish settlements over the next two decades with 30,000 new Jewish homes. Some minor progress was made on plans for a Gaza airport and a safe travel route for Palestinians between the Gaza Strip and the West Bank, but frustration is high among Palestinians.

At present, the Palestinians now have full or partial control over 27 percent of the West Bank. They'd hoped for another 60 percent from the promised three withdrawals At press time, negotiations are at an impasse, with the Palestinians willing to accept a 13% evacuation of the West Bank (one that would give them a contiguous block of land), and Netanyahu digging in his heels at 9% of segmented lands.

5. PLANNING YOUR TRIP

BEFORE YOU GO

If you contact the **Israeli Tourism Board**, *Tel. 800/596-1199*, a good few weeks before you go, they'll send you a full packet. Some of the brochures are just useless glossy pictures, but the maps are quite useful, and it's handy to have them before you get there. You can also call the **Royal Jordanian Tour Desk**, *Tel. 800/758-6878*, if you're planning to visit Jordan.

If you had a dime for every foreign phrase you intended to learn before taking a trip, you'd probably be living in the lap of luxury, but even if you don't become fluent in Hebrew and Arabic before taking off, familiarizing yourself (i.e. learning) the Hebrew letters will be an enormous help.

Destination signs and such suddenly provide information as they were meant to do when the blocky symbols of the Hebrew *Aleph Bayt* become meaningful. And, if you're planning much time in Arab countries, learning the Arabic numbers helps a great deal as well.

INTERNET RESOURCES

The Internet has web sites that provide a wide array of useful and pertinent travel information, from travel advisories to political commentary.
- **US State Department Consular Affairs**
  http://travel.state.gov
- **Israel Tourist Information**
  http://www.infotour.co.il
- **Welcome to Israel**
  http://www.israel-embassy.org.uk/london/web/pages/turisthm.htm
- **Welcome to the Israel Foreign Ministry**
  http://www.israel-mfa.gov.il/index.html

- **Politics – Israeli Culture Net Links**
  http://israeliculture.miningco.msub18.htm
- **Focus on Israel**
  http://www.focusmm.com.au/israel/is_anamn.htm
- **Guide to Mideast Peace Process**
  http://www.israel.org/peace/guide.html
- **ArabNet**
  http://www.arab.net
- **Akhbar.com**
  http://jordan-online.com

WHEN TO GO

If you have the choice of traveling whenever you want, spring and fall have the nicest weather, neither outrageously hot as it can get in summer nor as wet and cold as it can get in winter. Take note, however, of certain Jewish, Christian, and Muslim holidays, when places can be crowded or shut. **Passover**, typically in March or April, is a time when Israelis travel, hotels charge peak season rates, and reservations need to be made months in advance.

The same is true of the **High Holy days** in September-October. **Christmas** and **Easter** pack the houses in Jerusalem and Nazareth, and during **Ramadan**, Muslim restaurants are often closed during the day but open at night (See *Holidays* below for exact dates).

FAHRENHEIT LOW-HIGH AVERAGES

	December	April	August
Jerusalem	47°-56°	53°-69°	66°-86°
Tel Aviv	47°-66°	54°-72°	72°-66°
Tiberias	53°-68°	56°-80°	75°-99°
Haifa	48°-65°	55°-78°	70°-86°
Eilat	51°-74°	63°-87°	79°-104°
Amman	43°-64°	50°-78°	65°-90°

HOLIDAYS

The Jewish religious holidays all start at sundown the evening before the first day, and are called *erev* (evening of), as in Erev Pesakh.

HOLIDAYS OF ALL FAITHS

	1998	1999	Jewish Calendar
Tu B'Shvat -			
(New Year of Trees)	Feb 11	Feb 1	Shevat 15
Purim (Feast of Lots)	Mar 12	Mar 2	Adar 14 (or Adar II)
Passover (Pesakh)	Apr 10-17	Apr 1-8	Nisan 15-22
Holocaust Memorial Day	Apr 23	Apr 13	Nisan 27
Fighters' Memorial Day	Apr 29	Apr 20	Iyar 3
Israel Independ. Day	Apr 30	Apr 21	Iyar 4
Lag B'Omer	May 14	May 4	Iyar 18
Jerusalem Day	May 24	May 14	Iyar 28
Shavuot	May 31	May 21	Sivan 6
Tisha B'Av	Aug 2	Jul 22	Av 9
Rosh Hashana			
(Jewish New Year)	Sept 21-22	Sept 11-12	Tishri 1-2
Yom Kippur			
(Day of Atonement)	Sept 30	Sept 20	Tishri 10
Sukkot	Oct 5-11	Sept 25-Oct 1	Tishri 15-21
Simkhat Torah	Oct 12	Oct 3	Tishri 23
Hannukah	Dec 14-21	Dec 4-11	Kislev 25-Tevet 2

Christian Holiday	1998	1999	
Ash Wednesday	Feb 25	Feb 17	
Palm Sunday	Arpil 5	March 28	
Good Friday	April 10	April 2	
Easter	April 12	April 4	
Pentecost	May 31	May 23	
Christmas	Dec 25	Dec 25	

Muslim Holidays	1998	1999	Muslim Calendar
Ramadan	Dec 20	Dec 9	month of Ramadan
Eid al-Fitr	Jan 30	Jan 19	Ramadan 30
Eid al-Adhah			
(hajj to Mecca)	Apr 8	Mar 28	Zulhijjah 9
Ras as-Sana			
(Islamic New Year)	Apr 28	Apr 18	Muharram 1

WHAT TO PACK

It depends on when you go and who you are, but all variables aside, the general rule is as true as ever: take as little as possible without forgoing the important stuff. For **summer** (April-October), pack for heat. Take swimsuits and sandals, and plenty of changes of cotton shirts, socks (if you wear sneakers), and undergarments, as well as shorts or light skirts/dresses), plus a light jacket or sweater for the coolish nights in the hills. You'll also need a modest outfit for visiting religious sites, which means clothing to cover your legs and shoulders. Israel is fairly casual, but a nice outfit for a splurge meal is a good idea. With the sun in mind, take along a hat, sunglasses, and sunscreen. A water bottle is a good idea, or you can buy a thermal water bottle sling in Israel (which makes a nice souvenir and is easier to pack).

In **winter**, prepare for wet and cold, as well as the occasional warm and dry. Take a thin raincoat (under which you can heap up the sweaters when it's cold), an umbrella, and waterproof boots. Take a swim suit as well, for hot spring visits or Red Sea trips. Clothes that can be layered work best, as you never know in winter.

Clothing and season aside, it's the sundries that make the difference. Hotels generally provide towels, though many hostels don't, but a laundry bag is always useful. No matter when you travel, take a small **first aid kit** with plenty of aspirin, Band-Aids, corn pads, etc. to deal with blisters and pains from lots of walking. It's easy to catch a cold when traveling, and while it's not what you want to think about when packing, your favorite cough drops or cold capsules can be a comfort in the unhappy event. Personal toiletries are available in all the brands you're used to, but they aren't cheap, and earplugs come in very handy in all sorts of otherwise unbearable situations. A small flashlight is useful, as is the all-purpose Swiss army knife, and you may want a small spoon on picnics.

Binoculars come in handy on hikes, and swim goggles can take the place of a snorkel mask in a pinch (and they take less room to pack). Sunscreen is necessary, and you'll need a small day pack as well. And don't forget your driver's license, long distance calling card, and insurance card as well.

MAKING RESERVATIONS

Hotels and hospices appreciate reservations, and it's a good idea during peak seasons (July/August and the Jewish Holidays of Rosh Hashana and Pesakh, as well as Christmas and Easter in some cities). Faxing is probably the most convenient way to reserve (from the US, that is), but the phone will do as well, and the hotel clerks generally speak passable English.

Some hostels take reservations, but for many it's just a matter of showing up right after check-out for the best shot. There's plenty of turnover, and a little walking will get you a room or bed of some sort.

STUDY TOURS/LANGUAGE LEARNING PACKAGES

Ulpan is the place to go to learn Hebrew quickly and well. There are City Ulpan and Kibbutz Ulpan, and their goal is to provide students with a working knowledge of conversational Hebrew, to enable them to read simple Hebrew texts and newspapers, and to build a foundation for further study. The teachers are trained to teach Hebrew as a second language, and most of the students are *Olim* (people immigrating to Israel). Classes usually have 15-25 students, meet for 18-24 hours a week, and last four and a half to five months. For more information, contact the **Ministry of Immigrant Absorption** office, *2 HaKirya Building, Jerusalem, 91006, Tel. 02-675-2760.*

Jewish Agency for Israel, *3 Ben Shatach, Jerusalem, Tel. 02-623-1823,* also has information on less formal study programs for tourists. They're open Sunday, Monday, Wednesday-Thursday 8am-6pm, Tuesday 8am-4pm, and Friday 10am-1pm. Write them at the **Center for Ulpanim and Counseling for Young Adults**, *12 Kaplan, Tel Aviv.*

American Zionist Youth Foundation, *Tel. 800/274-7723 or 212/339-6941, Fax 212/775-4781,* in New York also arranges study, archaeological digs, University, and language programs in Jerusalem, Tel Aviv, Haifa, and Be'er Sheva. Their office is at the *University Student Department, Israel Action Center, 110 E. 59th Street, 3rd floor, New York, NY 10022.*

6. ARRIVALS & DEPARTURES

CUSTOMS & ENTRANCE REQUIREMENTS

You need a valid passport, and when you enter Israel you'll receive a three month visitor's visa free of charge (you can ask not to have your passport stamped if you so wish), and you can extend your visa for a nominal fee at any of the Ministry of the Interior offices in any of the main cities in Israel, the same place to apply if you want to work in Israel.

Israel's airports and the Rafiah Terminal have a **customs** clearance system featuring **the Green channel** (if you have no goods to declare) and the **Red channel** (if you do). You needn't declare any of the following items (and can therefore go Green): personal clothing, alcoholic drinks (up to two liters wine or one liter spirits for individuals 17 or older), perfumes (up to .25 liters per person), tobacco products (up to 250 cigarettes or grams for individuals 17 or older), and gifts, so long as they don't exceed the above limits or $150 in total value. You are also allowed items such as radios, tape recorders, musical instruments, and other such travel needs.

You must line up at the Red channel, however, if you possess any items to declare, such as a camcorder, personal computer, diving equipment, etc. For these and similar items, you'll have to pay a deposit for duties and taxes which will be refunded when you bring them back out of the country.

INTERNATIONAL ARRIVALS & DEPARTURES

By Air

Ben Gurion International Airport, *Lod, near Tel Aviv, Tel. 03-971-0000 or Tel. 03-971-0111, Fax 03-972-1217,* is the main airport in Israel, with scheduled flights from 24 international airlines. Ben Gurion Airport is near Tel Aviv but you can come to or leave from Jerusalem directly by shuttle, bus, or taxi. Flight information, *Tel. 03-972-3344*, on arrivals and departures is available in English.

El Al, *Center 1, 49 Yirmeyahu, Tel. 02-624-6726*, does advance check-in near Jaffa Road in Jerusalem. They're open Sunday-Thursday 1-10pm, Saturday one hour past sunset till 10pm. Other airlines may start soon – ask the airline for specifics. Otherwise, you'll need to check in at Ben Gurion two hours before you're scheduled to depart.

Confirm your departing flight at least 72 hours before you're scheduled to take off (don't neglect this – people have been bumped from international flights and their seats assigned to others).

The **departure taxes**, usually already added into the price of your ticket, are $13 from Ben Gurion, $7 from Jerusalem airport, $11 if you're going to Egypt, and zero from Eilat's airport. Due to the nature of the politics of the region, security is a serious issue at Ben Gurion (and other Israeli entry points). In-depth security checks are normal and necessary, and if you are selected for the experience, just take it in stride.

From/To the Airport

Nesher, *21 King George, Tel. 02-625-3233/5332*, has a taxi service that goes to Ben Gurion for NIS 32, including pick-up at your door and two pieces of luggage. Reserve one day in advance.

Egged Central Bus Station, *Jaffa Road, Tel. 02-530-4704*, has buses to Ben Gurion Airport.

By Land

Travelers wishing the most up-to-date border crossing information should contact the US Embassy in Tel Aviv or the US Consulate General in Jerusalem.

For further entry information, contact the **Embassy of Israel**, *3514 International Dr., NW, Washington, DC 20008, Tel. 202-364-5500*, or the nearest **Israeli Consulate General** in San Francisco, Miami, Atlanta, Chicago, New Orleans, Boston, Los Angeles, New York, Philadelphia, or Houston, or the US Consulate in Tel Aviv, email: acs.amcit-telaviv@dos.us-state.gov.

Israel-Jordan By Bus or Taxi

There are three land crossings between Israel and Jordan, evenly dispersed from north to south, but I'll skip the border crossing near Eilat since. From Israel to Jordan the **departure tax** is NIS 53 or NIS 103 (depending on where you cross), while Jordan's overland departure tax is JD4 or JD5, depending on where you cross (as compared to JD6 by sea and JD10 by air). There are buses and taxis to and from the crossings, but private cars are not allowed across. To Enter Jordan from Israel you need a Jordanian visa. You can obtain one at the Arava and Beit She'an crossings (JD15 for US, JD31 for Canada, JD23 for UK, JD5 for Ireland, JD4 for New Zealand, Australia and South Africa go free), but to enter via Allenby Bridge you'll need the visa in advance. You can get one at a Jordanian consulate before you leave home, or in Tel Aviv from its Jordanian Consulate, *14 Aba Hillel, Ramat Gan, Tel. 03-751-7722.*

The **Allenby Bridge**, *near Jericho and just 40 kilometers east of Jerusalem, Tel. 02-994-2302,* is the central and most regulated crossing between the two countries, with tons of security measures and steps, and an Israeli departure tax of NIS 103 (or Jordanian departure tax of JD5). The bridge is open Sunday-Thursday 8am-midnight, Friday, Saturday 8:00am-3:00pm, but it's better to get there as early as you can to make the transport hookups (the Jett bus is finished by 1:30pm, though taxis still wait for late arrivals) and straggle through customs. Unlike in Eilat, *you can not get a Jordan visa at the Allenby Bridge.* If you wish to use this crossing, get your visa in the US, Tel Aviv, or in Egypt.

Just to get there is a hassle. You can take an Egged bus (NIS 17) as far as the junction outside Jericho, from which point you'll need to hunt up a taxi. Special taxis cost a bundle. The best way to get there is via the American Colony taxi, *Tel. 02-628-5171,* for $30, but you need to call the day ahead and set it up.

Close to the border things start to get confused. The taxi may be stopped at the document checkpoint a few kilometers from the bridge, leaving you to board the Arab bus to customs for a few more shekels. Your best bet is to make certain in advance that your taxi is authorized to go all the way to the bridge. At the Allenby Bridge Terminal you get your passport stamped and get directed to the NIS 10 (or $3 or JD1.5) tourist minibus (separated from the Arabs in transit who get to board a local bus) to cross the bridge. On the mini-journey, the driver collects passports and you're off to Jordan's passport control, where you stand around and wait, and wait some more.

The Jordanian JETT buses are gone by 1:30pm or so, but there are other buses for JD1.5, and you can take a taxi to Abduli Bus Station in Amman for JD2 per person. Going to the bridge from Amman, the JETT buses leave daily at 6:30am, cost JD6, and take one hour.

The **Jordan River** (Sheikh Husseini Bridge) crossing, *north near Beit She'an, Tel. 06-658-6448, Fax 06-658-6421,* is open Sunday-Thursday 6:30am-10pm and Friday-Saturday 8am-8pm. Departure tax here is NIS 53, and you can get your visas here. Beit She'an city bus #16 leaves 8:15am, 9:20am, and 2:15pm for the border. This petite, Ottoman-built bridge sees a lot of traffic, so leave half a day for the ordeal. You can exchange money on the Jordanian side, then take a bus or share taxi to nearby Shona. From there you can catch a minibus to Irbid.

DOMESTIC ARRIVALS & DEPARTURES

By Air

Arkia Air operates domestic flights from Jerusalem to Rosh Pina ($46) and Eilat ($20). From Eilat you can fly to Jerusalem, Tel Aviv, and Haifa. And from Masada you can go to Tel Aviv.

By Bus

Egged Central Bus Station, *Jaffa Road, Tel. 02-530-4704,* is way west of downtown. You'll need to take a city bus (or taxi) to or from your hotel unless you're staying at the Holiday Inn nearby. It's a big station, with buses departing to all over the country (including Ben Gurion Airport). The 405 double decker goes from/to Tel Aviv, direct, for NIS 17. Bus 444 goes to Eilat via the Dead Sea for NIS 54, and bus 392 also goes to Eilat for NIS 47, and transfers in Beersheva.

Arab Bus Stations serve destinations within the Palestinian Authority. There is one station on Suleiman between Damascus and Herod's Gates for southern routes and another on Nablus serving northern routes. The 22 goes to Bethlehem when politics allow.

By Train

The **Train Station,** *Remez Square, Tel. 03-693-7515 (Tel Aviv),* is south of Moshe Yenim and Liberty Bell Park (buses 5, 6, 8, 14, 18, 21, 30, 31, and 48 all go there). Trains go to Tel Aviv Sunday-Thursday at 2:53pm, Friday at 11:56am (arriving two hours later) for NIS 17, continuing one hour more to Haifa for a total of NIS 33.5. Student discount is 25% off, and children 4-10 ride 50% off.

By Car

For now you can pass back and forth between Israeli and Palestinian Authority lands with just your passport without needing extra visas, but this may change so check for the latest updates.

7. GETTING AROUND JERUSALEM

BY CAR

There are lots of car rental agencies all over Israel, making for convenient (though not cheap) transportation, offering an ever-changing variety of deals and packages. Sometimes good deals can be arranged from the US before you go, but there's not much difference. If you leave it until Israel, shop around and pay attention to the ads in the tourist offices, but be aware that many of the touted prices don't include insurance fees. Winter rates are lower than summer, week-long rentals work out better than day-to-day, and unlimited mileage is worth the extra cost.

Rentals average around $40-$60 a day and $200-$300 a week for economy cars rented in Israel, and $25 (plus 25¢-55¢ a mile) to $33 (unlimited mileage) a day and $196-$420 a week if arranged from the US, plus insurance. To rent a car you need to be over 21 years old, have a US driver's license or an international driver's license, and have a major credit card.

Rules of the road: you drive on the right side of the road, there are lots of one-way streets, and when driving in the winter, keep your lights on, even during the day (required by law).

Parking zones: red & white means no parking ever; blue & white means you need a parking ticket 8am-7pm (they can be bought in most grocery stores or lottery kiosks); white lines mean free parking 8am-5pm; red & yellow indicates a bus stop and taxi station.

BY BUS

Egged (pronounced with two syllables) is the main intercity bus company in Israel, and except in Tel Aviv where Dan Company reigns supreme, they operate most of the intracity buses as well. Egged sells **Israbus passes** (available to tourists but not to locals) which give you unlimited bus use for the duration of the pass. Be warned, however, that they don't work on Dan buses, so they aren't such a hot idea if you're going to Tel Aviv.

They cost NIS 249 for 7 days; NIS 399 for 14 days; NIS 499 for 21 days; for more information, call Egged, *Tel. 03-527-1212.* Otherwise, transport costs within a city run you NIS 4.20 for each trip, and between cities it depends: Jerusalem to Tel Aviv costs NIS 17, to Haifa it costs NIS 34, and the five-hour jaunt to Eilat is NIS 56 (and student discounts are always available). Most buses don't run on Shabbat, and up-to-date information is available (after a patient wait) from *Tel. 03-537-5555* or *Tel. 04-854-9555* or *Tel. 02-530-4704.*

BY TRAIN

Israel's train line runs from Jerusalem to Tel Aviv and Tel Aviv to northern points such as Netanya, Haifa, Akko, and Nahariya. They are a little bit cheaper and slower than the buses, but the routes (especially up the coast to Haifa) are more scenic than the bus trip. They schedule fewer departures than the buses, however (especially the Tel Aviv -Jerusalem trip).

For the latest fares and information, call 03-693-7515 in Tel Aviv or 04-856-4154 in Haifa.

BY SHERUT TAXI

A sherut taxi is a shared taxi service that operates at a fixed rate between cities and on some urban routes as well. The ride can be more comfortable than buses, and the rates are competitive.

BY PRIVATE TAXI

Known as *special* taxis in Israel, they run on meters (insist on this) with 25% higher fares 9pm-5:30am, Shabbat, and holidays. There is also a fare surcharge for pick-up arranged by phone. Taxi-related complaints can be addressed to the **Controller of Road Transport**,*Tel. 03-532-1351 for Tel Aviv and the south, Tel. 02-531-9550 for Jerusalem, and Tel. 04-853-6711 for Haifa and the north.*

8. BASIC INFORMATION

BAR/BAT MITZVAHS

Bar and Bat Mitzvahs in Israel are big business, as arranged by a number of US-based agencies. At the Western Wall in Jerusalem or amid the stone ruins of the Zealot Synagogue on Masada, thousands of adolescents make the journey with families and friends in tow. **Tova Gilead**, *983 Port Washington Blvd., Port Washington, NY 11050, Tel. 800/242-8682, Fax 516-883-8383* arranges ceremonies at Masada for $2,200-$3,050 per person, including round-trip El Al air fare NY-Tel Aviv, 5-star hotel accommodations with some meals, and sightseeing trips of 8-15 days. **Travelcare**, *97-77 Queens Blvd., Rego Park, NY 11374, Tel. 800/233-1336 or 718/997-0090*, also features Masada or Wall ceremonies and 14 days of sightseeing for package deals from $4,900 (two adults and one child per room) to $7,000 (two adults, four children, two rooms), plus airfare.

If you want to do it on your own, contact the **Jerusalem Regional Office**, *Ministry of Tourism, PO Box 1018, Jerusalem, Tel. 02-675-4877, Fax 02-675-4974*, for an application form. A bar/bat mitzvah at the Western Wall is free (though donations are accepted). You can bring along your own rabbi or contact the Western Wall rabbi (*Rabbi Nahum, c/o Tzvi Hoffman, Hechal Shlomo, Moreshet Hotel, 58 King George St., Jerusalem, Tel. 02-624-7112 Fax 02-623-3620*. Note, however, that Western Wall services are all orthodox, so a bat mitzvah girl can't read from the Torah. Instead, her father or other male relative can read from the Torah during morning services.

Services for both genders can be arranged at **Masada**, *Ms. Nava Granitz, Tel. 07-658-4207, Fax 07-658-4464*, the **Neot Kedumim Biblical Landscape Reserve**, *Tel. 08-977-0770, Fax 08-977-0775*, or another synagogue of your choice.

BUSINESS HOURS

Stores are generally open Sunday-Thursday 9am-7pm, though some opt for mid-day breaks between 1-4pm. Stores usually close early Fridays and eves of Jewish Holidays. Muslim shops are closed on Fridays and Christian-owned stores close for Sunday.

COST OF LIVING & TRAVEL

Israel isn't cheap, but neither do you have to drop a pile of money; it depends on your budget and the level of luxury you want and are willing to pay for. Lodgings typically start at $7-$10 for dorm beds, you can get cheapish hotel rooms for $50-$80, and for 5 star luxury you should expect to pay $200-$400 (depending on the season and the city). Most hotels have different prices for the different travel seasons, with Low Season in mid-winter, Regular Season, and High or Peak Season including July-August and the Passover holidays.

For food there's more of a range. You can live very well for very little if you have a taste for falafel, hummus, and bagel, spending no more than $1-$2 for a snack or lunch, while local meat dishes (shishlik, shwarma) are a little more but still not what you'd call expensive at $4-$5 a pop. Full meals of local cuisine (Yemenite, Russian, etc.) start around $6, while if you yearn for fish or European cuisines you start paying bigger bucks at fancier restaurants, spending $20-$30 a meal.

Travel is cheaper by bus and train ($1 for city transit and $4-$9 between most cities), more expensive by rental car, which average around $40-$60 a day and $200-$300 a week for economy cars, and more expensive still by organized tours, typically $250 or so for a 3 day trip.

ELECTRICITY

Israel's electric current is 220 volts AC, 50 Hertz. Most Israel sockets accommodate the triangular three-pronged plugs, but they'll generally take the European round two-prong just fine. Electric shavers and such will need adapters, and you can buy these at any hardware store. Some of the finer hotels, however, have adapters built in to the bathrooms.

HEALTH CONCERNS

There are no vaccination requirements for entering Israel, though the usual precautions of hepatitis shots, polio boosters, and diarrhea pills are always advised. The most common health concerns typically involve reactions to heat and all that walking. Israeli camping supply stores sell nifty thermal slings just the right size for mineral water bottles, or bring your own favorite water bottles to take on all your hikes.

Call **101** anywhere in the country at any time for **emergency first aid** provided by Magen David Adom (the Red Star of David, Israel's version of Red Cross). The *Jerusalem Post* lists daily rosters of emergency hospitals, dental clinics, and all-night pharmacies.

Most US medical insurance isn't accepted right off the bat in Israeli hospitals. You generally need to pay them, and then get reimbursed later. **INS-CARE**, *9 Ben Yehuda, Tel Aviv, postal address POB 26136, IL 61261, Tel Aviv, Tel./Fax 03-517-1613*, offers services for insured tourists, meaning tourists who have taken medical insurance with them at the rate of $1.50 a day for a minimum of three months. For this fee you get an INS-CARE card providing access to their clinics (open 24 hours) and affiliated hospitals throughout the country. They offer a lot, including ambulance service, dental clinics, and specialist doctors such as internal, gynecological, and orthopedic.

In 1983, the Knesset banned **smoking** in public places such as buses, taxis, etc. A recent amendment bans smoking in all work places (except for closed, well-ventilated smoking rooms). It's not well adhered to, so if the smoke is bothering you, you can try saying something, or complain to the Ministry of Health, *Ben Tabai St. #2, Jerusalem, Attention: Occupational Health Service, Tel. 02-670-5705.*

Other Medical Services

Intensive care ambulances can be found in Jerusalem, *Tel. 02-562-3133.*

• **Shahal**, *Tel. 03-562-5555 or 177-022-1818*, is a private intensive care service for heart patients.

• **Eran Mental Health Hotline** can be reached in Jerusalem, *Tel. 02-561-0303*, or *Tel. 1201* anywhere in Israel.

• **Rape Crisis Line**: *Tel. 1202.*

MONEY & BANKING

Israeli currency is the **New Israeli Shekel (NIS)**, and its exchange rate hovers fairly steadily around 3.5 shekels to the American dollar, making each shekel worth about 29¢. The shekel contains 100 smaller units called *agorot.*

American Express (in Tel Aviv and Jerusalem) exchanges travelers' cheques with no commission or fee, whether you're a member or no. Banks change money, but many of them do so at usurious rates or with astounding commissions attached. And hotels change money, often at poor rates. Of the main banks (First International, Leumi Bank, Israeli Discount Bank, Mitzahi Bank, and Hapoalim Bank) Israeli Discount and Hapoalim generally give fair rates, but it changes dramatically from city to city.

GETTING MARRIED IN ISRAEL

*It is possible for non-Israelis to tie the knot in Israel, but it's neither simple nor easy. Not only must you be committed to one another, you need a strong desire to say your vows in Eretz Yisrael to persevere. First thing is to contact the **Marriage Rabbinut**. While there is such an office in all the major cities (in Tel Aviv contact the Tel Aviv Marriage Rabbinut, 33 King David St., Tel. 03-696-4181) most folks want to do the honors in Jerusalem.*

***Step 1**: Beit Hadin, 9 Koresh (a small street off Shlomtsion Hamalka), Tel. 02-623-3696, Fax 02-623-2396, open Sunday-Thursday 8:30am-1:30pm) is the Rabbinical Court, and this is where you both go to prove you are Jewish and single. Bring passport with valid visa, a letter from your home Jewish community rabbi attesting to your Jewish and single status, and if possible, a copy of your mother's ketubah (Jewish wedding certificate). Fill out a form and open a file (NIS 170 each). You also need to go to the Chief Rabbinate, Yirmeyahu Street, corner of Hamem-gimel Street, to get a stamp of approval that your rabbi is recognized. You must then bring that approval paper back to Beit Hadin, 9 Koresh, to get a court date (generally two-three weeks unless it's urgent).*

***Step 2**: Attend the court date (back at Beit Hadin), bringing two witnesses to swear you are single and Jewish. The witnesses should be relatives or friends – male, if possible (there have been cases where a female witness was not accepted). A few days later you should receive a letter attesting to your single Jewish status.*

***Step 3**: Take your letter to the Rabbinut Moatza Datit, 12 Hachavatzelet, off Jaffa, Tel. 02-625-6811, Fax 02-625-0600, open Sunday-Thursday 8am-12:30pm. There you open a file to get married (for NIS 500, but only NIS 250 if you're making Aliya). Bring your passport, the letter, and three pictures each.*

***Step 4**: They will give the woman a date to meet a counselor (Rabbinit) to set possible dates for marriage, depending on days of "purity".*

All these steps take time and should be done way in advance so you have time to plan the actual wedding.

Travelers' Cheques are the safest way to carry currency, but it's advisable to bring some hard US cash as well, $100-$200 in denominations of mostly 20s with a few 10s, 5s, and 1s. The cash is useful when banks are closed and you just need a few shekels to see you through. It's especially handy if you're traveling to Jordan and/or Egypt as well, and sometimes gets you a discount. It is illegal to change money on the street with individuals, though police look the other way. Still, it is a risk and you are likely to be ripped off.

Credit cards (Visa, Mastercard, Diners Club, and in some places American Express as well) are widely accepted by all major hotels, restaurants, shops, and car rentals. Plastic is a good alternative to coming laden with checks.

To have money sent, call **Western Union**, *Tel. 02-629-0447, or 177-022-2131, a toll-free number.*

POST OFFICE

You can mail letters, cards, and parcels from any postal branch around the country. Most are open all Sunday-Thursday 7am-7pm and Friday 7am-noon, but some of the branches close for a mid-day break.

The main city GPOs have **Poste Restante** sections (mail should be addressed to you, c/o Poste Restante, followed by GPO, the city, and Israel), and American Express (in Tel Aviv and Jerusalem, open Sunday-Thursday 9am-5pm, Friday 9am-1pm) holds mail (marked Hold for Client) for American Express card holders.

RETIRING IN ISRAEL & MAKING ALIYAH

There are an number of good resources for those wishing to **retire** in Israel. **A.A.C.I.** (Association of Americans and Canadians in Israel), *6 Mane, Jerusalem, mailing address: POB 30017, Jerusalem 93341, Tel. 02-561-7151, and 22 Mazeh, Tel Aviv ,Tel. 03-629-9799*, has a wealth of resources for North Americans moving to Israel, including seminars and info on personal financial planning and staying current with Social Security from abroad, doing business in Israel, finances and investment, and more. Membership (NIS 75 a year) entitles you to travel bargains, financial assistance, health insurance discounts, and social, educational, cultural, and employment information. You can also contact the **Ministry of Immigrant Absorption**, *2 Hakirya Building, 91006 Jerusalem, Tel. 02-624-1121*, for more information.

Making **Aliyah**, meaning literally to ascend and figuratively to leave your homeland and emigrate to Israel, is an age-old tradition among Jews, and one encouraged and supported by the Israeli government. In the Zionist pursuit of Jews returning to their homeland, the government will help sponsor it all, with Absorption Centers to help set you up and pick up part of the tab for moving, studying, and living.

The *Aliyah Pocket Guide* answers all the questions about customs, health care, employment, and more. To get the goods, contact the main **Israel Aliya Center** in the US, *110 E. 59th, New York, NY 10022, Tel. 212/339-6000, Fax 212/832-2597; or 20 Park Plaza, Statler Building, Room 1020, Boston, MA 02116, Tel. 617/423-0868, Fax 617/423-0468.*

STAYING OUT OF TROUBLE

It is easy to have a worry-free holiday in Israel, but in a country with as many sensitive political and religious issues as Israel has, you would do well to tread with care and avoid what dangers you can. Argument may be one of the Israeli national past-times, but people have lost friends and family, and emotions may run high. Some things are beyond your control, but there are a few precautions you can take.

Since many of you will be visiting other places in Israel, this advice goes beyond Jerusalem:

• Make a photo copy of the first page of your passport and keep it separate.
• Call Washington, *Tel. 202/364-5500*, for up-to-date information on the political situation before leaving the US.
• Don't go hiking on uncharted trails in the Golan Heights as there are still unexploded land mines up there, and don't go into orthodox neighborhoods dressed immodestly, as assaults have been known to take place.
• The best advice from embassy officials is to avoid power struggles with 18-year-olds carrying guns. Good advice in general, but in a country on edge from terrorism and war, arguing with youths in power isn't advisable. Remember this when some official is giving you the business in the airport, and keep cool.
• Recent advice from embassy folks in the know warned against travel in Gaza and Hebron. In Gaza there's a poor economy and it's getting worse, resulting in a hostile and frustrated populace. The West Bank is pretty calm and Jericho is open and anxious for tourists, but Hebron is still tense, and certain strike dates and anniversaries were observed such as the 23rd (anniversary of the Baruch Goldstein massacre), as well as the 9th and 17th. Wadi Kelt, a popular oasis near Jerusalem, has also been deemed unsafe lately. If you're taking an organized tour, the companies keep tabs on where not to go. If you're setting off on your own, contact the embassy in Jerusalem for the latest scoop, and if you're planning to go into occupied territory, it's a good idea to let the nearest embassy or consulate know.
• According to the Security Advisor in the Jerusalem Consulate, East Jerusalem, Bethlehem, Jericho are all fine to visit, but it's not a great idea to wander around at night, not so much because of trouble but because things close up after dark so you stand out on the streets. They also advised tourists to veer clear of Arab bus lines because they are more prone to break downs and reckless driving.
• While the nature of terrorism is such that you never know where and when it's going to hit, a number of the recent suicide bombings have targeted public buses carrying soldiers returning to duty or leaving base for the weekend.

• If you get in difficulties (jail, lost passport, etc.) while in Israel, call the US Embassy, *Tel. 03-517-4338*, during business hours, *Tel. 03-517-4347*, after hours.

The police stress that you should keep an eye on your belongings, do not accept gifts from strangers, make use of hotel safes, and take all the usual common sense precautions. In Israel, an unattended bag is considered a potential terrorist bomb, and the authorities don't fool around on this issue.

Anywhere in the country, **100** will reach the **police** and **102** will get you the **fire** department.

TAXES

There is a $17 airport departure tax, but it's usually included in your ticket. If you're not sure, ask your airline.

Israel's 17% **VAT** (**Value Added Tax**) is levied on all goods and services, but if you (the foreign tourist) pay in foreign currency you are exempt from paying VAT on hotels, tours, car rentals, domestic flights, and hotel meals. You'll often see store signs boasting the VAT reduction for foreign currency purchases. In addition, if you pay with foreign currency for an item worth $50 or more (when shopping at Ministry of Tourism recommended stores – you'll see the seal of approval), you're entitled to a 5% discount and a VAT refund when you leave the country.

Not applicable to tobacco, electrical or photographic purchases, your item must remain in its sealed see-through bag so you can show it to officials in Bank Leumi (in Ben Gurion Airport) and get your money back. If you leave from elsewhere in Israel, customs officials will stamp your invoice and the refund will be mailed to you back home.

TELEGRAMS

The central telegraph office is open 24 hours a day at *23 Jaffa Street*, providing telegraph, telex, and fax services. **Solan Telecom** (see below) also sends telegrams and is open 24 hours.

TELEPHONES

• **Phoning/faxing Israel and the Palestinian Authority from the US**: *dial 011-972*, the city code (just the single digit, no "0"), then the number.
• **Phoning/faxing direct to the US from Israel**: *dial 001 or 013 or 012*, and the area code and number; to charge the call to your long-distance **MCI** account, *dial 177-150-2727*, **AT&T** *is 177-100-2727*, and **Sprint** *is 177-102-2727* (don't give up, it may take a long time to get through).

Or, go to one of the **Solan Telecom Centers** in Tel Aviv or Jerusalem.They are open 24 hours a day, every day, and place discount international telephone calls. They also can send faxes and provide modem hookups.

• **Phoning/faxing within Israel**: use the two-digit city code (0_) and the phone number if you're phoning another district; use just the phone number without the two-digit area code if phoning within the district. The prefix "050" indicates the number belongs to a cell phone.

Public phones, available in post offices, on the street (often quite noisy), and in many hotel lobbies (generally the quietest place to make a call) operate by tokens sold at the post office, by shekel, and most convenient of all, by phone card (sold at post offices, Solan Offices, and vendors).

The **phone cards** are sold in denominations of 20 (NIS 10.5), 50 (NIS 23), and 120 units (NIS 52), and they make long-distance (within Israel) calls much easier. The cost of a call varies greatly by time of day, with one unit lasting 72 seconds from the 8am-1pm slot, 144 seconds from 1pm-8pm, and 15 minutes from 10pm-7am.

TELEVISION & RADIO

• **English TV news**: Channel 1 at 6:15pm except on Shabbat, and at 4:30pm Erev Shabbat.
• **English Radio news**: Kol Yisrael 927 kh in north, 954 in Jerusalem and central, 7am, 5pm, 8pm.
• **BBC Radio news**: 130 AM with hourly news reports and other English programs

TIME

Given relative to Greenwich Mean Time (GMT) and US time zones, Israel is two hours ahead of GMT, 7 hours ahead of Eastern Standard Time, and 10 hours ahead of Pacific Standard Time. So in the summer when it's 7pm in Israel, it's 5pm in London, noon in New York, 11am in Chicago, 10am in Denver, and 9am in San Francisco.

TIPPING

Ten to fifteen percent in general is expected in nice restaurants. Side street nooks and market restaurants aren't as sophisticated. Look at the tables around you to get a sense of what the locals are doing.

FOR MORE INFORMATION...

Call **Israeli Tourism**, *Tel. 800-596-1199*, for maps and a general tourist packet, but good luck getting more specific help.

Jewish Literacy by Rabbi Joseph Telushkin is a magnificent source of insight into the Jewish religion and culture.

Dictionary of Jewish Lore and Legend, compiled by Alan Unterman, further explains Jewish terms, traditions, and practices.

The Joys of Yiddish by Leo Rosten may not provide practical daily vocabulary, but it's most amusing, and the Jewish culture really comes through the definitions and anecdotes.

A Concise History of the Middle East by Arthur Goldschmidt does an excellent job explaining the history and growth of Islam as well as the political and cultural shifts through the ages in the Middle East.

Jerusalem Walks by Nitza Rosovsky details a variety of Jerusalem routes.

Israel, a Phaidon Art and Architecture Guide by Prentice Hall Press is full of architectural and Archaeological details about sites throughout Israel.

The Source, a fictional historical novel by James Michener, provides an entertaining introduction to archaeology and the region's history.

Islamic Monuments in Cairo - A Practical Guide by Richard Parker does a good job with Cairo.

Khul-Khad - Five Egyptian Women Tell Their Stories by Nayra Atiya is well written and is an in to the flavor of Egyptian culture.

Nine Parts of Desire: the Hidden World of Islamic Women by Geraldine Brooks takes a personal, personable, and provocative look behind the Middle East's back door.

WEIGHTS & MEASURES

Israel uses the metric system.

inches to centimeters	x 2.54
centimeters to inches	x 0.39
feet to meters	x 0.30
yards to meters	x 0.91
meters to yards	x 1.09
miles to kilometers	x 1.61
kilometers to miles	x 0.62
acres to hectares	x 0.40
hectares	x 2.47
Centigrade to Fahr.	x 1.8 plus 32
Fahr. to Centigrade	minus 32 then x .55
meters to feet	x 3.28
ounces to grams	x 28.35
grams to ounces	x 0.035
kg to pounds	x 2.21
pounds to kg	x 0.45
US tons to kg	x 907
gallons to liters	x 3.79
liters to gallons	x 0.26
British tons to kg	x 1016
British tons	= 2240 lbs
US tons	= 2000 lbs

9. FOOD & DRINK

The cuisine of Israel is one of the major pleasures of a trip here, or it can be if you venture away from the hotel dining room and sample some of what the locals eat. If you're looking for American style food, however, you'll probably be disappointed. It exists, but the quality is nowhere near what you can find in the foods people have been making here for centuries.

There are lots of ethnic cuisines to choose from, and they've got some exquisite specialties to offer. Arabic (aka oriental or Mediterranean) food predominates with its falafel and hummus, but there's also Moroccan and Tunisian, Yemenite, Russian, Kurdish, Hungarian, and what's loosely called Jewish food, which is really Ashkenazi Jewish cuisine. Most of the restaurants are kosher, some are glatt kosher (see kosher under Religion in Chapter 3, *Land & People*), and a few aren't kosher at all.

ARABIC OR ORIENTAL CUISINE

The **falafel** reigns supreme; it's good, nourishing, cheap food, and when it's done just right it can be sublime (but done poorly it's a mushy, boring affair). Made of mashed chick peas and spices and then deep-fried, it's the staple food stall snack stuffed in a pita with a variety of salad toppings (note: Israelis define "salads" much more broadly than do Americans or Europeans).

Hummus, a dip made from chick peas and olive oil, is another standard, and restaurants in Jerusalem war over who has the best (see the Jerusalem section for the answers). Served with a basket of pita bread (unleavened disk-shaped bread that can be opened to form a pocket) it can make a light lunch by itself, but it's also used to line the pita for falafel and other pita pocket sandwiches. **Tehina**, another favorite falafel sandwich addition, is a dip made from sesame paste and olive oil, and **baba ghanoush** is a smoky eggplant-based dip with tehina mixed in.

Fuul (pronounced fool, and sometimes spelled that way, too) is made from fava beans, sometimes mashed with garlic and lemon, sometimes whole. Also in the snack or quick meal department is the ubiquitous **shwarma**, a sandwich of sliced grilled meat (carved off a rotating, grilling chunk that's meant to be lamb but is usually turkey, packed like pressboard with old meat ends). The meat goes in a pita (or a larger flat bread rolled like a burrito) and filled with all the same salad options as the falafel. **Labane**, a goat cheese and olive oil dip, is another light lunch or dinner appetizer option. Order a **mezza** and you'll get a whole plate with tastes of salads, **dolma** (stuffed grape leaves) and pita. **Majadera** is a rice and lentils side dish, and **kubbeh** is ground spiced meat stuffed in a cracked wheat casing and deep fried. For more substantial meals, there are a variety of grilled meats such as **shishlik** (meat chunks grilled on skewers), and **kebab** (spiced minced meat, also grilled on skewers). They can both be very tasty, but kids tend to distrust the kebabs because they're not familiar with the spices.

And for dessert, there's honey-sweet **baklava**, a flaky pastry with honey and a variety of possible extras like pistachio nuts, for example, that can be heavenly, or just sweet and viscous.

While this food can be found all over Israel, not to mention Egypt and Jordan, it's worth it to seek out a truly fine restaurant (try East Jerusalem) at least once to see what this cuisine is like at its very best.

EASTERN EUROPEAN CUISINE

The standard Ashkenazi appetizers are **chopped liver**, **gefilte fish**, and **stuffed cabbage** (or other vegetables, they're stuffed with a mix of meat, rice, nuts and spices). Not everyone's cup of tea but no less authentic is **pickled herring**, **patcha** (jellied calf foot), and **kishke** (stuffed stomach lining).

Soup is the specialty of this cuisine, starring **chicken soup**, **kneidlach** or **kreplach soup** with dumplings (some filled with meat), as well as **borsht** (beet soup, hot with meat and cabbage or cold and meatless), and a **goulash soup** that changes shape from venue to venue. **Schnitzel** is a popular main dish, a bit lacking in pizzazz though perfectly adequate as a meal. Other sturdy but zipless meals include roast or boiled chicken and pot roast.

Tcholent is a ground up heavy meaty stew, usually including some innards, and traditional for Shabbat. Other organ meals include hot potted **tongue**, **pupiks** (chicken gizzards, *pupik* means belly button), **spleen**, or **lungs** in gravy. At dairy restaurants (kosher and with no meat) **blintzes** are popular, stuffed with either cheese or fruit.

YEMENITE CUISINE

A delicious and often overlooked cuisine, many of the dishes are similar to other Arabic standards. Hummus, tehina, and baba ghanoush are all available, though the hummus with egg is a different treat. **Mellawach** is unique, however. It's a kind of baked unleavened bread (different than pita) that is either covered with a sauce or filled with meat or vegetables, and it's a traditional Yemenite dish.

Also traditional, though not always found at restaurants that cater to tourists, are the **soups**. **Lung** soup, **brain** soup, **testicle** soup, and **stomach** soup, all are exceptionally delicious if your appetite overrides your trained cerebral reactions. They also have a **rice and okra** (*bamya*) dish that's very tasty and filling, and lots more.

NORTH AFRICAN CUISINE

The best known North African food is **couscous**, a tender small grain served with a variety of sauces and meats or vegetables. There is also a stew called **tangine** that can be quite tasty. The appetizers and soups that accompany can vary from place to place, but lemon flavored soups are common, as are **cigars** (a deep-fried tube of spicy ground meat, common in Yemenite restaurants as well).

Mint tea is a regional treat, and the platters of gooey flaky **baklava** go without saying.

VEGETARIAN

Israel's a fairly easy place to be vegetarian. Falafel stands are everywhere, dairy restaurants are guaranteed by kosher law to serve no meat, and the Black Hebrew restaurants (one in Tel Aviv and one in Dimona) are vegan with a vengeance, serving no animal products, meat, or dairy.

There are also lots of markets with a plenitude of fresh fruit, vegetables, yogurt, and a variety of cheeses. **Hummus** can be purchased at street markets, along with pita for a fine picnic.

FAST FOODS & SNACKS

Burekas are flaky pastries stuffed with a variety of fillings, though white cheese or potato are the most common. Cheap (around NIS 3) and tasty (though not a diet item), they make an easy snack if you're on the move, and are available in bakeries and supermarkets. **Arabic style pizzas**, usually topped with egg or olive oil and za'atar (ground thyme) are filling snacks. There are also **American style pizza** slices, mediocre but edible, and poor quality burgers from the **Burger Ranch** chain.

And then there are **bagels**. They're different from what Americans are used to, but once you accept this, they're quite good and a cheap snack that's not dripping with oil. The Israeli bagel is round, soft, and studded with sesame seeds, and the Arab version, larger and oval, is always available on the streets of the Old City in Jerusalem, where they sell them with little folded packets of za'atar (ground thyme-based spice) to dip it in. **Seeds** and **nuts** are very popular, and lots of little shops sell nothing but paper bags of these treats. **Pickles** are also an Israeli specialty, and any deli or market will have a full selection of half sour, full sour, pickled cabbage, pickled eggplant, and pickled etcetera.

DESSERTS & SWEETS

Baklava, as described above, is a buttery, flaky pastry (or toasted shredded wheat) with or without pistachios, and soaked in honey – Akko has some fine examples. **Katayeef** and **kanafe** are more oriental sweets with cheese in a flaky pastry and sugar syrup over all (it can actually be quite good if the proportions are right).

Halvah, a traditional dessert, is a dense, sweet loaf made from sesame seeds ground fine and crumbly. It can round off a meal nicely, but just a little bit will do you. If it's **ice cream** you're after there's good old Ben & Jerry's as well as the local Dr. Lek chain, all very good. And all the **cafes** dish up sublime cake, pastry, and pie concoctions that'll bust your bank and diet, but might be worth it anyway.

OTHER CUISINES

There are other cuisines to chose from as well, especially in the larger cities like Jerusalem, Tel Aviv, and Eilat. El Gauchos is an **Argentinean** steak chain that's beloved by those pining for a big slab of meat. There are plenty of Italian and French restaurants, and some of them are quite good. With Kurdish food and Hungarian, Chinese, Thai, and Indian, there's not the dearth of cuisines people used to complain about.

ISRAELI BREAKFAST

A concept popular with (and created by) hotels and kibbutzim, it's a big buffet of cheeses, cereals, salads and eggs, and whatever else the establishment cares to throw in. Ask your average Joe (or Shlomo) on the street what an Israeli Breakfast is, however, and you'll get a blank look. Some of these spreads really are magnificent, others are just some Laughing Cow cheese triangles and bug juice, so when a hotel promises the world and a "full Israeli Breakfast" you might want to ask what exactly theirs has.

ISRAELI BEER

Israel brews its own beer, with **Maccabee** and **Goldstar** being the two local brands you see most often. They're both okay, though Goldstar is a little darker and more flavorful, and generally more popular with travelers. You can also purchase imported brands, but you'll pay a lot more for them.

ISRAELI WINES & SPIRITS

Israel isn't known for boozing, but there is a booming wine business and any self-respecting Israeli prides himself on knowing the best Yarden, Carmel, and Gamla vintages, even if he doesn't drink the stuff himself.

There are lots of decent wines put out by Israel's three main vintners, but the following are very fine, good for a picnic, gift, or souvenir: Note: prices greatly subject to change.

- **Yarden Blonde Blanc** - a good champagne
- **Yarden Brut** - around NIS 64
- **Gamla Chardannay** and **Cabernet Sauvignon** - NIS 37
- **Yarden Chardannay** and **Cabernet Sauvignon** - NIS 46
- **Yarden Mt. Hermon** red and white - NIS 32
- **Barkan Cabernet Sauvignon Reserved '88**
- **Yarden Cabernet Sauvignon '89**

The local brandies and other spirits are not remarkable other than for the hangovers suffered by unwary travelers, but the orange and chocolate flavored liquor **Sabra** is special. Not only does it come in a bottle that looks like it might contain a genie, it's a tasty liquor and unique to Israel. A small bottle is NIS 24 and a 750 ml bottle is NIS 39.

NON-ALCOHOLIC DRINKS

Israeli tap water is safe to drink, but if you have a sensitive stomach it might be a good idea to get bottled water (available everywhere), as foreign microbes aren't always welcomed wholeheartedly by your stomach.

Coffee is an extremely popular drink, and the quality isn't bad. Most cafes have espresso and cappuccino, European Nescafe and the Israel concoction called *café hafukh* which is espresso and milk and quite good. Asking for it will not only earn you the respect of the coffee maker, it'll net you a fine and relatively inexpensive cup of coffee as well.

Soft drinks are ubiquitous here, as they are worldwide.

10. JERUSALEM'S BEST PLACES TO STAY

THE AMERICAN COLONY HOTEL, *Nablus Road. Tel. 02-627-9777, Fax 02-627-9779, is a 10 minute walk from Damascus Gate. Superior and Deluxe rooms cost $115-$230 a single and $175-$275 a double, while suites go for $350-$380. Children younger than seven stay free, those between seven-twelve can stay in their parents' room for $20, while additional adults are $40. Breakfast is included, and half board is available.*

The American Colony more than lives up to its reputation for beauty and elegance. The 98 rooms, some modern and some traditional, vary in form and decor depending on whether they're in the original or the added wing. The old wing rooms are wonderful, with Turkish carpets, old stones, and painted ceilings. And the suites in this wing are enormous and lovely and opulent. One of the most fabulous hotels in Jerusalem, this former Pasha palace oozes ambiance and history. From the Cellar Bar done in Mid-East weaves to the verdant oasis of the Palm House Garden, the attention to detail is impressive. The Courtyard is open in summer for dining, there's a luxurious outdoor pool, and the Cellar Bar, with its low ceilings and stone walls, feels like it should figure in some Humphrey Bogart movie.

There are the usual room amenities of air-conditioning, direct-dial phones, cable TV, and hotel facilities like parking and restaurants. Then there are the unusual pleasures of star-watching (the long list of famous guests includes Ingrid Bergman, T. E. Laurence, and Graham Greene, and Marc Chagall, Ed Koch, Lauren Bacall and Joan Baez, to name a few) or reading up on the hotel's history that started with the Pasha in 1860. If it's in your budget it's worth a stay. Reservations months ahead are suggested.

KINGS HOTEL, *60 King George. Tel. 02-620-1201, Fax 02-620-1211, is a big white block of a hotel with cubit balconies on one side. Just next to the Great Synagogue, the Kings Hotel has 217 rooms, all with airconditioning, bath, radio, and phone (TV and mini-bars available for the asking), for $115 a single and $145 for doubles, breakfast included, plus 15% service charge.*

This hotel has a synagogue, Shabbat elevators, and a variety of kosher eateries. On top of that, it's friendly, helpful, and very quiet. Built in 1954, opened in 1956, and renovated in 1988, they clearly try to keep it nice.

The rooms are pleasant, clean and modern, but you should specify one with a balcony when you make your reservations. The decor is easy on the eyes, with soft, muted colors, the phones all have voice-mail, and the views from the higher floors are sensational. Downstairs, there's a piano bar in the lobby (from 7:30pm) and an attractive sun terrace. They also offer safe deposit boxes, fax services, private parking, and have a doctor on call. Even better, they're a mere 15 minute walk to the Old City, and 10 minutes to Jaffa Street. Kings does a good job of combining kosher, comfortable, quiet, and convenient.

HOTEL PALATIN, *4 Agrippas. Tel. 02-623-1141, Fax 02-625-9323, is a family-run hotel one block up from King George, in the center of West Jerusalem; they charge $85 a single and $89 a double year round, including a big breakfast.*

The 28 rooms are comfortable, carpeted, and cozy, with color cable TV, radio, phone, shower, air conditioning, heat, and hairdryer (one room has a balcony as well). The owners run it with care, maintaining a home-like milieu with a European pensione feel. Another thing the owners do well is collect modern art. The bedrooms and hallways are decorated with quality colorful paintings. They're uplifting to the spirit, and give the hotel a museum look.

They serve an immense Israeli breakfast in their dining room, with more of their superb art on the walls. Located centrally in West Jerusalem, you can walk as easily to the Old City as to the Mahane Yehuda street market. It's also near major bus lines. From a Jaffa Street bus you can get off at King George and walk a couple blocks, and the #9 bus comes even closer.

SAINT GEORGE'S CATHEDRAL PILGRIM GUEST HOUSE, *20 Nablus. Tel. 02-627-7232, Fax 02-628-2575, is on the corner of Salah Eddin about eight minutes from Damascus Gate. A single is $120-$135, a double costs $160-$175, and breakfast is included.*

The Saint George's Guest House is a lovely sight. Just off the old cathedral and courtyard, it's a beautiful stone complex of 22 rooms in a house that has offered lodgings to travelers (both pilgrims and tourists) since the early 1900s. The rooms are quite comfortable, all renovated with phones and enormous bathrooms, and distinctive looking with their Jerusalem stone walls and floors.

There are amenities beyond the attractive rooms, too. The Anglican Cathedral, built in 1898 in Gothic style to be the Mother Church of the Diocese of Jerusalem, has services daily. There's fax service available at the reception, and the lounge is an appealing place, full of inviting old chairs. Meals – a variety of European and local cuisine – are served in the dining room, and in the summer a cafeteria offers meals in the garden. The cloistered garden is especially lovely, with olive trees, shaded tables, and an intimate atmosphere. And there's a small archaeological museum as well. They recommend you be in by 11pm, but there's no curfew as such.

JERUSALEM INN GUEST INN, *7 Horkanos. Tel. 02-625-2757, Fax 02-625-1297, has 22 rooms, costing $62-$68 a single and $76 a double (breakfast is $4 extra). There's also a dorm with beds for $14, plus $2 for breakfast for youths aged 28 years and younger.*

The Guest Inn has a lovely lounge with white walls, dark wood, cozy tables, and a piano. It's a nice place to plan your day or relax at day's end, and jazz or classical music is often performed on Thursday evenings.

The rooms are small but classy, with private bathrooms, balconies and marble floors. There's a family feel to the inn, homelike and helpful. Very clean, it's on a quiet street near the center of West Jerusalem, surrounded by good restaurants and nightlife, and just seven minutes from the Old City. For location, atmosphere, and reasonable prices, it's an excellent choice.

11. WHERE TO STAY

WEST JERUSALEM HOTELS

THE KING DAVID, *23 King David. Tel. 02-620-8888, Fax 02-620-8882, has 237 rooms (35 of which are suites), costing $228-$416 for a single and $248-$436 for a double, depending on the season and the type of room. Suites range from $356-$480.*

This is the Dan's best known hotel and the most prestigious in Jerusalem. For elegance and grandeur and all those good things, not to mention superb views and history-soaked ambience, this is a one-of-a-kind place. The Garden rooms have patios, and are in great demand in summer. The decor was designed in 1931, with Italian marble lights and Victorian study lamps, and an amazing staircase on the fourth floor. While renovated and kept up, the original decor and tradition for the most part has been maintained. The Reading Room is especially lovely. The original parquet floor remains, and its big heavy table was borrowed for the signing of the Jordan/Israel Peace Treaty. Nixon, Ford, and Clinton have all stayed here. Behind the hotel is a lovely garden and terrace, and there is also a good fitness center (with sauna and steam room) that manages to keep the look of Old Jerusalem while incorporating all modern equipment.

Even if you don't stay here, you can take in the special feel with a drink in the dark woody bar room or hang out on the terrace and listen to classical music 5-7pm in summer (starting after Passover).

JERUSALEM HILTON, *7 King David. Tel. 02-621-1111, Fax 02-623-6844, US Tel. 800-445-8667, is a new hotel charging $185-$290 a single and $215-$340 a double, depending on grade of room and time of year.*

This spanking new hotel, just opened in January 1998, boasts a fine Mamilla location near Yemin Moshe and the Old City, plus all the amenitites of outdoor pool (heated in winter), steam room, saunas, jaccuzi, and tennis courts.

LAROMME JERUSALEM HOTEL, *Liberty Bell Park. 3 Jabotinsky, Tel. 02-675-6666, Fax 02-675-6777, is across from the Jerusalem Theater.* Rooms cost $131-$271 a single and $148-$288 for doubles, depending on season and type of room. Suites start at $265 in low and $385 in peak seasons.

Their 294 air conditioned rooms all come with private bath, cable TV, phone and phone mail, mini-bar, and breakfast. The Maximum rooms are truly beautiful and elegant, with marble bathrooms, king-sized beds, and lots of nice touches, and the Regulars are luxurious as well. The double windows ensure quiet, the carpets are plush, and the Jerusalem Post is delivered to your room. The hotel provides Shabbat elevators and clocks, a synagogue, dairy and meat restaurants, outdoor pool (heated in winter), sauna and fitness room, and parking.

HOLIDAY INN CROWNE PLAZA, *Givat Ram. Tel. 02-658-8888, Fax 02-651-4555, across from the central bus station, charges $178-$215 a single and $212-$249 a double, breakfast included, 15% service added on.*

The tallest building in Jerusalem is a landmark people negotiate by, though not one of the prettiest. With 21 floors, 397 rooms, 18 suites, and a business center, it makes up in convenience what it lacks in charm, especially if you're attending a function at the Binayanei Hauma Convention Center across the street. The rooms, all air conditioned and with balconies, phone, TV, and bath, are pleasant and have good views. The building has gift shops and hairdressers, car rental, parking, and a bank. There's a pool, sauna, fitness equipment, tennis court, Kids Club, even miniature golf. Among their loads of restaurants, Kohinoor Kosher Indian restaurant attracts most notice. The hotel is about five minutes from City Center (by bus) just across the way from the central bus station, their free shuttle bus goes to and from Jaffa Gate Sunday-Thursday 9am-6pm.

DAN PEARL JERUSALEM, *Zahal Square. Tel. 02-622-6666, Fax 02-622-6600, is just 300 meters from Jaffa Gate, facing David's Citadel and Mount Zion. The 34 guest rooms cost $144-$200 a single and $164-$220 a double, while the suites range from $240-$650, all depending on the month and view, plus 15% service charge, breakfast included. Time shares available.*

This luxury extravaganza opened January 1996 with the hottest of locations, where West Jerusalem meets the Old City. Beyond their fully accessorized rooms and suites, the Pearl has an indoor pool, health club, jacuzzi, steam room, sauna and massage. There are a variety of restaurants, coffee shops, and bars, plus room service, a synagogue, a mikveh, laundry and dry cleaning, outlets for taxis, travel agencies, galleries, gift shops, and an underground parking lot with valet service. There's even a multi-purpose amphitheater, and a glass roofed atrium. More a city than a standard hotel, the Pearl sits as close to the Old City as a hotel can get and still be in West Jerusalem.

RADISSON MORIAH PLAZA, *39 Keren Hayesond. Tel. 02-569-5695, Fax 02-623-2411, has 292 rooms and eight suites on 10 floors, costing $140-$200 for a single and $175-$270 a double.*
The rooms all have heat/air conditioning, direct-dial phone, cable TV, and are fairly nice and big, but they don't compare with those in the Laromme. The hotel offers parking, a rooftop pool with sundeck, a health club, synagogue, and babysitter and doctor on call.

KING SOLOMON HOTEL, *32 King David. Tel. 02-569-5555, Fax 02-624-1774, charges from $84-$181 a single and $98-$194 a double, based on season and room grade; breakfast is included, but the rates are subject to 15% service charge. In the US, call 800-345-8569 for information or reservations.*
There's an elegant lobby and 150 pleasant rooms, all with air conditioning, cable TV, mini fridge, and direct-dial phone. The restaurants here are all glatt kosher, and the pool (open in summer) overlooks the hills of Judea. Newly renovated, the hotel is quite sedate.

MITZPEH RAMAT RACHEL, *Talpiot district. Tel. 02-670-2555, Fax 02-673-3155, is a kibbutz to south of Jerusalem (bus 7 goes there), with rooms for $152 a single and $174 a double, breakfast included.*
They have 93 rooms, all with air conditioning, radio, phone, TV, and bath. They've many reacreational facilities, such as a swimming pool (heated in winter), water slide, sauna, fitness room, and tennis courts. In addition, there's a synagogue, guided tours showing kibbutz life, and a museum with 1948 War exhibits. The guest house closes for one month out of the year for maintenance – check for exact dates.

THE SHERATON, *47 King George. Tel. 02-629-8666, Fax 02-623-1667, is set a bit from the street overlooking the green of Independence Park. They charge $143 a single and $153 a double, breakfast and 15% service included.*
The 300 rooms and suites have all the usual five-star amenities like cable TV and direct-dial phone and the hotel provides restaurants, sauna, and outdoor pool. They're comfortable and large with big balconies, and red roses grace the bathrooms. Next to Henry Wolf Park and across from the Great Synagogue, it's about a 10 minute walk from Jaffa Street.

JERUSALEM TOWER, *23 Hillel. Tel. 02-620-9209, Fax 02-625-2167, charges $100-$115 a single and $120-$150 a double, breakfast included.*
Their 120 rooms with TV and phone are small and tidy, neither crummy nor fancy.

KINGS HOTEL, *60 King George. Tel. 02-620-1201, Fax 02-620-1211, is a big white block of a hotel with cubit balconies on one side. Just next to the Great Synagogue, the Kings Hotel has 217 rooms, all with air conditioning, bath, radio, and phone (TV and mini-bars available for the asking), for $115 a single and $145 for doubles, breakfast included, plus 15% service charge.*

The hotel has a synagogue, Shabbat elevators, and a variety of kosher eateries. It's a friendly, helpful place, and very quiet. Built in '54, opened in '56, and renovated in '88, they clearly try to keep it nice. The rooms are pleasant, but you should specify one with a balcony. There's a piano bar in the lobby (from 7:30pm) and a sun terrace. It's a 15 minute walk to the Old City, and 10 to Jaffa Street.

HOTEL TIRAT BAT-SHEVA, *42 King George. Tel. 02-623-2121, Fax 02-624-0697, has 70 rooms for $66-$110 a single and $88-$144 a double, breakfast and service charge included.*

A hotel for 30 years, there's a pleasant lounge, and the rooms have twin beds, desk, phone, radio, TV, and bath. It's a clean, solid hotel across the street from Rondo Park, in between mid-range and luxury.

THE PARADISE, *4 Wolfson. Tel. 02-655-8888, Fax 02-652-5521, charges $90-$1116 a single and $110-$140 a double.*

The hotel has pleasant, attractive rooms, swimming pools (inside and out), tennis courts and connecting rooms for families. It's a 10 minute walk from the Knesset and the Israel Museum, and 10 minutes by bus from city center.

THE YMCA 3 ARCHES HOTEL, *26 King David. Tel. 02-569-2692, Fax 02-623-5192, has 56 rooms that cost $103 for a single, $126 a double, and $161 a triple, breakfast included.*

Located in one of the more remarkable buildings in Jerusalem, this not your run-of-the-mill YMCA. Across the street from the King David and set off by its magnificent 152 feet high granite tower, the reception area is quite grand, and the rooms are small but beautiful, with marble-topped desks and more. The hotel has a swimming pool, tennis courts, squash courts, and a fitness room, a fine coffee shop and restaurant, and a feel of quiet, simple elegance. They also have occasional evenings of Arab and Jewish Folklore – call *Tel. 02-624-7281* for information.

THE WINDMILL HOTEL, *3 Mendele, Tel. 02-566-3111, Fax 02-561-0964, has 133 rooms with breakfast, with prices for singles $85-$100, and $95-$120 for doubles. During Passover and Sukkot reservations must be made for half-board at $145 a single and $170 a double, 15% service charge added to all rates.*

All the rooms have air conditioning, direct-dial phones, cable TV, and bath or shower. They are adequate but a little dingy and drab. The hotel has parking, a Shabbat elevator, a synagogue, and a sun deck. On a side street off Keren Hayesod, it's fairly quiet while still near Liberty Bell Park. They pride themselves on their traditional religious atmosphere, and offer special Bar Mitzvah packages. They welcome children and have a Family Plan, providing babysitting and a doctor on call.

PARK PLAZA HOTEL, *2 Wolfson. Tel. 02-652-8221, Fax 02-652-8423, is off Herzl. Rooms cost $109 a single and $120 a double, breakfast included, 15% service charge added.*

Another in a series of big modern hotels, their 217 rooms are nice and roomy, with couch and sitting area, phone and TV. The hotel, a 10 minute walk from the Knesset, provides a synagogue, parking, and for families, baby sitting and a doctor on call.

THE HOLYLAND HOTEL, *Bayit Vagan. Tel. 02-643-7777, Fax 02-643-7744, charges $90-$100 a single and $100-$120 a double, breakfast included, plus 15% service charge.*

This hotel is not close to anything except their over-hyped Second Temple replica. There are 115 rooms, with phone and TV. They have tennis courts and a pool, miniature golf and shuffle board, but are a good drive and irregular bus service (#21) away from the city of Jerusalem. There are better, friendlier accomodations available in the city for less money.

THE NOTRE DAME OF JERUSALEM CENTER, *opposite New Gate. Tel. 02-627-9111, Fax 02-627-1995, is in the grand complex by the striking Notre Dame Statue. Rooms cost $79 a single and $98 a double, including breakfast. Special prices and winter discounts sometimes apply.*

Along with the cathedral and the location, this Vatican-owned hospice offers 150 adequate but bland rooms. Built for French pilgrims in 1885, the building incurred heavy damage during the fighting in 1948 and became an Israeli bunker in no-man's land. By 1978 Notre Dame was repaired and opened to the public, and now it functions as a pilgrims' hospice.

HOTEL PALATIN, *4 Agrippas. Tel. 02-623-1141, Fax 02-625-9323, is a family-run hotel one block up from King George, in the center of West Jerusalem; they charge $85 a single and $89 a double year round, including a big breakfast.*

The 28 rooms are cozy, with cable TV, radio, phone, shower, air conditioning, heat, and hairdryer (one room has a balcony as well). The owners run it with care, decorate it with modern art, and maintain a homelike feel. From a Jaffa Street bus you can get off at King George and walk a couple blocks, and the #9 bus comes even closer.

MENORAH HOTEL, *24 King David. Tel. 02-625-3311, Fax 02-624-2860, during regular season the rates are $58 per single and $78 per double, breakfast included.*

The Menorah boasts a "homely atmosphere" and they aren't far off, especially the 64 drab rooms in basic brown (all of which have the standard private bath, phone, and heating). Some of the rooms have air conditioning, and TVs can be hired. It's got a great location however, just across from the King David Hotel and close to the Old City and the Great Synagogue. They've got their own synagogue as well as laundry service, parking and a Shabbat elevator. Credit cards not accepted.

JERUSALEM INN GUEST HOUSE, *6 HaHistadrut. Tel. 02-625-2757, Fax 02-625-1297, has 22 rooms that are small but with balconies, and marble floors, costing $62-$68 a single and $76 a double (breakfast costs $4 extra). There's also a dorm with beds for $14, plus $2 for breakfast for youths aged 28 years and younger.*

There's a lovely lounge with white walls and dark wood, with jazz or classical music on Thursdays. Very clean, it's on a quiet street (although some readers report rooms with balconies are noisy) near fine restaurants and nightlife, and seven minutes from the Old City.

RON HOTEL, *44 Jaffa. Tel. 02-622-3122, Fax 02-625-0707, charges $77 a single and $82 a double, breakfast included. There is a 15% service charge added on, but if you present your Open Road guide they will waive it.*

This is a beautiful old building that unfortunately hasn't been kept up. The 22 rooms are up the circular staircase, but they are just okay, with TV, phone, and shower/toilet. Founded by Warshavsky in 1926, Menachem Begin made his first speeech after coming out from the Underground from their balcony on March 8, 1948. It's centrally located in West Jerusalem, but the hotel isn't all it could be or all it once was.

HOTEL MERCAZ HABIRA, *4 Havatzelet. Tel. 02-625-5754, Fax 02-623-3513, is across from Zion Square. They have 30 rooms, costing $50 a single, $80 a double with shower, breakfast included.*

This hotel has been newly remodeled, with an entrance of white marble and a new elevator. The quiet rooms are spacious, all have phones, cable TV, private toilets, some with shower and others with bath, and many come with balconies. In addition, up on the roof is a wrap-around patio for lounging and relaxed city viewing.

BEIT SHMUEL, *6 Shama. Tel. 02-620-3456, Fax 02-620-3467, is just off King David. The prices depend on the season and number of people per room, all include breakfast, and the maximum stay is two weeks. Singles are $70, doubles $76, and triples $102, single sex only.*

Run by the World Union for Progessive Judaism in the Hebrew Union College complex, most meals cost $13, while Shabbat dinner is $16.

HOUSE 57, *57 Midbar-Sinai. Tel. 02-581-9944, Fax 02-532-2929, are Guest Houses, charging $50 a single, $72 a double, breakfast included.*

This two-story stone building for up to 14 guests with views of Jerusalem and the Judean Hills is in Givat Hamivtar, a residential neighborhood above Ramat Eshkol shopping center, 10 minutes from downtown.

HOTEL ZION, *10 Dorot Rishonim. Tel. 02-625-9511, Fax 02-625-7585, is just next to Rimon Cafe – walk up Luntz off Jaffa and bear right; they've 26 rooms that cost $44-$65 a single and $61-$74 a double, breakfast included.*

Located right on the *midrahav* (pedestrian walkway) and with a pleasant lounge/bar area, but no elevator, the rooms are clean and fresh, and some have balconies overlooking all the cafes below, while all come equipped with TV, phone, and radio, some with showers and some with baths. There's an attractive breakfast room with white arches and windows over the square.

HOTEL GOLDEN JERUSALEM, *40 Jaffa. Tel. 02-623-3074, Fax 02-623-3513, has 21 rooms, at $50 a single and $70 a double ($64 when slow), with continental breakfast.*

Located in the thick of downtown. The rooms are cheery and clean, not fancy but good for the price; all have heat and cable TV, and some have phones, air-conditioning, and balconies. This used to be the offices of marriage and divorce under the Chief Rabbi, but since 1992 the only activities in those departments have been behind closed doors. The location couldn't be more central, but some travelers have complained of noise off the street and from other guests.

SAINT ANDREW'S, *past the foot of King David. Tel. 02-673-2401, Fax 02-673-1711, is near the railway station and Bethlehem Road. Singles are $43, doubles $65 and triples $83, Scottish breakfast included. There are discounts for seven day stays.*

This hospice is a building of exceptional beauty and warmth, with blue tiles, green plants, and all the best of Scottish hospitality. Set on top of the ridge over Hinnom Valley near the British Consulate, Saint Andrew's Scots Memorial Church and Hospice was opened in 1930 in memory of the Scots who died fighting the Turks in WWI. With 14 rooms and 34 beds, the hospice welcomes all and provides comfortable singles, doubles, and family rooms. Every Sunday at 10am the church has services, followed by tea and coffee in the lounge, and there are often vocal concerts, *Tel. 02-561-2342*, held at night. It's centrally heated, has a cozy lounge, and stunning garden. In addition to the concerts, there's Scottish country dancing the first Saturday of every month. Coffee and tea are always available, and credit cards are accepted.

KAPLAN HOTEL, *1 Havatzelet. Tel. 02-625-4591, Fax 02-623-6245, is just off Jaffa in downtown. They have 16 rooms that rent for $50 a single and $60 a double, breakfast not included.*

The rooms are comfy and small, with phone, TV, art on the wall, and clean bathrooms. Some have noisy balconies as well. The hotel is atop a nice old circular stone staircase, has been run by the Kaplan family for three generations, and has a pleasant feel. You can use the washing machine for free, and should make reservations in advance.

ROSARY SISTERS CONVENT GUEST HOUSE, *14 Agron. Tel. 02-625-8529, Fax 02-623-5581, is right next to the US Consulate. They've 22 rooms, at $30 a single and $60 a double, breakfast included.*

Lovely and clean though without frills. They all have phones, rugs, and charm. To gain admittance you have to be buzzed through two large and imposing doors, with the outside bell positioned for the very tall. The Rosary Sisters are dedicated to the education of Arab girls; the mother house was built in 1892 and the church, which holds daily masses for pilgrims and locals, was built in 1937. There's a curfew of 10pm.

GOOD MORNING JERUSALEM, *Binayanei Hauma Convention Center. Tel. 02-623-3459, Fax 02-625-9330, the reservation center in the Convention Center is in the behind the central bus station, open Sunday-Thursday 9am-5:30pm, Friday 9am-1pm.*

This service will set you up in someone's home in a nice neighborhood. For last minute service at night, call *Tel. 05-051-3989*. They'll ask you some questions and match you up, or you can fax them your particulars, including the number of people, grade of accommodations (2-4), dates, and credit card number and expiration date. The houses and locations vary but the prices are set, depending on the grade (2-4) of the place. Singles go for $40-$55 and doubles are $50-$75, plus $13 for an extra bed.

MAMILLA'S VILLAGE – BED & BREAKFAST INN, *4 King David. Tel. 02-625-0075, Fax 02-625-1820, can be reached with bus 6, 13, 18, 20, or 21. There are 10 rooms costing $45 a single, $54 a double, and $153 for a room of six beds, breakfast included.*

The private rooms are pleasant, though their balconies presently overlook a hotel construction site. The hostel room is nicer than most with three wood bunks, heat, a table, bathroom, and balcony. It's a lovely old building with nice tiles, it's close to Jaffa Road, and there's no curfew. Visa/Mastercard accepted.

HOTEL ERETZ ISRAEL, *51 King George. Tel. 02-624-5071, just past Ha-Rav Avid'a – the dilapidated path and signs do in fact lead to this homey little hotel with six rooms that go for $25 a single and $40 a double.*

A small, family-run hotel, you get coffee/tea and cakes in the morning and warm attention and personal loving care from the Barmatz couple round the clock. The rooms are not fancy but they are clean, and though the bathrooms are down the hall, each room has a sink. Eretz Israel, started by Josuf Barmatz' father, has been in the family for 70 years and in its present location for 40. It's a homey place, and since it's off the road there's no traffic noise. Run by an adorable old couple who speak some English as well as Yiddish, Hebrew, Arabic, and German, their sitting room feels like your grandmother's old living room. Midnight curfew.

WEST JERUSALEM HOSTELS

LOUISE WATERMAN-WISE HOSTEL, *8 Rehov Hapisga, Bayit Ve-gan. Tel. 02-642-0990, Fax 02-642-3362, is an IYHA off the beaten track. Beds cost $23 for members, and $21 for non-members.*

They have 300 beds, as well as a sports facility, kitchen, and park. You can get there by bus 18, 20, 40, or 39, but once you're there in what's generally considered a fine hostel, you're not near much.

BERNSTEIN YOUTH HOSTEL, *1 Keren Hayesod. Tel. 02-625-8286, Fax 02-624-5875, is a centrally located IYHA in a century-old stone building. Open Sunday-Thursday 7-9am and 3pm-midnight, Friday 7-9am and 2pm-midnight (curfew midnight), the 15 rooms are clean, and some have showers in the room. A bed (five per room) costs $21, big breakfast included.*

There's a cafe, and a TV room, and it's across from a Supersol and King's Hotel. Transport there is easy on buses 7, 8, 9, 14, 31, 32, and 48.

JERUSALEM FOREST HOSTEL, *Mount Herzl. Tel. 02-641-0060, Fax 02-641-3522, has 140 beds for $21 each.*

This IYHA is beautifully situated on the western slopes of Mount Herzl with tremendous views of the Judean Hills. They have a sports facility and swimming pool as well. Not easily reached by bus, you'll need to taxi or drive here.

HADAVIDKA GUEST HOUSE AND YOUTH HOSTEL, *67 Hanevi'im. Tel. 02-538-4555, Fax 02-538-8790, is in Liberty Square. A dorm bed costs $20.50 ($18.50 for members), a single is $40.50, and a quad is $94, breakfast included.*

A new three-story building just near Jaffa and King George streets, with 60 rooms of two-six beds each, all with cubbards, desk, heat/air conditioning, and private bath. There's a cafeteria and rec room with a TV, and no curfew. To bus there, 27, 34, 35, 36, and 39 stop on Hanevi'im and the 3, 18, 20, 21, and 23 stop nearby on Jaffa.

JERUSALEM INN HOSTEL, *6 HaHistadrut. Tel. 02-625-1294, has dorm beds for $16 and private rooms for $38 a single, $48 a double.*

Perhaps the finest hostel in West Jerusalem, it was renovated in 1997, and is safe and quiet with dorms, private rooms, and clean bathrooms. The attentive, friendly, care of the manager makes staying here a special experience. There are heaters and fans, a bulletin board, with a deposit you can have a key, and you can wash or dry laundry for $5 each. It's right near all the cafes and all the bus lines of the new city and just minutes away from the old.

EIN KAREM YOUTH HOSTEL, *Ma'ayan Street. Tel. 02-641-6282, is an IYHA that's away from the center. A dorm bed goes for $11.*

Up in the hills and near Mary's Spring in pretty Ein Kerem, bus 17 gets you there, and it's not far from Yad Vashem. They have 100 beds in a charming old stone building, and there's a TV room as well.

EAST JERUSALEM HOTELS

THE AMERICAN COLONY HOTEL, *Nablus Road. Tel. 02-627-9777, Fax 02-627-9779, is a 10 minute walk from Damascus Gate. Superior and Deluxe rooms cost $115-$230 a single and $175-$275 a double, while suites go for $350-$380. Children younger than seven are free, those between seven-twelve can stay in their parents' room for $20, while additional adults are $40, breakfast included, and half board available.*

The American Colony more than lives up to its reputation for beauty and elegance. The 98 rooms, some modern and some traditional, vary in form and decor depending on their location in the original or added wing. The old wing rooms are wonderful, with Turkish carpets, old stones, and painted ceilings. And the suites in this wing are enormous, lovely, and opulent. One of the most fabulous hotels in Jerusalem, this former Pasha palace oozes ambiance and history. From the Cellar Bar done in Mid-East weaves to the verdant oasis of the Palm House Garden, the attention to detail is impressive.

There are the usual room amenities of air conditioning, direct-dial phones, cable TV, and hotel facilities like parking and a pool. Then there are the unusual pleasures of star-watching (the long list of famous guests includes Ingrid Bergman, T. E. Laurence, Graham Greene, and Joan Baez to name a few) or reading up on the history that started with the Pasha in 1860. If it's in your budget it's worth a stay. Reservations a month ahead are suggested.

HYATT REGENCY, *32 Lehi, Mount Scopus. Tel. 02-533-1234, Fax 02-581-5947, has prices ranging from $126-$212 a single and $139-$235 a double, including breakfast and service charge.*

A remarkable example of modern luxury seven-level architecture high atop Mount Scopus, the hotel is landscaped into the hill and the main entrance and reception is on the sixth floor. Termed a "Conference Resort," it caters to business and tourism alike. There are 501 rooms of differing grades depending on view and luxury. They are pleasant rooms, with writing desk, central heat/air conditioning, and mini-bar, and the private balconies of Deluxe rooms have magnificent views of the Old City. The lounge is outstanding, with leather settees, a fountain, and modern sculpture, and the level of sumptuous luxury and convenenience is unsurpassed, especially compared to the prices at the King David.

The restaurants are superb though pricey (Valentino's is well-known for its Italian cuisine, and costs NIS 85 for all-you-can-eat), and the Castel lounge menu features international cuisines from $4.50-$13. The Jerusalem Spa is enormous and state-of-the-art, with fitness machines, trainers, and Dead Sea treatments. There's tennis, a swimming pool, and massage as well. There's a synagogue, Shabbat clock, and elevator. The Orient Express Night Club is a fun disco with a touch of elegance, and free shuttles tranverse the route from hotel to Jaffa Gate to King George.

SAINT GEORGE'S CATHEDRAL PILGRIM GUEST HOUSE, *20 Nablus. Tel. 02-627-7232, Fax 02-628-2575, is on the corner of Salah Eddin about eight minutes from Damascus Gate. A single is $120-$135, a double costs $160-$175, and breakfast is included.*

It's a beautiful stone complex of rooms off the old cathedral and courtyard. There are 22 comfy rooms, all with phones and enormous bathrooms, Jerusalem stone walls and floors, in a house that has offered lodgings to travelers since the early 1900s. The Anglican Cathedral, built in 1898 in gothic style, has services daily. The lounge is full of inviting old chairs, the cloistered olive tree garden is especially lovely, and there's a small archaeological museum as well. They recommend you be in by 11pm, but there's no curfew as such.

PILGRIMS PALACE HOTEL, *Sultan Suleiman near Damascus Gate. Tel. 02-627-2135, Fax 02-626-4658, costs $70-$110 a single and $80-$130 for doubles, breakfast included.*
There are 100 spacious air conditioned rooms with private facilities and phone, and TV. The lobby has more comfy couches than you can shake a stick at, plus inexpensive drinks and snacks, and nice views of the old city. The restaurant serves Middle Eastern cuisine, and the gift shop sells local handicrafts.

MERIDIAN HOTEL, *5 Ali Ibn Abitaleb. Tel. 02-656-3175, Fax 02-628-5214, charges $52-$85 for a single, and $74-$125 a double, breakfast included, 15% service charge added.*
Behind the square facade with balconies is a somewhat empty mid-sized hotel. The 72 rooms all have air conditioning, phone, radio and the ubiquitous '50s furniture.

CHRISTMAS HOTEL, *1 Ali Ibn Abitaleb, off Salah Eddin. Tel. 02-628-2588, Fax 02-689-4417, has 24 rooms for $55-$72 a single and $70-$102 a double, no credit cards accepted.*
It's neither fancy nor grotty, and the rooms are small and clean, with phone and shower or bath. They have a pleasant lounge and garden.

HOTEL 7 ARCHES, *Mount of Olives. Tel. 02-627-7555, Fax 02-627-1319, charges $90 for singles and $110 for doubles, breakfast included.*
A stunning hotel with a winning view of the Old City. While the elegant lobby and Bistro are decked out in sumptuous tones, the rooms (200) are a bit drab, though comfortable, with direct-dial phone, air conditioning, and TV. It's close to the Old City, but not an easy walk.

PILGRIMS INN HOTEL, *Rashid, Tel. 02-628-4883, Fax 02-626-4658, is on the street east of and parallel to Salah Eddin, near Herod's Gate. Singles cost $55-$75 and doubles are $65-$110, breakfast included.*
It's a family-oriented hotel with 16 air conditioned rooms done in 50s style decor, but not because it's in vogue. They are open most of the year but are usually closed in January.

AMBASSADOR HOTEL, *Nablus. Tel. 02-582-8515, Fax 02-582-8202, is beyond the American Colony, up the Scopus hill, charging $85 a single and $100 a double, breakfast included and 15% service charge added.*
The rooms are nice enough, with phone, TV, and large clean

bathrooms. The lounge has an engaging view, the terrace is pleasant, and there's a restaurant and bar.

CAPITOLINA HOTEL, *29 Nablus. Tel. 02-627-7964, Fax 02-627-6301, rented from the YMCA Jerusalem, has 57 rooms with 113 beds at $69 a single and $92 a double, full breakfast included, and 15% service added on.*

Rooms are comfortable, clean, simple, and small, with phone, radio, heat and air conditioning; some have lovely balconies. The dining room on the fifth floor has a swell view of the city; the YMCA sports facility, Tel. 02-627-1793, with swimming pool, gym, and squash courts, can be used by guests. This big building tends to be used mostly be pilgrims, and there is no curfew.

HOLY LAND HOTEL EAST, *6 Rashid. Tel. 02-628-4846, Fax 02-628-0265, near Herod's Gate, they charge $70 a single and $90 a double, breakfast included, plus 15% service charge.*

Not to be confused with the rip-off Holy Land with the temple model, their 105 rooms have private bath, heat, and phone, and most have balconies. The rooms are a bit chintzy, but adequate and very clean. The hotel provides parking as well as laundry, room service, and a friendly staff.

NATIONAL PALACE HOTEL, *4 Azzahra. Tel. 02-627-3273, Fax 02-628-2139, is on the street at the end of Rashid and Salah Eddin. They charge $65 a single and $90 a double, breakfast included.*

There are 105 small, comfortably pleasant rooms with small clean bathrooms, direct-dial phone, and attractive lamps. Not the promised palace, but they do have marble stairs, nice wall trim, and lots of European groups.

RITZ HOTEL, *corner of Ibn Batuta and Ibn Khaldoun. Tel. 02-627-3233, Fax 02-628-6768, has 103 rooms with heating and air conditioning, for $70 a single and $85 a double.*

For your money you get breakfast, parking, and a snooty attitude.

AZZAHRA HOTEL, *13 Azzahra. Tel. 02-628-2447, Fax 02-628-2415, near the National Palace Hotel, costs $60 a single and $80 a double.*

The fifteen rooms come with phone, heat, air conditioning, and big gorgeous bathrooms with bidet and tub. This century-old stone building is on a quiet side street off Azzahra, with lovely stone walls and steps, and tall ceilings. Three of the rooms have balconies, but no credit cards are accepted.

JERUSALEM HOTEL, *Nablus Road. Tel./Fax 02-628-3282, is on the road across from Damascus Gate, charging $49-$55 a single and $75 a double, rate including breakfast.*

A very lovely place, with 13 rooms, big windows, curved walls, stone and tile floors, and lovely Arabic touches. A lot of care has obviously gone into bringing out the beauty of this old19th century stone house, and the result is charm, comfort, and ambiance. There is a small Arabic style restaurant with rugs and cushions, and entertainment here Thursday and Saturday nights as well. The only drawback is its proximity to the Arab bus station, with its noise and fumes.

MOUNT SCOPUS HOTEL, *Mount Scopus. Tel. 02-582-8891, Fax 02-582-8825, has singles for $55 and doubles for $74, breakfast included, 15% service charge added.*

This large boxy hotel has 65 comfortable rooms with private bath, phone, TV, patterned spreads and old lamps, and the rooms facing south have great views from the balconies. It's ugly outside but pleasant and friendly within, and you get a lot for your money. Bus #23 stops out front.

NEW REGENT HOTEL, *20 Azzahra. Tel. 02-628-4540, Fax 02-626-4023, has singles that cost $40-$50 and doubles for $50-$70, breakfast included.*

It's a small hotel with 26 sparsely furnished rooms, all with heat, bath, and phone.

RIVOLI HOTEL, *3 Salah Eddin. Tel. 02-628-4871, Fax 02-627-4879, is half a block from Herod's Gate, with rooms for $40 a single and $60 a double.*

Its Persian carpeted lobby appears to be decorated straight out of the 50s. All 31 rooms are nice and spacious, and they've all got private baths and phones.

METROPOLE, *6 Salah Eddin. Tel. 02-628-2507, Fax 02-628-5134, is just up from the Rivoli, with 29 rooms that cost $35 a single and $60 a double, breakfast included.*

The management is rather unfriendly, so this isn't your best bet for a pleasant haven.

NEW METROPOLE, *8 Salah Eddin. Tel. 02-628-3846, Fax 02-627-7485, near Herod's Gate, has 25 rooms that cost $30 a single and $60 a double, breakfast included.*

The rooms are fusty, dusty, and quaint, decorated in old-lady style, and some are graced with bird-dropping bedecked balconies.

EAST JERUSALEM HOSTELS

THE PALM HOSTEL, *6 HaNevi'im. Tel. 02-627-3189, has dorm beds (4-10 a room) for NIS 18, and private rooms for NIS 80.*

The Palm has a pleasant sitting room and atmosphere despite the atrocious green trim, with old dilapidated sofas, nice stone walls, and tea and coffee (NIS 1). They offer tours to everywhere, have no lockers, but do have a safe. There's a furnace in reception, but that's the only heat in the house. This old building was constructed in the late 1800s and was one of the first built outside the old city walls. Buses 27 and 23 go there from the bus station.

RAMSES HOSTEL, *20 Hanevi'im. Tel. 02-627-1651, is just outside Damascus Gate, the last stop for bus 27. It's got private rooms for NIS 60 a single and NIS 80 a double. The dorm is $10 each but is only for groups of six.*

The Ramses has small basic rooms with high ceilings, very clean and quiet, and beautiful blue tile bathrooms. There's a lounge and TV room, hot showers and central location, laundry service for NIS 10, midnight curfew, and space to park outside.

THE NEW RAGHADAN HOSTEL, *HaNevi'im. Tel. 02-628-3348, opposite Damascus Gate, charges $5 a bed and $17 a private room.*

The prices are cheap, and you get what you pay for.

THE FAISAL HOSTEL, *4 HaNevi'im. Tel. 02-627-2492, near Damascus Gate, costs NIS 15 a bed, or NIS 9-11 in the outside room, and a private is NIS 60.*

The two main dorms have balconies and eight bunks squished together, while the two smaller rooms are roomier, without bunks or balconies. With washing machines, a kitchen with tea and coffee, and a big balcony, the Faisal is seedy, run down, and depressing. Reservations accepted.

THE CAIRO HOSTEL, *21 Nablus. Tel. 02-627-7216, near the American consulate and across from the mosque, is accessable from bus 27. A dorm bed costs NIS 15 and a private room (just a room with beds) is NIS 60.*

The Pink Panther greets you, and their six dorms, with 3-10 beds each, have tile floors and balconies overlooking the street. It's fairly clean, has a nice kitchen, free tea, luggage storage, and movies nightly. They organize trips to Masada, etc., and give travel information as well.

THE OLD CITY: NEAR THE DAMASCUS GATE

(take bus 23 or 27)

For Old City hostels and hospices: the prices quoted apply for most of the year, but during Christmas the rates skyrocket at most hostels.

ARMENIAN CATHOLIC HOSPICE, *41 Via Dolorosa (third station). Tel. 02-628-4262, Fax 02-627-2123, has reopened. They charge $12 a dorm bed and $45 a private single, no breakfast.*

Inside you'll find beautiful wood furnishings and tile floors, quality mattresses and crisp linens. And all the rooms are properly appointed with TVs, phones, and hair dryers in the pristine bathrooms.

AUSTRIAN HOSPICE, *37 Via Dolorosa. Tel. 02-627-1466/3, Fax 02-627-1472, has dorm beds (8-12 per room, no bunks, one storage unit per bed) for $12, singles for $44, doubles for $68 per, and triples $96, two night minimum required. Prices include breakfast, and half board's available for $5 more. Get buzzed in one gate and then another, proceed up the stairs to the Madonna, and continue all the way up for the office. Write to POB 19600, 91194 Jerusalem.*

It's in a beautiful, well-kept building. The rooms are immaculately clean, the bathrooms are beautifully tiled, the ceilings arch loftily and serenely, and the doors shut firmly at 10pm, but keys are available with deposit. There is a lovely garden, and a beautiful view from the terrace. Staffed mostly by volunteers from Austria and Germany, you can apply to volunteer (stay at least one month, be 19 or older, cover your own airfare) for full board, lodging, and pocket money. There are lifts and wheelchair access, and if you want to be met at Lion's Gate to be helped with luggage, phone ahead.

ECCE HOMO CONVENT YOUTH HOSTEL & GUEST HOUSE, *Eastern Via Dolorosa. Tel. 02-622-7292, POB 19056, is just past Ecce Homo Arch, turn left on Via Dolorosa from El Wad coming from Damascus Gate. They have dorm beds for NIS 30 in the Youth Hostel, Guest House cubicles for $18 with breakfast, and private rooms for $30 a single and $55 a double, with breakfast.*

Bang the brass hand and the door mysteriously opens on another world, one of beautiful stone floors, columns, and lofty arching ceilings. The Youth Hostel and Guest House are separate and operate under separate rules, though the facilities look similar. They both have rows of little cubicles complete with bed, wardrobe, and sink, made semi-private with wooden walls and cloth curtains for doors. The Youth Hostel cubbie (for girls only) doesn't include breafast, has a sitting area and kitchen, and heat in winter, a lockout from 10am-12pm, a curfew of 11pm, a maximum stay of 10 days, and no access to the Guest House section. In the Guest

House, the cubicle arrangement (available to both men and women) and charmingly referred to as "boxes," includes breakfast and access to the beautiful terrace, has no lockout, but does share the 11pm curfew. The Guest House prices do not include the 10% service tax. Reservations taken for Guest House only, no credit cards. Once you get past all these rules and distinctions you are left with a lovely, safe place. In the Jerusalem world of youth hostels, the cubicles give a sense of privacy and let you unpack and spread out a bit without costing much more than the dives. And there are lockers available at no extra cost.

HASHIMI HOSTEL, *73 Khan el-Zeit. Tel. 02-628-4410, is nearly across from Al-Arab. Dorm beds (only four-six beds in room) cost NIS 15, doubles are NIS 50-80, NIS 90 a triple, roof beds are NIS 10, and if you stay seven days, you get the eighth free.*

Each room, including the dorms, has its own toilet/shower, hot water 24 hours, and all appears fresh and quiet. Staying in the dorms, however, is no picnic. The bunk mattresses are on slabs of plywood that tilt and shift if you turn over or sit up, and the dorm toilets aren't the cleanest. There is a kitchen, and from the roof you have a great view of the mosque. Basel, the owner, is aiming at still more improvements to upgrade to two star quality. Right now the prices match the nearby hostels but the aura is different. You'll find it quieter, with lots of friends and family of the management rather than the frenetic college party atmosphere of some nearby hostels.

AL-ARAB HOSTEL, *Khan el-Zeit. Tel. 02-628-3537, has dorm beds (5-15 per room) for NIS 15, small private rooms for NIS 50, and roof mattresses in summer for NIS 11. Enter Damascus Gate, take street on right, and it's about 100 meters on the left.*

This place is chock-a-block with scraggly lounging backpackers and the walls are covered with summer of love style flowers. Entertainment includes hanging out with other travelers, comparing travel war stories, and nightly videos at 9pm. There are clean showers, a kitchen, free tea, and a curfew of 1:30am. Tours offered to Masada, refugee camp, and more.

AL-AHRAM YOUTH HOSTEL, *Al-Wad. Tel. 02-628-0926, is left from the Damascus Gate, with dorm beds (five-six a room) for NIS 15 (NIS 18 with heat), and private rooms with shower, toilet, and balcony for NIS 60. Roof top beds are NIS 10 (you'll need a sleeping bag in winter).*

This place is drab but not disgusting, they offer kitchen use, and have a midnight curfew. Treat it as a back-up if everything else is full.

BLACK HORSE HOSTEL, *28 Aqabat Darwish. Tel. 02-628-0328, has beds for NIS 13 and private rooms with toilet and shower down the hall for NIS 60. It's near Via Dolorosa Street #14, turn left towards Herod's Gate at the Black Horse sign, or better yet enter the city at Herod's Gate and walk 400 meters.*

A relatively new addition to the lodgings scene, with dorm beds 12 to a room, it's very close quarters but very clean. They've got a bar/coffee shop area with beautiful pine tables and a happy hour (7-8:30pm) with Maccabees two for NIS 10. It also has a beduin tent hang-out popular with the young and groovy crowd, with rugs, pillows, shoes off and hushed tones. It's a neat place to feel with-it and special and compare prices with other travelers. Amazing big, clean bathroom. The private rooms, in a separate building, have many nice touches, and the large bathrooms are spotless. There's no curfew, and there is a washing machine, TV, tours and information.

THE OLD CITY: NEAR THE JAFFA GATE
(take bus 13, 6, or 20)

GLORIA HOTEL, *33 Latin Patriarchate. Tel. 02-628-2431, Fax 02-628-2401, is left on Latin Patriarch after entering Jaffa Gate. Rooms for $60 a single and $75 a double, breakfast included. No credit cards, no curfew.*

Inside you'll find a clean tile entrance and vaulted faux stained glass windows. Most guests are from France so you can practice your French with them or fall back on English. The rooms are standard.

CHRIST CHURCH GUEST HOUSE, *just inside Jaffa Gate to the right. Tel. 02-627-7727, Fax 02-627-7730, charges $40 a single, $72 a double, $84 a triple, and $96 per quad, less during regular and low season, more during Jewish holidays, breakfast included, credit cards not accepted.*

There's an old wing and new, and both are very nice and very, very clean, with a beautiful dining room, stone arches, and sweeping lines. Tours include Life & World of Jesus, Roots of the Faith, and unmarried couples can't stay together.

LUTHERAN HOSPICE GUEST HOUSE, *Saint Mark's. Tel. 02-628-5105, Fax 02-628-5107, is in the same complex as the Lutheran Youth Hostel, but upscale. They charge $40 a single and $66 a double during peak season, less during regular and low, full breakfast and 5% service charge included, no credit cards accepted.*

The rooms are quite nice, and it's best to book ahead as they are often full.

LARK HOTEL, *8 Latin Patriarchate. Tel. 02-628-3620, is just up the road from the Gloria and next to the Latin Patriarch Church. They charge $30 a single and $60 a double, with bathrooms in each room and continental breakfast included.*

This is a small mediocre place with an 11pm curfew. Downstairs an Armenian Restaurant run by the same family has funky grottoesque decor, chicken soup that tastes Cambells all the way with cinnamon on top, and 17% VAT on top of the low prices.

THE MARONITE CONVENT, *25 Maronite Convent Street. Tel. 02-628-2158, Fax 02-627-2821, has 20 beautiful stone rooms with vaulted ceilings and clean bathrooms for $29 a single and $50 a double, breakfast included.*

The building, purchased in 1893 by the Bishop (and later the Patriarch) Elias Hoyek, had been a hospital before Hoyek took it over. Recently restored, there's the chapel, the Maronite parochial church of Jerusalem, and a section that's been turned into a home for pilgrims. The bedrooms are appealing, the chapel is lovely, and the courtyard through the stone arches gleams in the sun. The only catch is the 10pm curfew.

NEW IMPERIAL HOTEL, *inside Jaffa Gate. Tel. 02-628-2261, Fax 02-627-1530, has singles for $25 and doubles for $40.*

Dingy but clean, with vaulted arches that have seen better days, it's open 6am-midnight, after which ringing the bell will get you in.

LUTHERAN YOUTH HOSTEL, *Saint Mark's. Tel. 02-628-5105, Fax 02-628-5107, not far past Citadel, has dorm beds for NIS 24.*

Though the dorms are large (40 beds in the girls' dorm, 20 in the boys'), they are great all the same, with high vaulted stone ceilings, and private nooks and partitions separating the bunks. There's an age limit of 32, but it's only enforced during crowded peak times. With a nice kitchen, lockers, and pleasant garden, it's spotlessly clean, safe and well-tended. There is a 9am-noon lockout for cleaning and a curfew of 10:45 (you can get permission to return later, but by no more than a couple of hours).

PETRA HOSTEL, *David Street. Tel. 02-628-6618, is straight into the shuk after entering Jaffa Gate, with dorm beds for NIS 20 and private rooms for NIS 70-120.*

A somewhat dilapidated, once beautiful old building, but each dorm room has a balcony overlooking the square, and there is no curfew.

CITADEL YOUTH HOSTEL, *20 Saint Mark's. Tel./Fax 02-627-4375, has dorm beds (five per room, no bunks) for NIS 20, and private rooms (small) for NIS 75, NIS 90 with views – discounts with weeklong stays and students available.*
There's a clean kitchen to use, little sitting/eating areas, a roof, and laundry lines. There's a midnight curfew but no lockout, and you can get a key. This is a likable place with a nice feel to it.

NEW SWEDISH HOSTEL, *29 David Street. Tel. 02-589-4124/02-627-7855, has dorm beds for NIS 15 and private rooms for NIS 40-50, pay six nights in advance, get the seventh free. Roof mattresses (NIS 10) should be in place by summer.*
The dorms rooms are claustraphobic, and as you wend your way through slung towels and back packs you might disturb united couples. The private rooms are, well, more private. The cheap one is very small and its entrance is through the dorm. Those upstairs, however, are cute with curved ceilings and walls, and have their own entrances. The bathrooms are clean, though as of now they are only downstairs. Lockers are NIS 3, laundry NIS 7 a wash or dry, and tea/coffee is free. In winter the curfew is 3am, in summer there's no curfew. They also arrange tours (see Tour section). They take no reservations during peak time – the best time to come by is 10am-1pm.

THE OLD CITY: THE JEWISH QUARTER
(take bus 1, 2, or 38)

OLD CITY YOUTH HOSTEL, *3 Dorot Rishonim. Tel. 02-628-8611, is off Saint Mark's, with dorm beds for $13 or NIS 45, including a full Israeli breakfast, spiffy clean toilets/showers, and small, clean dorms with sinks.*
The kosher breakfast is 8-9am, the hostel is closed 9am-4pm (5pm in summer), and curfew is 11pm. There's no heat in the winter, a shame in a big old stone building. The airy, spacious halls, lofty ceilings, and stone floors have been around for a while, starting out as a Protestant Missionary from 1833-1856 and a bikkur holim hospital from 1867-1948 before becoming a hostel. Reservations over the phone may or may not be accepted, and the phone may or may not be answered.

EL-MALAK YOUTH HOSTEL, *18 Jewish Quarter. Tel. 02-628-5362, is between Ararat and El-Malak. A dorm bed costs NIS 30, and a private room is NIS 70.*
You can take bus 1, 2, or 38 to the Jewish quarter or 3, 13, 19, 20, or 30 to Jaffa Gate and walk in from there. There's a TV room and use of the kitchen, as well.

HERITAGE HOUSE, *Men's: 2 Ohr HaChayim. Tel. 02-627-2224, Women's: 7 HaMelakh. Tel. 02-628-1820, has its Heritage office at at 90 Habad, Entrance B, Apt. 14, Tel. 02-627-1916, and has dorm beds available for traveling Jews at no charge.*

A Jewish community-sponsored hostel offering free lodging for young traveling Jews interested in their roots (or a bed). There are no strings attached, though Judaism evening lectures (8:30pm, free) and Shabbat programs (including candle lighting, prayer at the Western Wall, and dinner with a local family, lecture, Saturday tour of the city, and final communal meal for NIS 26) are available. They provide a clean, comfortable, warm atmosphere (the women's dorm is especially nice) and though they prefer you not stay longer than a week, the rules can be bent if you're involved in spiritual growth or learning. The hostels are closed from Saturday-Thursday 9am-5pm daily, but you can drop your bags at the Student Center of the hostel. The curfew is 12-1am. The women's dorm, with 28 beds, has a sitting area and a nice kitchen; to get there, go up some stone winding stairs to the cozy charming dorm of comfortable wood bunks, shelves, and curtains.

The men's dorm has 60 beds but no curtains. Clean and spare, but not as cozy, there is also one room for a married couple. They don't accept everyone, depending on how they feel you'll fit in. Though they are funded for and cater to Jewish guests, they won't deny lodging to a non-Jew who's part of a Jewish group. If they can't take you, however, they'll try to place you at a hostel nearby.

To get there, take bus 1, 2, or 38 into Jewish Quarter, or bus 3, 13, 19, or 30 to Jaffa Gate, walk down David, turn right on Armenian Patriarchate and right again on Saint James. The men's dorm is straight ahead (Saint James turns into Ohr HaChayim). Or, keep going straight and turn right on Habad to find the Heritage Office.

12. WHERE TO EAT

WEST JERUSALEM: JAFFA STREET

KIKAR HA'IR, *19 Jaffa. Tel. 02-625-0795.*
This is a kosher Kurdish restaurant that's open Sunday-Thursday 9am-6pm, serving fast food in pitas or sit-down meals. Snacks and light meals like hummus, mejadarra (rice and lentils) and stuffed vegetables go for NIS 9-16.

MA'ADAN, *35 Jaffa. Tel. 02-625-5631.*
Ma'asan specializes in kosher grilled meat and fish. They have tasty goulash for NIS 25, entree platters for NIS 9-15, and fish meals for NIS 25-45.

PIKNIC, *57 Jaffa. Tel. 02-625-4195.*
Open Sunday-Thursday 8am-7pm, Friday 7am-3pm, they serve good traditional Jewish food to eat in or to go. Sample prices include soups for NIS 8-15, chopped liver or shnitzel for NIS 15, and a piece gefilte fish is NIS 10.

MISHKENOT SHA'ANANIM, *below the Montefiore Windmill. Tel. 02-625-4424.*
This is an exclusive French eatery. The elegantly antique neighborhood and splendid views of the Old City enhance the fine French and Moroccan food, and make the lofty prices seem a bit more reasonable. With a bottle of wine from their extensive cellar, a lunch might cost $30 and dinner might start at $40. However, there is also a smaller room (four or five tables) with the same food but much cheaper, within the residence. They're not always open to the public, but it's worth checking.

> ## INTERNET CAFE
> *There is a newly opened Internet cafe, called **The Netcafe** at 9 Helene Hamalka Street near the Russian Compound, Tel. 624-6327. The rates are 7 NIS for 15 minutes, 14 NIS for 30 minutes and uses AOL for e-mail. You can buy pastries and coffee while e-mailing or surfing the web.*

WEST JERUSALEM: YOEL SALOMON WALKWAY

PIPO, *16 Yoel Salomon. Tel. 02-624-0468.*

Located down toward the end of the street, Pipo is open Monday-Friday 10am-11:30pm, Saturday 11:30am-1am. Serving Argentinian food to occasional Argentinian music, it's a very popular Saturday spot. A friendly place with white walls, lots of stone, and tightly packed tables, they dish up quantities of meat and luscious desserts. Light meals (salads, empanadas) go for NIS 20-35, pastas are NIS 25-35, and the main dishes are NIS 45-65.

OSTERIA PAPAS, *3 Rivlin Street. Tel. 02-625-6738.*

An Italian restaurant open Sunday-Friday 9am-midnight, Saturday noon-midnight, it's packed on Shabbat. With a small, cozy dining room, white walls and nice paintings, there are also tables out on the walkway. Focaccio costs NIS 8, soups and salads are NIS 17-24, and main dishes go for NIS 35-49.

WEST JERUSALEM:
BEN YEHUDA PEDESTIAN MALL & NEARBY

VILLAGE GREEN, *10 Ben Yehuda. Tel. 02-625-2007.*

This is a vegetarian restaurant on the Pedestrian Mall. There's another branch at *1 Betsalel, Tel. 02-625-1464.*

FINK'S BAR AND RESTAURANT, *2 HaHistadrut. Tel. 02-623-4523.*

FInk's is on the corner with King George, open Saturday-Thursday from 6pm, and it's busiest 8-10pm. Rightly ranked by Newsweek as "One of the best bars in the world," their food is equally noteworthy. The ever-charming Moulli (son-in-law of the late owner Dave Rothschild) runs the joint. With a bar and just six tables, it's big in status and quality alone. If you want to dine at a table, you'd best make reservations (you can call during the day). The chef has been cooking up Moshe Fink's goulash for 40 years, as well as tafelspitz, cordon bleu à la Fink, chopped liver, and a very succulent pepper steak, priced NIS 22-63. But you needn't eat.

There's fine beer, wine, and more, and even a Fink's Special (aka The Hammer) of gin, vodka, Bacardi, and Triplesec, to melt away your tourist aches and pains.

A SPECIAL PLACE: FINK'S

Fink's has been called the restaurant equivelent of the Sabra: a plain, unlovely outside belies the warmth and goodness within. Founded in 1933 by Hungarian emigré Moshe Fink, the restaurant/bar served as a hidden arsenal and secret post office for the Haganah. In the pre-war years Fink's was popular with both British Mandate officers and members of the Haganah, creating an interesting dynamic and lots of eavesdropping. Today, Fink's still attracts a mixed bag of diplomats, artists, journalists, Likkud and Labor parliament members, and diverse travelers.

Zubin Mehta, Isaac Stern, and Pablo Casals have bellied up to the polished bar. Golda Meir used to frequent the place as well, but was adamant about wanting no special treatment (in fact she got mad at Rothschild when once he tried to seat her before her turn). Less democratically inclined, when Kissinger wanted to visit in 1973, he had certain conditions: notably that everyone else leave the premises. And here Rothschild didn't play favorites, saying Kissinger was certainly welcome, but no more so than his regular customers. And despite the fancy names and magazine write-ups, it's the regulars who make Fink's. As much a club as a restaurant, it's a place people come back to, it's a family people want to join.

OTHER DOWNTOWN RESTAURANTS

ANGELO, *9 Horkanos. Tel. 02-623-6095.*

Located off Havazelet, parallel to Jaffa, and open Sunday-Thursday noon-4pm and 6:30pm-midnight, Saturday from the end of Shabbat. Angelo serves what might be the best kosher Italian food in Jerusalem, in a cozy setting run by a lovely couple. True, you probably didn't come to Israel for pasta, but the authentic Roman cuisine (Angelo's home before emigrating to Israel), rivals the best of New York, San Francisco, and Rome. Business lunches cost NIS 45. There's an innovative anti pasta buffet, and everything is homemade, and the *cecio e pepe* is a real treat. The red wine is good, the espresso is strong, and your bill is sweetened with a complementary glass of dessert wine. There's smoking and non-smoking sections, and they're setting up sidewalk tables as well.

THE TICHO HOUSE CAFE, *7 Harav Kook. Tel. 02-624-4186.*

This cafe is also known as Beit Ticho, open Sunday-Thursday 10am-midnight, Friday 10am-3pm, Saturday from sundown to midnight, and is a serene, lovely, and popular kosher place to dine. Breakfasts (served 10am-noon) cost NIS 15-25. For lunch or dinner, there are salads (NIS 20-30), soups (NIS 14), entrees (NIS 27-43) and sumptuous desserts (NIS 14-18). The tile tables are decorated with fresh flowers, the cutting boards are laden with fresh brown bread, and the fish soup is delicious. The white walls and vaulted ceilings frame this beautiful little room, and all that's lacking is a non-smoking section. The food is enough of a reason to come here, but the main focus is Anna Ticho's drawing exhibit and Dr. Ticho's menorah lamps.

YEHUDA BISTRO, *Laromme Jerusalem Hotel, Liberty Bell Park, 3 Jabotinsky. Tel. 02-675-6666, Fax 02-675-6777.*

They provide a kosher dinner accompanied by candlelight and classical guitar. Laromme sometimes gives out 10% discount vouchers.

OCEAN, *7 Rivlin. Tel. 02-624-7501.*

Ocean serves – not surprisingly – fish, and lots of it, generally prepared au Francais. It's not cheap, and you should be prepared to pay NIS 85 for a business lunch and NIS 100 for their fixed dinner menu.

SHUK MAHANE YEHUDA

HASHLOSHA, *68 Agrippas. Tel. 02-625-3876.*

This is a reliable Oriental foods standby, open Sunday-Thursday 10am-8pm in winter and 10am-11pm in summer. They sell appetizers like hummus, stuffed veggies, and beans with rice for NIS 8-11, and goulash, fish, and grilled meats for NIS 25-45.

SIMMA, *82 Agrippas. Tel. 02-623-3002.*

Open Sunday-Thursday 10am-2am, Friday 10am-4:30pm, Simma is well known for its cheap Mediterranean food and good hummus. It's so well known, in fact, that the food it serves is no longer that cheap, and its fame seems to have gone to its head. Simple fare like hummus or shak-shuka are NIS 10, and a main dish will run you NIS 33-50.

RAKHMO, *5 HaEshkol. Tel. 02-623-4595.*

This place serves up a more authentic, inexpensive meal. Open Sunday-Thursday 8:30am-5pm and Friday 8am-1:30pm, an institution in these parts for 42 years. Just off Agrippas, they sell fine, simple foods (self-service) for pittance. Hummus is NIS 7, beans and rice costs the same, and the kubbeh soup is much admired. A light meal will cost you around NIS 7, a full more-than-you-need meal won't run above NIS 20. It's not fancy, but it has its charm, with formica-topped wooden tables surrounded by old men talking politics and eating well.

HASHIPUDIA, *6 Hashikma Street. Tel. 02-254-036.*
Open Sunday-Thursday noon-midnight, Saturday from the end of Shabbat until midnight, they serve the usual kebabs, stuffed veggies and salads for NIS 10-20, bull's testicles, fish, and spinal cord for NIS 17-38, and desserts for NIS 6.
Not far past Hashlosha but across the street is a popular stall selling grilled innards and meats in a pita (NIS 16-22).

BAGEL BAKERY, *125 Agrippas.*
Just past the stall mentioned above, you can get fresh, fine bagels hot from the oven.

IMA, *189 Agrippas. Tel. 02-624-6860, Fax 02-625-5693.*
Open Sunday-Thursday 10am-10pm, Friday 10am-3pm, Ima serves kosher Kurdish food in an old white stone house all the way down Agrippas, past the market and further still. The complimentary pickled cabbage is well-spiced, and a meal here is filling and good. Appetizers of mejadara, hummus, or stuffed veggies are NIS 9-13, main courses run NIS 30-48, and the take-away menu is 10% less. The fried eggplant and stuffed cabbages are especially good, and a big feast can be had in this cozy place for NIS 19. There's smoking and non-smoking sections, and you can rent one of the dining rooms for parties. You can order half portions, and hot sauce is available too, for the asking.

FURTHER AFIELD

PUNDAK EIN-KAREM, *13 Hama'ayan. Tel. 02-643-1840.*
Pundak Ein-Karem bills itself as a bar-cafe garden restaurant. It's near Yad Vashem, and though you may not have much of an appetite after visiting there, this restaurant has a pleasant garden atmosphere, with colorful paintings and dark wood. The food is moderately priced, with light meals starting at NIS 19.

KOHINOOR, *Holiday Inn Hotel building. Tel. 02-653-6667.*
This is a kosher Indian restaurant, open Sunday-Thursday noon-4pm and 6pm-midnight. They serve Tandoori cuisine in a classy Indian setting. Appetizers cost NIS 4-11, entrees are NIS 22-32, and the business lunch is NIS 41.

BLUES BROTHERS, *3 Lunz. Tel. 02-258-621.*

Open 10am-1am and specializing in substantial (though not inexpensive) steaks and kebabs.

WEST JERUSALEM CAFÉS

CAFÉ ATARA, *15 Ben Yehuda, Pedestrian Mall. Tel. 02-625-0141.*

This cafe has history, good coffee, and incredible desserts. Established in 1938 and long-time hangout of Jerusalem Post (previously Palestinian Post) writers, were closed for a year but have happily reopened. The coffee is good though not cheap, and it's a swell place to sit and sip, people watch, and indulge in their luscious, worth-the-fat-and-shekels desserts. If you like chocolate you shouldn't die without first

---

WEST JERUSALEM FAST FOOD & SWEETS

TA'AMI, 3 Shammai, Tel. 02-622-5911, off HaHistadrut, serves basic local items to basic local workers, dishing up plates of hummus, rice and macaroni, kebabs, and goulash for NIS 9-20. The decor isn't much to speak of, but around lunch time there are plenty of hungry men slurping up simple, good food. Not as charming or cheap as Rakhmo's, but the same sort of fare. The pita here isn't free (it's 50 agorot each), and the service isn't doting, but the fresh lemonade is great, and it's a fine mid-town option if you tire of the cafe scene.

For good, cheap, fast food there are bakeries all over town:

KHEN BAKERY, 30 Jaffa, not far up from Tourist Information, is open Sunday-Thursday 8am-5pm and has excellent cheesy burekas for just NIS 4.

CHEZ PARIS, 35 Jaffa, open nearly round the clock, is another good bakery, but more western in its outlook and baked goods, with cookies and muffins as well as burekas.

MISEDIT GAZIT, 39 Jaffa, lacks an English sign, but serves a vegetarian omlet in pita (called khavita emerakot in Hebrew or eeja in Arabic) for just NIS 6. Dressed up with hummus and salads, it makes a tasty alternative to the ubiquitous falafel.

AMI PIZZA, Emek Refdim, Tel. 02-563-0469, has servicable pizza for NIS 6 a slice. Open Sunday-Thursday 9am-midnight, and Saturday after Shabbat till midnight, a slice makes a fine snack.

BEN & JERRY'S, 5 Hillel, Tel. 02-624-2767, is off King George and open Sunday-Thursday 10am-midnight, Friday 10am-2pm, Saturday from the end of Shabbat till midnight. Same good ice cream, at NIS 5 a scoop.

experiencing the Mozart Chocolate cake with hot chocolate sauce on the side (NIS 14).

Café Atara is more down to earth than many of the abundant cafes in the zone, with marbled floors, plain wood tables, utilitarian chairs. Supposedly a spot for local politicians and intelligentsia, even if you can't recognize any of the patrons you might as well believe you are surrounded by fame, sit back, and enjoy your dessert. They also have lunch/light dinner fare, and in the mornings folks sit over coffee and newspapers. The back room is no-smoking.

CAFE TA'AMON, *27 King George. Tel. 02-625-4977.*
Open Sunday-Thursday 6am-midnight, Friday 6am-4pm, Saturday 5pm or 6pm to midnight. In operation for 42 years, they're not fancy or charming but they serve a good, relatively inexpensive cup of coffee and draw an interesting crowd. Popular with writers, artists, and retired left-wing scholars, the walls are decorated with pictures painted by the late Abraham Offick; fresh flowers and intently reading, smoking men inhabit the tables. It's not chic, but what it lacks in marble table tops it makes up for in history and integrity.

CAFE RIMON, *Luntz. Tel. 02-624-3712.*
A popular cafe, full of chipper Israelis and travelers in their 20s and 30s, drinking somewhat pricey cappuccinos and eating fancy desserts.

OLD CITY:
EATING IN THE CHRISTIAN & MUSLIM QUARTERS

If you hunger while traipsing the alleys of the Old City, you generally want food without a wait; the heat and crowds of the narrow lanes do something to normally tolerant, patient folk.

If you want a light snack and put off the real meal till later, one of those omnipresent long oval sesame-seeded bagels (*ka'ak*) is a fine choice. It's cheap (3 NIS), and bound to be good. Ask for *za'atar* to go with it and they'll dish up some tasty green spice in a square of newspaper for you to add to your snack (it's very tasty and middle eastern). Generally speaking, the falafels in the Old City are disappointing, especially compared to the fine quality available just blocks away in East Jerusalem.

ABU SEIF, *just inside Jaffa Gate.*
You can get hummus for NIS 9 and falafel for NIS 5. The falafel satisfies your hunger but is boring. If you can, hold out for better fare outside Damascus Gate.

THE COFFEE SHOP, *next to Christian Information near Jaffa Gate. Tel. 02-626-4090.*
A bright and cheery place with nice tile-topped tables, tempting desserts, and lunches for around NIS 15-20.

ABU SHUKRI, *63 Al-Wad. Tel. 02-627-1538.*
Features Taha's deservedly famous hummus (NIS 9), which is better than the labaneh. He also serves falafel, salads, soda and mint tea (NIS 4) to refresh and refuel you in your Old City wanderings.

ABU ASSAB, *Khan Ez-Zeit.*
This is a fine juice stand. It's on your right coming from Damascus Gate and has wonderfully refreshing and reasonable fresh squeezed juice (orange/grapefruit/carrot) for NIS 4.

ROTISEREE CHICKEN, *Khan Ez-Zeit.*
Sells half a chicken to go NIS 10 or eat in with salads, pita, and yummy green hot sauce ("felfel" in arabic) for NIS 13. There are lots of chicken joints on the strip, and English signs generally boost the price quite a lot. Make sure to ask how much before ordering.

Shuk Khan ez-Zeit assaults you with trays and trays of gooey flaky treats dripping honey and pistachio nuts that look scrumptuous but may be disappointing. **ZALATIMO'S**, *Khan Ez Zeit*, is an exception. Near the Coptic Church and the ninth station of the cross, it makes the real thing. The cheese filled moutabak is their specialty, but there's lots more to choose from if that isn't the treat you yearn for. It's open daily in the morning till 11:30 or whenever the pastry's gone.

OLD CITY: EATING IN THE JEWISH QUARTER

QUARTER CAFE, *corner of Tife'eret Yisrael and Ha-Sho'arim, on the second story. Tel. 02-628-7770.*
Open Sunday-Thursday 8:30am-6:30pm, Friday 8:30am-3:30pm, with a rooftop terrace and a terrific view. It's self-service, the salads are NIS 9-16 and full meals NIS 38; the food's good, the prices average, and the view of Mount of Olives superb.

Off Cardo Square is food option lane. **HAHOMA RESTAURANT** is a sit-down proper place (credit cards accepted), with salads for NIS 9 and entrees for NIS 33. To the right is a **SHWARMA JOINT** with pita sandwiches for NIS 9-15, and to the left is a hole-in-the-wall **BAKERY** with za'atar pizzas for NIS 5.

Across the lane is **ROMI'S PIZZA** (open Sunday-Thursday 7am-midnight), with regualr pizza as well as malawach, soup, spagetti, and fresh carrot juice, too.

EAST JERUSALEM

AL-QUDS RESTAURANT, *23 Sultan Suleiman. Tel. 02-627-2052.*
Located opposite the post office, across from the Old City, and about a block down from the Damascus Gate, this is a self-serve gem. A big shwarma or kebab pita costs just NIS 7. Muscle past all the people in line and pay the cashier, get your ticket and take it to the meat man of your choice (shwarma, kebab, or chicken). Get the pita, help yourself to chips and salad toppings, and enjoy. The roast chicken, NIS 17 for a whole one and NIS 8 for half, are also very tasty. The front of the restaurant is always thronged with locals, attesting to the continuing popularity of this neighborhood place.

PETRA RESTAURANT, *11 Rashid. Tel. 02-628-3655, Fax 02-628-6008.*
Petra is open daily noon-midnight. They serve oriental food in one room and sea food in another. The decor is standard, checkered table cloths and such, neither shabby nor dazzling. Prices are reasonable, and NIS 25 gets you a sampler of salads and dips, while NIS 30-40 buys a big spread of meat main dishes.

AL-QUDS, *Azzahra, around the corner from Rashid.*
Open daily 7am-6pm. A small cafe with four tables and excellent, inexpensive Arabic food, this isn't the Al-Qud's of shwarma and kebab fame, but the quality is equally fine. The hummus is terrific, better than Abu Shukri's, and only NIS 6 for a plateful (and NIS 3 for a pitaful). The reyani (a spinach-stuffed triangle) is good, as is the falafel (NIS 3) and ojay (an eggs and onion dish). And, if you're willing to be gastronomically adventurous, the brain sandwich (NIS 8) is delicious.

CAFE EUROPE, *9 Azzahra. Tel. 02-628-4313.*
Cafe Europe jumps out of the pages of colonial decor. Rattan chairs with flowered cushions surround pink table-clothed tables. If you (or the kids) have been yearning for a burger and fries (NIS 18-27) like they make back home or a thick milk shake (NIS 11), this is the place to go. There are chops, steak, and cheeseburgers (this is not a kosher restaurant), and coffee drinks aplenty. This is also a fine spot to hang out over elaborate cocktails – the social hub starts around 5pm.

PHILADELPHIA, *9 Azzahra. Tel. 02-628-9770.*
Opposite Al-Quds Cinema and open every day from noon-midnight, is an Arabic restaurant of deserved local and international fame. Since 1970, this has been a restaurant that adheres to tradition. The result: food of exceptional quality, service of a standard that is an endangered species, and a stubborn resistance to new-fangled inventions like fax machines and credit cards. And with food this good, who cares how you pay? Certainly not the endless list of famous visitors whose signatures grace the leather-bound guest book. Jimmy Carter ate here, as did Edwin Meese III, Geraldo Rivera, and many more, though most of the guests come from the community – perhaps a greater tribute to its quality. I can honestly say I've never had oriental food as superbly prepared, as delicious, and all the little touches that keep standards high are just honey on the baklavah.

The decor is proper without being ornate, the red table clothes and napkins have been the style since the day they began, and every morning before they open a man rattles an incense pan in all the corners and booths to add to the food aromas the "smell of the Middle East." And with all this, the prices are reasonable. Appetizer salads are NIS 9 each, stuffed foods are NIS 14, and grilled meats are NIS 30-40. For $20, you can get a feast so vast and delectable you won't soon forget it, beginning with an enormous spread of 15 dips and salads, kubeh, stuffed veggies, and falafel that enters the category of gourmet, followed by mixed grill and rice pilaf, then assorted baklava, tea or coffee, and fruit. After such a meal, you will waddle out a very happy person, thankful that Philadelphia Restaurant also provides a free shuttle to anywhere in Jerusalem. Reservations are a good idea, especially if you plan to dine at peak times, around 2pm for lunch or 8-9pm for dinner.

KANZAMMAN, *Jerusalem Hotel, Nablus Road. Tel./Fax 02-628-3282.*
This is a lovely small Arabic subterranian restaurant, awash with rugs and cushions. Cozy and pleasant (with a garden setting in summer), they serve appetizers for NIS 5-7, vegetarian dishes for NIS 10-15, and meat dishes for NIS 20-29. On Saturdays at 8pm there's a special Lebanese buffet, and on Thursdays they have jazz night.

For **sweets**, try one of the bakeries on HaNevi'im, near the Old City.

13. SEEING THE SIGHTS

THE OLD CITY: THE WALLS & GATES

The walls that now stand were built by **Suleiman the Magnificent** in 1534-40. There had been walls before, but Al Muazzan demolished them in 1219 so the Crusaders wouldn't win a fortified city, and no walls were rebuilt for over 300 years. The Old City walls have eight gates, all with varying names (English, Hebrew, Arabic) and histories; of the six built by Suleiman, only the Jaffa, Zion, and Damascus gates survive in their original form.

Jaffa Gate is one of the old gates to the Old City. There's been one here since 135 CE, but the present gate dates from 1538, though some of the stones in the gate are from Crusader and Mamluk times. The left-hand turn you have to make to enter (a mark of an old-time gate) was to deter armed people on horseback from storming the city. It opens into the Christian and Armenian quarters of the city, and stands at the beginning of the former trade route to Jaffa. In 1948 the area in front of Jaffa Gate (what used to be a market and industry zone) became no-man's-land. The gate is now the most used entrance to the old city, and many buses (3, 6, 13, 19, or 30) stop here.

New Gate opened in 1889 to ease the way to the Christian Quarter. This gate gave the patriarchs direct access to their Christian Quarter residences.

Damascus Gate, facing East Jerusalem and where the Sultan had his palace, is the largest and grandest of the eight gates. The Cardo Maximus started here, there was a statue of Caesar (the body in permanent bronze, the head conveniently changable), and columns from a Roman Arch of Triumph stood there as well. The walkway entrance, added in 1980, was meant to be an auditorium, but it is used as a shuk instead. The gate now separates the Christian and Muslim quarters.

Herod's Gate is east of Damascus Gate, and is another entrance from East Jerusalem. The gate got its name because Jesus was led to Herod's palace along the street passing through this gate.

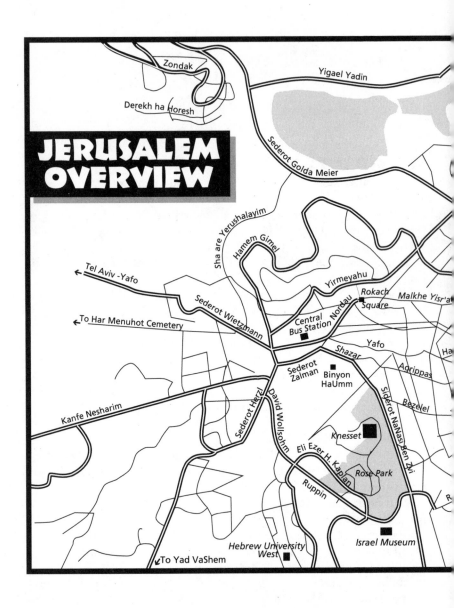

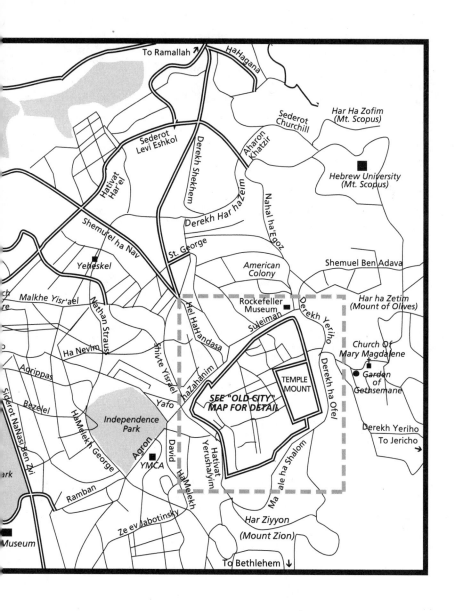

To Ramallah

HaHagana

Sederot Churchill

Har Ha Zofim (Mt. Scopus)

Sederot Levi Eshkol

Derekh Shekhem

Aharon Khatzir

Hebrew University (Mt. Scopus)

Hativat Har'el

Derekh Har haZeim

Nahal ha'Egoz

Shemuel ha Nav

St. George

Yeheskel

American Colony

Shemuel Ben Adava

Malkhe Yisr'ael

Nathan Strauss

Hel HaHandasa

Rockefeller Museum

Derekh Yeriho

Har ha Zetim (Mount of Olives)

Ha Nevim

Suleiman

Church Of Mary Magdalene

Agrippas

Shivte Yisrael

haZahanim

Garden of Gethsemane

Bezalel

Yafo

TEMPLE MOUNT

Derekh ha Ofel

Siderot NaNasi Ben Zvi

HaMelekh George

Independence Park

Agron

YMCA

David

HaMelekh

SEE "OLD CITY" MAP FOR DETAIL

Hativat Yerushalyim

Derekh Yeriho
To Jericho

ark

Ramban

Ze ev Jabotinsky

Ma ale ha Shalom

Museum

Har Ziyyon
(Mount Zion)

To Bethlehem

Lion's Gate is a gate of many names. It gets its Lion name either from the two Mamluk lions on both sides of the gate built by Sultan Baybar, or due to the legend that Suleiman built the walls and gates around Jerusalem after he had a dream which told him to do so or be torn apart by lions. The Christians call this **Saint Stephen's Gate** (and it's the beginning of the Via Dolorosa) because according to tradition Saint Stephen was led through this gate to be stoned. Muslims call it **Bab Sitti Maryam** (**Mary's Gate**) to honor Mary's birthplace as marked by the nearby Church of Saint Anne, and Jews refer to it as **Jehoshaphat Gate** from the Valley of Jehoshaphat (also known as Kidron Valley). This is the gate Israeli paratroopers entered in 1967.

Up the hill, **Golden Gate** once opened onto the east side of the Temple Mount but is now blocked up. It's believed to have been built either by the Byzantine emperor Theodosius II in 444 CE or by the Persians after they captured Jerusalem in 614. It was walled off for good after the Crusaders were driven out in 1187 CE. Since the Messiah is supposed to come from the east, the Arabs blocked it so the Jewish messiah couldn't get into the old city. Tradition has it that Jesus descended from the Mount of Olives and entered the Old City through the Golden Gate on the Sunday preceding his death, and ceremonies used to process through here on Palm Sunday before it was closed off.

Dung Gate (first mentioned in 445 BCE by Nehamiah) enters the Old City near the Western Wall. Its flavorful name comes from a medieval belief that dumping refuse here was a salubrious act. It's been changed a lot over the years, and the lintel shows how small the gate used to be. Buses 1, 3, and 38 enter there into the Jewish Quarter.

Zion Gate connects the Armenian Quarter with Mount Zion. "Zion" as a term first was applied to the Temple mount, and from there it was generalized to Jerusalem, and then to all of Israel. Built in 1540, it was one of the last to be constructed in the old city. Like Jaffa Gate, it has many Crusader stones in its structure, and was really hammered by the pre-independence fighting; the stones are covered with bullet marks.

The Ramparts Walk, *Tel. 02-625-4403*, takes you on a path along the top of the Old City walls, providing you with terrific views of Mount Scopus, Mount of Olives, rooftops, and the shiny heads of tourists. Tickets (NIS 8 for adults, NIS 4 for students) are sold at Jaffa Gate, Damascus Gate, and the Citadel, and they grant you unlimited access for two days after purchase. The entrance to the Ramparts at Damascus Gate entails first descending before you enter the gate. Walk under and keep going throught the old carriageway to the left of the plaza. It's open Saturday-Thursday 9am-4pm, Friday 9am-2pm – but it's not a good idea for women to walk up there on their own.

At the rampart entrance is also the entrance to the **Roman Square Museum**, and its Aelia Capitolina (second century Roman period) excavations. Open Saturday-Thursday 9am-4pm, Friday 9am-2pm, admission is NIS 2 for adults, NIS 1 for students. In the central plaza is a replica of the 1,400 year old Madaba map, the oldest mosaic map of Jerusalem that shows the Cardo in its glory days. There's a hologram of the 22 meter pillar that used to stand here which gave Damascus Gate its Arabic name of **Bab al Amud** (*Gate of the Pillar*). There are two towers built by Hadrian, and in the eastern one there's a staircase leading up to the Ramparts Walk.

Just inside Jaffa Gate is **Tower of David**, *Tel. 02-627-4111, Fax 02-628-3418*, an important fortress spot from First Temple times, and now a museum of the History of Jerusalem. It was named so by Christian pilgrims even though David's city was on the other end of the Old City. Open Sunday-Thursday 9am-5pm (an hour later in summer), Friday-Saturday 9am-2pm (you can usually stay an hour later before being kicked out), it costs NIS 24 for adults, NIS 17 for students and seniors, and NIS 12 for youth.

In this reconstructed citadel that was first built by Herod 2,000 years ago, history lessons of Jerusalem are portrayed through diaramas, relics, and explanatory texts. The maze-like layout is confusing, but if you don't mind not proceding chronologically through the ages, you can't go wrong by just wandering around. To help guide you, a number of paths have been set up. Follow the red line, the green line, or the blue line, depending on how much time you set aside (it takes a good two to three hours to "do" the red line) and your interests (some paths focus on archaeology, others on history, etc.).

There is a guided tour in English leaving the main entrance Sunday-Friday at 11am, or there's a headset with recorded lecture you can rent for NIS 5, but they're in the process of improving the system. Soon they'll have a computerized disk that will elaborate on the exhibits as you come to them, rather than requiring you to follow a set path. And on Saturday nights at 9pm there's a special Whodunnit feature that's popular with kids, finding the murderer of the High Priest Aristobulus III. There's also a spring and summer sound and light show in English Monday & Wednesday at 9:30pm and Saturday at 9pm.

The Shuk (or *souk*) is the market, the bazaar, the heart of the Old City with the sights, sounds, and smells of the Middle East; it's the gauntlet that frays the nerves and patience of the most saintly. It spans the Muslim, Christian, and Armenian quarters, running principally along David Street, Khan ez-Zeit, and El Wad. For souvenirs, bargaining is the rule, and time, patience, and a sense of humor the tools of the trade. Banter is fine, but don't stand for harassment, sexual or otherwise, and take down the name of the proprietor (or at least the store) if you're subjected to unwarranted nastiness.

The **Old City Police** branch, *Tel. 02-622-6222, ext. 33*, is inside Jaffa Gate to your right, and has a tourist desk. But this isn't to say the shuk is a bad time. It's a wonderful place, especially in the morning when the day, the food, and people's smiles are still fresh.

THE TEMPLE MOUNT

The southwestern corner of the Old City is enormously sacred to Jews, Muslims, and Christians, and that's where nearly all agreement ends. By the **Temple Mount**, called *Har Bayit* in Hebrew and *Al-Haram ash-Sharif* in Arabic, scores of military stand ready to keep the peace among the hordes of the faithful. All agree that this was the biblical **Mount Moriah**, the spot where the Patriarch **Abraham** was called upon by God to sacrafice his son (Isaac according to Jews and Christians, Ishmael according to Muslims). This is the site that **Solomon** chose for his Temple in 950 BCE, and it's here that the **Holy Ark of the Covenant** was given its permanent home.

Destroyed by the Chaldeans under **Nebuchadnezzar** in 587 BCE, the **Second Temple** was built when the Jews returned from Babylon in 538 BCE. In 19 BCE Herod put his two cents in, tearing down the old and putting up a Herodian Temple complex, vast and elaborate, in its place. This, in its turn, was mostly destroyed in 70 CE by Titus following the Great Revolt, and Hadrian ordered the final razing of the Temple in 132 CE after the Bar Kokhba Rebellion. After the Second Temple was destroyed in 132 CE, Hadrian ordered a Temple of Jupiter to be built upon the Temple Mount. Emperor Constantine the Great had this torn down in the third century, and he allowed Jews to pray there once a year on the 10th of Ab in memory of the destroyed Temple. Emperor Julian the Apostate organized the rebuilding of the Temple in 361, but this activity was halted by an earthquake and Julian's death in 363.

In the southwest corner of the Old City, today's Temple Mount is a walled area within the Old City walls and administered by the **Supreme Muslim Council**, with eight entrance gates for Muslims. But while you can exit through any, only two entrances are accessible to non-Muslims: **Moor's Gate** south of the Western Wall and **Chain Gate** at the end of Bab el-Silsila. **Al Haram** and the nearby **Islamic Museum** are open to the public Saturday-Thursday 8am-noon and 1:30-3pm (approximately – the down time is based on the Muslim prayer schedule, which varies from month to month) and 7:30-10am during Ramadan.

While entrance to Al Haram is free, you need to buy a ticket to enter the mosques, and it gains you admission to the Islamic Museum as well.

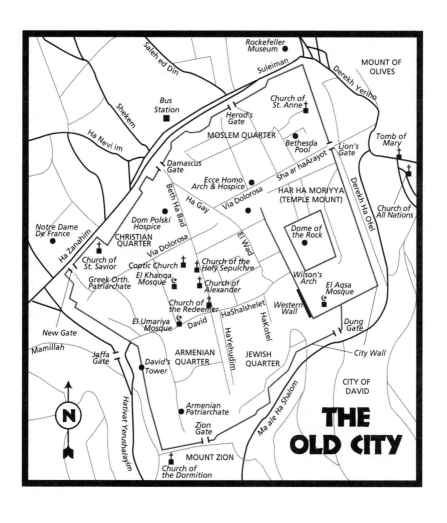

Tickets cost NIS 16 for adults, NIS 10 for students, and the ticket booth is between Al Aqsa Mosque and the museum. To enter the mosques you must be dressed modestly, and you'll have to take off your shoes. The Haram guards have very little sense of humor when it comes to tourists breaking rules. Entrance hours are strictly adhered to, and if areas are marked off-limits, don't test the boundaries. The Western Wall which abuts this complex is under different jurisdiction and has its own entrances and regulations (see below).

The Dome of the Rock (*Qubbet es-Sakhra*) is an extraordinary sight, with its gold dome, marble base, and many thousand tiles; it is also one of the best preserved example of early Islamic architecture. The dome was at one time solid gold, but the caliph's debts had to be paid, and lead replaced gold for a time. In 1958 lead was recapped with aluminim-bronze, but in 1993 the dome received a thin coat of gold. Of the tiles with their Koranic verses, many date back to Suleiman the Magnificent's time, but some were added by Jordan's King Hussein in 1950-1960. Inside it's equally beautiful, all white and gold.

The Holy Rock is associated with **Abraham** and **Ishmael** (Abraham's son by Hagar, whom the Muslims believe was the son to be sacrificed), and also with altars used for burnt offerings in the First and Second Temples. There are also sacred relics with the imprints of prophets' footprints and Angel Gabriel's fingerprints from when he held the rock steady when Mohammed rode into heaven. In the cave below is the "souls' well" where the souls of Elijah, Abraham, David, and Solomon meet twice weekly for prayer.

When the Caliph Omar conquered Jerusalem in 638 CE, he prayed at the rock of Temple Mount and recalled Abraham's call to sacrafice. In 688, Caliph Abd al-Malik had the Dome of the Rock built over the Rock of Abraham, oriented toward Mecca, and Jerusalem became a Muslim pilgrimage site. The Knights Templar took up residence there for a time while the Crusaders held the city, but Sultan Saladin took Jerusalem back in 1187, and the Dome of the Rock has been in Muslim hands ever since. After the Ka'bah in Mecca and the Prophet's tomb in Medina, it is the third holiest Islamic site.

Arab tradition has it that from this rock the **Prophet Mohammed** took off on his horse el-Buraq for his miraculous night journey to heaven, and that this was the motivation for building the mosque. Islamic scholars note, however, that the nearby **Dome of the Ascension** honors that trip, and that the drive to build the Dome of the Rock was far more compli-cated. It was a message to the Byzantine Empire and Jerusalem's Christians that Islam was there to stay, and a political message directed to Muslims in Mecca and Medina, with a competitive third Holy Shrine.

Between the Dome of the Rock and al Aqsa mosque is **El Kas** (*The Cup*) a fountain where Muslims wash before prayer. Built in 709 CE, the fountain is connected to the vast underground system of cisterns.

Al Aqsa Mosque is domed in silver rather than gold, and is the largest mosque in Jerusalem. Its name (meaning "the farthest") refers to the Koranic verse 17:1 which tells of Mohammed's trip to Heaven from the Holy Rock, "the farthest" point from his journey from Mecca, but to Jews it's known as Midrash Shlomo (the School of King Solomon). Right after the conquest of Jerusalem in 638 CE, Caliph Omar ordered the mosque built, but construction didn't begin until Abd al-Malik initiated it in 710 (probably in wood, and probably on the old site of a sixth century Crusader Church of Saint Mary); it was rebuilt many times after many earthquakes.

WEST JERUSALEM FAST FOOD & SWEETS

TA'AMI, 3 Shammai, Tel. 02-622-5911, off HaHistadrut, serves basic local items to basic local workers, dishing up plates of hummus, rice and macaroni, kebabs, and goulash for NIS 9-20. The decor isn't much to speak of, but around lunch time there are plenty of hungry men slurping up simple, good food. Not as charming or cheap as Rakhmo's, but the same sort of fare. The pita here isn't free (it's 50 agorot each), and the service isn't doting, but the fresh lemonade is great, and it's a fine mid-town option if you tire of the cafe scene.

For good, cheap, fast food there are bakeries all over town:

KHEN BAKERY, 30 Jaffa, not far up from Tourist Information, is open Sunday-Thursday 8am-5pm and has excellent cheesy burekas for just NIS 4.

CHEZ PARIS, 35 Jaffa, open nearly round the clock, is another good bakery, but more western in its outlook and baked goods, with cookies and muffins as well as burekas.

MISEDIT GAZIT, 39 Jaffa, lacks an English sign, but serves a vegetarian omlet in pita (called khavita emerakot in Hebrew or eeja in Arabic) for just NIS 6. Dressed up with hummus and salads, it makes a tasty alternative to the ubiquitous falafel.

AMI PIZZA, Emek Refdim, Tel. 02-563-0469, has servicable pizza for NIS 6 a slice. Open Sunday-Thursday 9am-midnight, and Saturday after Shabbat till midnight, a slice makes a fine snack.

BEN & JERRY'S, 5 Hillel, Tel. 02-624-2767, is off King George and open Sunday-Thursday 10am-midnight, Friday 10am-2pm, Saturday from the end of Shabbat till midnight. Same good ice cream, at NIS 5 a scoop.

It wasn't till 1033 under **Fatimid Caliph az-Zahir** that it took on its present appearance. The last major renovation took place in 1938: The central marble columns were donated by Italian dictator Benito Mussolini, and Egypt's King Farouk funded the ceiling paint job, while the stained-glass and carpets add further color to the interior.

The **Qait-Bey fountain**, built in 1487, was funded by the Egyptian Sultan Qait Bey (but supervised by a Christian constructor), and it's based on cisterns that were there long before. Many of the cisterns on the Temple Mount were at one time routes leading directly to the Temple for priestly access, but were later converted into reservoirs. According to Jewish tradition, the Holy of Holies in the Temple was on the spot now occupied by the Qait-Bey fountain.

Dome of the Chain (*Qubbet es-Silsileh*) is is an open pavilion which looks like a smaller version the Dome of the Rock to the west. The Jews refer to is as David's place of Judgement, and Muslims view it as the site where the good will be separated from the evil on the Last Judgement Day by means of a chain hung from Heaven to be grasped by the righteous. It stands in the precise middle of the Temple area, and was probably built by Caliph Abd al-Malik (685-705), who's said to have used the dome to hold his treasure. For a time the Crusaders turned it into a chapel dedicated to Jacobus. Back in Muslim hands, Sultan Suleiman the Magnificent donated the ceramic facing in the 16th century.

Nearby, the **Islamic Museum** admits those with a mosque ticket. Exhibits include architectural designs, textiles, creramics, manuscripts, coins, and weapons. The so-called **Stables of Solomon** near the al-Aqsa mosque are an enourmous underground complex of 13 aisles and 88 pillars holding up the vaults. It is believed that sacrificial animals were housed here in Solomon's day (hence the name), and it's known that some of the structures date to Herod's time. A shell-shaped niche from Roman days is referred to as "Christ's Cradle," and the Virgin Mary is said to have stood here when presenting her child in Temple (Luke 2:22). At times this site is off-limits due to terrorist fears.

The Temple site is also important to Christians in New Testament accounts. Luke tells how John the Baptist's birth was announced there by the Angel Gabriel (1:5-25), how Jesus was consecrated to the Lord there (2:22), and how some years later Jesus stayed behind in Jerusalem and was rediscovered by his parents studying in the temple courts (2:42). Jesus was tempted by the Devil there (4:9) as well. Matthew (21:12-17) tells how Jesus drove from the Temple the wheelers and dealers, calling them robbers.

And John tells of Jesus teaching at the Temple (7:14-53), and (8:2-11) how in the Temple Jesus tells those who have not sinned to cast the first stone. It is also in the Temple that Judas throws down his 30 silver coins

(Matthew 27:2-10) and after Jesus dies, Matthew (27:52) recounts that the Temple curtain was torn in two.

But, though it figures in Christian theology, it's not as important a site to them as it is to Jews and Muslims. The major impact of these connections is that when Crusaders held sway here in 1099, they left the Dome of the Rock mostly unaltered because they considered it to have been the place where Jesus taught (hence their renaming of it as *Templum Domini*, or Lord's Temple).

THE WESTERN WALL & THE JEWISH QUARTER

All that survives of the Second Temple is the **Western Wall** (*Kotel haMa'aravi*, or just *Kotel* in Hebrew), called the **Wailing Wall** by some due to the grief expressed there mourning the destruction of the Temple. The site is open to all, 24 hours a day, after passing through tight security entering from Dung Gate or along El Wad from the Old City. As a relic of that ancient and holy site, the Western Wall is held sacred among Jews.

The cracks between the big old stones brim with wads of paper holding reams of special wishes and prayers. Over the years the scraps pile up, however, and from time to time the the notes are removed and buried according to Jewish Law. At night the Wall's spectacularly lit, and it's also wonderful to watch the Orthodox welcome Shabbat with prayer, song, and dance as the sun sets Friday evening.

Not surprisingly, the largest portion of the wall is set aside for the men, rocking and chanting in their black robes and yalmakahs (there are cardboard ones available if you wish to approach the Wall and didn't bring your own), while a lesser section is aportioned to the women, who cover their heads and pray more modestly on their side. Monday and Thursday mornings are popular times for Bar Mitzvahs to be held here, and they are festive events.

Though the area is open to all, certain attitudes of decorum should be respected, such as modest dress (no shorts, no overly exposed flesh). Photographs are okay, but only during the regular week; the praying Hasidim may look photogenic, but it's not appreciated during Shabbat. If you're here in the summer, an interesting time to visit the Western Wall is Friday from 3:30pm to about 6:30pm.

FAX-A-PRAYER TO THE WAILING WALL!

*Tradition embraces modern innovation in odd combinations throughout Israel, and a fine example is the sevice **Bezek** offers. You can fax your message to them at 02-661-2222 and your prayer will be dutifully wedged in.*

Excavations have been done in the vicinity of the Wall, and **Wilson's Arch** is one of the finds. Named after the archaeologist who found it, it's in a large, arched room to the left of the Wall. It used to be part of a water-supply system in the Maccabean period, and spanned Tyropoeon (Cheesemakers') Valley, letting Jewish priests cross to the Temple from their homes. If you look down the shafts you'll get a sense of the wall's original height. The room is open to men only, and just on Sunday, Tuesday, Wednesday 8:30am-3pm, Monday and Thursday 12:30-3pm, and Friday 8:30am-noon. There are tunnels under the Western Wall area, and you can take tours of them from a number of companies (see *Tours*).

The Yitzhak Ben-Youssef Archeological Garden/Ophel, *Tel. 02-625-4403*, named for the complex built on the Ophel Hill in First Temple days, is open Sunday-Thursday 9am-4pm, Friday 9am-2pm and costs NIS 9 for adults, NIS 4.5 for youth. Near Dung Gate and extending from the foot of the Southern Wall to the southern part of the Western Wall, the site contains structures from King Solomon's days in 10th century BCE to the time of Suleiman the Magnificant who built the Old City walls in 16th century CE, including remains such as *mikvaot* (Jewish ritual baths), sections of **Robinson's Arch** (the oldest crossover in the world), and parts of the Caliph's palace. Tours help take it all in, and Archaeological Seminars does a three and a half hour tour on Sunday, Tuesday, Wednesday, and Friday at 9:30am.

In the southeast of the Old City, the **Jewish Quarter** offers sacred sites, Roman ruins, synagogues, history, and tiny winding stone streets. Step off the main plaza, stray from the Cardo complex and the tour groups in full-throated explanation and you can easily find yourself completely lost among old houses, cobbled paths, and Hasidic boys coming back from yeshiva. There are many yeshivas and small synagogues in and about the alleys and courtyards of the quarter, and you are generally welcome to stop in, visit, and learn. This was the ritzy Upper City in Second Temple times, but after Jews were driven from the city in 135 CE, a Jewish community didn't begin to reestablish itself here till the late 1400s (when Jews were kicked out of Spain).

In 1800 the Jewish community held 2,000 people; by 1865 that number had grown to 11,000, and Jews started looking outside the city walls for housing. By British Mandate times, the Jewish Quarter had become an overcrowed slum, a problem soon solved by fierce fighting between Jews and Jordanians. This section of the city was devastated by the fighting, and few of the buildings survived. When the Jordanians took the Old City, the remaining Jews were evacuated. Now, about 650 families live in the fairly pricey Jewish Quarter, mostly Orthodox (and many American in origin). After Israel reclaimed this quarter following the Six Day War of '67, the rubble of destruction was cleared and a lot of building went on, incorporating gracefully what remained of the old, and leaving room for excavations to delve into the older still.

A section of the Roman **Cardo Maximus** (think 'heart' of the city) has been uncovered off David Street near Jewish Quarter Road. The Cardo was Jerusalem's main artery in Roman and Byzantine times, and it appears on the sixth century Madaba mosaic map of the city (a copy of which is on display). You can see part of the original street, flanked by pillar remains, as well as remains of the city walls from First and Second Temple days, though the site is a bit overshadowed by the nearby complex of overpriced boutiques and shops and galleries.

The Cardo is open till 11pm, and illuminated nicely after dark. **One Last Day**, *Tel. 02-628-8141*, is an interesting exhibit in the Cardo complex. It shows a sereis of photographs taken by John Phillips the day the Jordanians took the Jewish Quarter in 1948. Open Sunday-Thursday 9am-5pm and Friday 9am-1pm, it costs NIS 5 to get in.

The Hurva and Ramban Synagogues are just off Jewish Quarter Street near the southern end of the Cardo, built over the ruins of the Crusader Church of Saint. Martin. A stored stone arch stands over what's left of the ruins of the **Hurva Synagogue**, recalling the synagogue built by followers of Rabbi Yehudi the Hassid in 1700. It was demolished by Muslims 21 years later, giving the synagogue and surrounding courtyard the name of Hurva (which means "ruins"). This important Ashkenazi community synagogue was rebuilt in 1856, and was destroyed once more by Jordanian explosives in 1948.

Next to Hurva stands **Ramban Synagogue**, named after Rabbi Moshe Ben-Nahman (his acronym formed 'Ramban,' but he was also known as Nachmanides). He was considered a great sage, and inside is the letter he wrote in 1267, the year he arrived from Spain, describing the poor state of the Jewish community he found in Jerusalem. The synagogue is believed to have originally stood on Mount. Zion, but was moved to its present site around 1400. The minaret was built in the 1400s by the mother of someone who converted to Islam after arguing with neighbors. In the 1500s when Jews were forbidden to pray here, the building served as a workshop, and later (during the British Mandate) as a cheese and butter shop. Today it's back to being a synagogue

Next to the synagogues is the **War of Independence Memorial**, paying tribute to those Jews who died in battles here in the 1948 War of Independence.

The Old Yshuv Court Museum, *6 Or HaChayim, Tel./Fax 02-628-4636*, is up the steps at the southern end of the Cardo – cross over, and up the other side. The exhibits how things were in the quarter before 1948, with rooms set up to reflect various aspects of Jewish life. Open Sunday-Thursday 9am-2pm, it costs NIS 8, NIS 5 for students.

More city history is available through the **Jerusalem Multi-Media Presentation**, *1 Jewish Quarter Road*, shown Sunday-Thursday at 11am, 2pm, and 5pm in English near the parking lot. The show lasts 35 minutes and costs NIS 12.

Not far from the southern end of Jewish Quarter Road – take a left on HaTuppim, left again, and down the stairs – are the four **Sephardic Synagogues**. The Sephardic community built these synagogues underground in the late 1500s because laws of the time forbade synagogues to be built taller than the surrounding buildings. The large chambers beneath the street allowed a sense of loftiness otherwise unattainable in those times. These synagogues (named Rabbi Yohanan Ben-Zakkai, Elijah the Prophet, the Central, and the Istanbuli Synagogues) were used by the Jordanians as sheep pens, but were restored using remains of WWII damaged Italian synagogues. Still vital to the Sephardic community, services are held twice daily. They are open to viewers Sunday-Thursday 9:30am-12:30pm and additional hours 12:30-4pm Wednesday-Thursday, and admission is free.

Batei Machseh Square was once the quarter's largest square, and in the 19th century this was the site of an independent Jewish neighborhood. The **Shelter Houses** here were built to provide for the poor. During the last 10 days of fighting in 1948, hundreds of Jews hid in the basements, close to the nearby Jewish military headquarters. One such was Rothschild Building A, built in 1871 by the Baron Wolf Rothschild of Frankfurt.

Tife'eret Yisrael Synagogue (*Glory of Israel*) was dedicated in 1872 as the twin brother of the Hurva Synagogue. Its tall frame and dome served as a well-known quarter landmark till it was demolished in 1948. This was once the largest Hassidic center in the Old City. Its ruins stand on Tife'eret Yisrael Road, near the northeast corner of the courtyard behind the Hurva Synagogue.

Burnt House, *east on Tife'eret Yisrael and next to the Quarter Café, Tel. 02-628-7211*, is open Sunday-Thursday 9am-5pm, Friday 9am-1pm, and costs NIS 7.5 for adults, NIS 6 per child and student (the combo ticket, including the Israelite Tower and Wohl Archaeological Museum, costs NIS 16, NIS 13 for students). They have shows every half hour 9am-4:30pm describing how this once luxurious house in the Second Temple era's Upper City was destroyed by the Romans in 70CE following the Great Revolt. They set fire to all of Upper City and killed the inhabitants after first razing the Temple. Excavations of this house gave direct evidence of this, what with the severed bones and carbonized spears they found.

Saint Maria of the Germans, *Misgav Ladakh*, is a 12th century church, hospital, and hospice, just east of the Quarter Café.

The Wide Wall, *at the western end of Tife'eret Yisreal and north on Plugat Ha-Kotel,* is what's left of the Israelite wall that once circled the City of David, the Temple Mount, and the Upper City. King Hezekiah built it in 701 BCE, along with his tunnel, to defend his city and its water access against Assyrian attacks.

The Israelite Tower, *east of the Cardo on Shonei HaLakhot (corner of Plugat Hakotel)*, is the tower of the northern wall gate from the Babylonian seige when the First Temple was destroyed in 586 BCE. Open Sunday-Thursday 9am-5pm and Friday 9am-1pm, it costs NIS 7.5 for adults, NIS 6 per child and student, or get the combo ticket including the Burnt House and Wohl Archaeological Museum for NIS 16, NIS 13 for students.

The Rachel Ben-Zvi Center, *across from the Israelite Tower, Tel. 02-628-6288*, is open Sunday-Thursday 9am-4pm and Fridays by appointment, admission costs NIS 8. This institute focuses its research on the history of Jewish communities. Of more interest to most visitors is their model of Jerusalem in First Temple days, along with archaeological findings from King David's rule (the water system as shown by the model is pretty elaborate).

New Church was the New Church built by Justinian in 543. Its southern apse sticks outside the city wall, and after the Holy Sepulcher it was once the city's second grandest church. When Justinian extended the Cardo, he did so in all likelihood to connect up with this church.

The Siebenberg House, *35 Misgav Ladakh, corner of HaGittit, Tel. 02-628-2341*, is an archaeological museum. Open Sunday-Thursday 9am-5pm, and costing NIS 10, it features a Hasmonean cistern and aqueduct parts that may once have connected Solomon's Pools to the Temple.

The Wohl Archaeological Museum, *off the Jewish Quarter's main square, Herodian Quarter, Tel. 02-628-3448*, is around the corner the Yeshivat Ha-Kotel and is open Sunday-Thursday 9am-5pm, and Friday 9am-1pm, costing NIS 10 for adults, and NIS 9 for students. A combined ticket with the Israelite Tower and Burnt House costs NIS 16, NIS 13 for students. This vast complex shows renovated mansions built for the Temple's high priests, and illustrates how the wealthy Upper City folk lived in Herod's day. The Cohanim and Temple servants lived quite well, as shown by the frescoes, stucco reliefs, fancy furniture, and floor mosaics on display.

CHRISTIAN & MUSLIM QUARTERS

These two quarters take up the northern portion of the Old City, and within its quadrant are many sites holy to Christians, such as the Church of the Holy Sepulchre and the Via Dolorosa, and Muslims too, as well as densely packed shuk alleys catering to (perceived) tourists' needs.

The **Via Dolorosa** (literally, *The Way of Suffering*) is believed to be the route Jesus took as he carried his cross to Skull Hill. Divided into the Via Dolorosa and Via Dolorosa East (with a turn left then right connecting the two), the street starts from the east in the old Muslim Quarter near Saint Stephen's Gate and ends west in the Church of the Holy Sepulchre. All along the way the **Stations of the Cross** are honored on this route, mounted at intervals on church walls or placed in outdoor shrines, though some are hard to find, and others are mobbed by large flocks of tourists being herded from one to the next.

VIA DOLOROSA: THE STATIONS OF THE CROSS

*As with many Christian holy sites, the faith that this **Via Dolorosa** is the path goes back to the Byzantines, who traced Holy Thursday processions from Gethsamane to Cavalry, pretty much along the path now marked out as Via Dolorosa, though minus the official stops. Over the years, the routes taken were changed and argued about. As Christianity became more divided, church locations (they all had their own) complicated procession routes, one saying the Praetorium was on Mount Zion, and another saying that no, it was to the north.*

The idea of the stations emerged during the Middle Ages, when they developed as a devotional substitute for actually following the Via Dolorosa, the route in Jerusalem that Christ followed to Calvary. By the 14th century, the Franciscans mapped out a walk including some of today's stations but starting at the Holy Sepulchre. This became the accepted route for nearly 200 years till the European pilgrims started adding to the eight stations, following more gospel stops, and totaling 14. The Jerusalem Way of the Cross as we know it now came into use in the 1800s, and probably has little in common with historic reality, as best as scholars can figure.

The 14 Stations of the Cross (eight of which are mentioned in the Gospels) can be seen with tour groups, or on your own with guide book and map. Or you can join the Franciscan Friars' processions (often complete with carried cross) Fridays at 3pm starting at Station 1.

The **1st Station**, *200 meters west of Saint Stephen's Gate*, is near Saint Anne's Church – see the following section of *Other Sites along the Via Dolorosa* – in the courtyard of **Al Omariyeh College**, *through the door at the top of the ramp east of the Ecce Homo Arch*, and it's closed 1-3pm. *Gabbatha* in Hebrew (meaning elevation) and *Lithostrotos* in Greek (meaning stone pavement), this is where Pilate sat in judgment and condemned Jesus to death on the cross (Saint John 19:13). This building was once Turkish military barracks on the sight of the Herodian Antonia fortress. Aside from historic and religious significance, the main attraction is the view of the Temple Mount.

The **2nd Station**, *marked by a board across from the Omariyeh College*, signifies where Jesus took up the cross. To the right of the station is the **Chapel of Flagellation** where Jesus was scourged by Roman soliders; open daily 8am-noon and 1-5pm, the dome is decorated with a crown of thorns and the windows depict the witnessing mob. To the left is another Franciscan building, **Condemnation Chapel**, built on the foundations of a Byzantine church.

Continuing along the Via Dolorosa you come to the Ecce Homo Convent, Arch, and archaeological remains (see the following section of *Other Sites along the Via Dolorosa*). The **3rd Station**, where Via Dolorosa intersects with El-Wad, is where Jesus first fell while carrying the cross. A small Polish chapel built in 1947 marks the spot with a relief in the arch above the lintel showing Jesus falling under the weight of the cross.

Just past the Hospice is the **4th Station**, where Jesus saw his mother in the crowd. Commemorated by the Chapel of the Swooning Virgin (built around 1950) and the Armenian Catholic Church of the Virgin Mary's Sorrows (built 1881), this event is not mentioned in the New Testament.

The **5th Station** *requires a right turn on Via Dolorosa* to where Simon the Cyrene (from modern day Libya) helped Jesus carry the cross. A Franciscan chapel built in 1881 with signs on the door mark the spot.

Fifty meters on is the **6th Station** where Veronica wiped Jesus' face with her cloth (*sudarium* in Latin). Neither Veronica nor sudarium is mentioned in the bible, but the holy relic of the cloth, complete with imprint of Jesus' face, is revered by the Catholic Church; it's on display at the Greek Orthodox Patriarchate in the Christian Quarter.

The **7th Station** is for Jesus' second fall, honored by a Fransciscan chapel built in 1875 and by *signs on the wall west of Shuk khan ez-Zeit*. In the first century this marked the edge of the city with a gate, a fact used to substantiate the argument that the Church of the Holy Sepulchre is the true location of Jesus' crucifixion.

The **8th Station** represents where Jesus said to the lamenting women "Weep not for me, but weep for yourselves, and for your children..." (Saint Luke 23:28-30). This is a difficult one to find. Cross Khan ez-Zeit and ascend Aqabatel-Khanqa. *Just past the Greek Orthodox Convent on the left* is the stone with a cross and the inscription IC XC NIKA (Jesus Christ is victorious) to mark the station.

For the **9th Station**, there are remnants of a pillar back on *Khan ez-Zeit by the Coptic Church*, marking the point where Jesus fell for a third time. The remaining stations are all in the Church of the Holy Sepulcher, so retrace your steps back to the main street and head there.

For the **10th Station**, enter the Church of the Holy Sepulcher and climb the steep stairway on your right. The chapel has two naves, and the entrance to the one on the right, the Franciscan one, is where Jesus had his clothes stripped from his body. At the far end of this same chapel is the **11th Station** where Juseus was nailed to the cross. The other nave is the Greek Orthodox Chapel, and in there is the **12th Station** where Jesus was crucified and died. To mark the spot there hangs a life-sized Jesus amid flowers and the flames of oil lamps and candles.

The **13th Station**, between the 11th and 12th, is where Jesus was taken down from the cross and received by Mary, as commemorated by a statue of a bejeweled Mary with a silver dagger stuck in her breast. And lastly the **14th Station**, down in the Holy Sepulcher, is where Jesus was buried. Walk down the stairs past the Greek Orthodox Chapel to the ground floor. In the center of the rotunda is a large marble complex surrounded by candles, the Holy Sepulchre, within which is the actual tomb. Beyond the Chapel of the Angel is the Tomb of Jesus, amid still more candles. Around the back of the Holy Sepulchre is the Coptic Chapel where pilgrims come to kiss the wall of the tomb.

Not the prettiest church, **The Church of the Holy Sepulcher** is definitely one of the most sacred of Christian sites, standing above Cavalry (also known as Golgatha), the spot most agree was where Jesus was crucified, where he died and was entombed, and where he rose again. The church is open daily from 4:30am-8pm in summer and to 7pm in winter, but only to those in suitable modest dress. The guards don't mess around, and hold no truck with bare shoulders, legs, or midriffs. Shorts are not acceptable, even in summer. *The main entrance is in the southern courtyard, accessable from Christian Quarter Road or Dabbaga Road off Shuk Khan ez-Zeit.*

The area around **Cavalry** rock was revered by Christians as early as the first century CE, following the Jewish tradition of the time of praying at the tombs of holy people. When Hadrian kicked the Jews out of Jerusalem following the Bar Kokhba Rebellion of 135 CE, he did his best to surpress the budding Christianity and its significant sites as well. The place of the Crucifixion and Resurrection was targeted, and a temple to Venus was erected in its place.

Nearly two centuries later in 326 CE Helena (Emperor Constantine's mother) visited the Holy Land and went around locating and naming the holy sites. Makarios, the Bishop of Jerusalem, showed her where Jesus had been crucified. She initiated some excavations and came upon a tomb (which she identified as the tomb of Joseph of Arimathea) and three crosses, confirming her belief in the holiness of the spot. Shortly thereafter Constantine issued an order to pull down the Venus temple and in its stead build a basilica. It was consecrated in 335 as Anastasis (the Church of the Resurrection); it was destroyed in 614 by the Persians, and later rebuilt. The Caliph al-Hakim demolished it in 1009, leaving little, and a new church was built by the Crusaders in 1149, the church that is there today, though it's buttressed by some of Constantine's foundations. Given its religious importance (five of the 14 stations of the cross are located within), all the Christian communities and divisions have angled for as much Church of the Holy Sepulchre terrain as possible. In 1852 the Ottomon Empire passed the **Law of the Status Quo** (and the law still stands today), declaring who got what. So the Church of the Holy Sepulcher, the rotunda, the chapel of the Holy Sepulchre, and the anointment stone all belong jointly to the Greek Orthodox, the Armenian, and the Roman Catholic churches, while the Copts, Syrians, and Ethiopians get only individual chapels. This feuding has injured the church a bit in that it's not kept up as it should be. There were fires in 1808 and 1949 and an earthquake in 1927, but the cooperation hasn't existed to pool resources and funds and make all the necessary restorations.

The church is a conglomeration of chapels and alters and stations of the cross. Once in the church, the **Anointment Stone** is the first holy site you come to. The reddish-brown limestone slab is regarded as the place where the body of Jesus was anointed before he was entombed. Underneath the Golgotha chapel is the Greek Orthodox **Chapel of Adam**, where a skull was found, and the claim is that it's the skull of Adam.

Above the Chapel of Adam is **Golgotha Rock**. Golgotha is interpreted to mean "place of a skull," probably from the Aramaic *gulgulta* meaning skull, whereas Cavalry derives from the Latin *calvaria* which means brain case or skull. The argument in Byzantine times ran that the name was given to the rock because Adam was buried here, but some scholars nowadays figure the most likely interpretation is that Golgotha was a skull-shaped hill outside the walls of Jerusalem which was used as a place of execution and burial. By this definition, both the Holy Sepulchre and the Garden Tomb (see *East Jerusalem Sights*) fit the specifications.

The rotunda's 165 foot high dome spans the **Holy Sepulcher**, and is the primary focus of faith and candle-lit glow. The portico of the chamber is called the **Angel Chapel** because tradition has it that the angels were sitting here when they announced to the women that Christ had risen. The body of Jesus lay in the burial chamber on the bench now faced in marble.

Behind the Holy Sepulcher is the **Chapel of the Copts**, which boasts a part of the rock tomb which can be seen (and kissed) at the alter in back. And to the right of the Sepulcher is the **Chapel of Mary Magdalene**, celebrating where she, along with two others, discovered the empty tomb on Easter morning. She is also believed to be the first to have seen the Risen Christ. The church holds many more chapels to wander through. There's the **Chapel of the Appearance** (where Jesus appeared to his mother), the **Prison of Christ** (where Jesus and other criminals were supposedly held prisoner), the **Seven Arches of the Virgin Mary**, the **Crypt of the Invention of the Cross** (where Helena is said to have found the cross Jesus died on), and more.

The **Ethiopian Monastery**, *up some stairs on Khan ez-Zeit*, is right over part of the Church of the Holy Sepulchre, and since the Ethiopians weren't alloted any of the church itself they value their access to the Holy Sepulcher roof. This pleasant monastery with green doors also has access to the Church of the Holy Sepulcher through the Ethiopian Chapel.

Next to the Holy Sepulchre are two mosques. The **Khanqah Salahiyya** is to the north. Built in the late 1100s but with a minaret added in 1417 during restorations, the Khanqah mosque is on the site of the Crusader Patriarch of Jerusalem's palace. The **Mosque of Omar** to the south was built in 1193, and its minaret was also added later in the 1400s. The mosques are not open to non-Muslims, and the minarets are a puzzle. Seemingly meant to match (note the design and material), it has also been pointed out by someone good at geometry that the mid-point of an imaginary line drawn between the two minarets would be the entrance to the Tomb of Jesus in the Holy Sepulcher. Merely coincidental? Many think not, though the intent remains mysterious.

In the east of the Christian Quarter is an area called **Muristan** (named for the Persian word for hospice), after a ninth century hospice built here by Charlemagne. Sultan Abdulhamid II in 1896 gave the east section to the German state and the west to the Greek Orthodox. **Saint Alexander's Church**, a block east of the Church of the Holy Sepulcher on Dabbaga, attends to the Russian mission in exile. With its restored triumphal arch dating from Hadrian's times, there is also a part of the pavement from Hadrian's Temple to Venus that replaced the first Church of the Holy Sepulcher. Open for sevices Thursdays at 7am when prayers are said for Tsar Alexander III, its excavations are open Monday-Saturday 9am-1pm and 3-5pm and cost NIS 2 – ring the bell to be let in.

Kaiser Wilhelm II's **Lutheran Church of the Redeemer**, *across the street from Saint Alexander's Church, Tel. 02-627-6111*, is open Monday-Saturday 9am-1pm and 1:30-5pm. To climb the tall white bell tower and feel like Quasimodo, enter on Muristan and climb the spiral staircase to the top. There's also a nice medieval door with zodiac signs.

The Greek Orthodox **Church of John the Baptist**, *Christian Quarter Road*, is nearby. It's the oldest surviving church in Jerusalem, or at least the lower level is. Built by the Byzantines in the fifth century, it serves as a base for the more recent 12th century Crusader addition.

Greek Orthodox Patriarchate Museum, *Greek Orthodox Patriarchate Street, Tel. 02-628-9112*, is open Tuesday-Friday 9am-1pm and 3-5pm, and Saturday 9am-1pm, and costs NIS 1 to get in. It contains gifts from pilgrims and early Patriarchate printings in a recontructed Crusader building. It also features the imprinted cloth with which Veronica wiped the face of Jesus (see *Station of the Cross #6*).

OTHER SIGHTS ALONG THE VIA DOLOROSA

Saint Anne's Church by Lion's Gate (also known as Saint Stephen's Gate) is one of the best-preserved Crusader churches in Israel. It is traditionally viewed as the site of Saint Anne, the Virgin Mary's mother. The basilica, built in 1140 on some fifth century ruins, resembles a castle. It was used as a mosque for some 700 years after Saladin captured Jerusalem. Next to the church is the **Pool of Bethesda**, an archaeological excavation of an eary Roman pool where Jesus healed a crippled man (Saint John 5:1).

Ecce Homo Convent archaeological remains, *Via Dolorosa, Tel. 02-627-7292*, is open Monday-Saturday 8:30am-12:30pm and 2-5pm, and costs NIS 5 for adults and NIS 3 for students. The excavations here, funded by the Sisters of Sion, showcase the **Struthion Pool**, some Roman pavement, and the **Ecce Homo Triumphal Arch**. The convent is believed to be just north of where Herod's Antonia Fortress stood, surrounded by a moat. Herod had it built in 30 BCE, destroying part of the canal (built by the Hasmoneans in second century BCE to provide water to the Temple Mount cisterns) when the moat was dug. A reservoir (the Struthion Pool, a part of the moat) replaced the canal to serve the fortress. The pool was later vaulted over by Hadrian (second century CE) and turned into a cistern.

Much of the convent is built over the cistern remains. The Roman pavement was laid above the cistern and seved as a plaza. Hadrian's triple Truimphal Arch formed a gate to the plaza, and the largest one was known as Ecce Homo Arch. This arch now marks the spot the church remembers for Jesus' trial before Pilate (John 19:5) and his words "Behold the man" (*Ecce Homo* in Latin).

ELSEWHERE IN THE MUSLIM QUARTER

The architecture is Ayyubid and Mamluk, the area is the largest, the population is the densest, and the quarter is the least well-explored by travelers. Near the entrance to the Temple Mount is **Bab el-Silsilah**, a street built on what used to be part of the Mamluk route over the Tyropoeon (Cheesemaker) Valley and leading to Chain Gate. It eventually becomes David Street deep in the core of the tourist markets and exits out by Jaffa Gate.

Near the beginning of the street is the **Khan as-Sultan**, a well-preserved Crusader caravansary which lodged merchants and donkeys.

Farther down and to the right (just past Misgav Ladakh) is the **Tashtamuriya Building**. It holds the tomb of none other than the builder himself, Tashtamuriya (d. 1384), and used to be an Islamic college.

If you follow Bab el-Silsilah to its intersection with HaKotel you'll come to the **Kilaniya Mausoleum** (1352) and its Mamluk half-dome. Further on are the **Tomb of Lady Turkan** (Turba Turkan Khatun, 1352) and **Turba Sadiyya** (1311). And at the end of Bab el-Silsilah on the right is the **Tankiziya Building**, built in 1328 by a Mamluk with a varied career. He started out as a slave, rose to Governor of Damascus, and then fell back down to imprisonment and execution. This building is on the site of what used to be the Sanhedrin, and is now occuupied by Israalis for its strategic location near the Western Wall and Temple Mount.

Aqabat et-Takiya is a small street that intersects with El Wad. On it stands the old palace **Serai es-Sitt Tunshuq** (1382) which is now an ophanage. Across the street is the domed tomb **Turbatt es-Sitt Tunshuq**, built by and for the lord of the palace. On the corner with El Wad is an old pilgrim's hospice **Ribat Bayram Jawish**; built in 1540, it's one of the last examples of Mamluk architecture.

Tariq Bab en Nazir is another main route to the Temple Mount, and as with the others, it's named after the gate (*bab*) at the end. The gate has two names: Gate of the Inspector and Gate of the Prison. The former refers to the founder, and the latter to the Turks who used Ribat Mansuri (built in 1282 and once a hospice) as a prison. Nearby is **Ribat Ala ed-din el-Basir** (built in 1267 as a hospice and the first Mamluk builing in the city). Next to the gate is the **Supreme Muslim Council** office, the grandly decorated place to plead you case (probably futiley) if you want access to a Muslim site not currently open to tourists.

Tariq Bab el-Hadid leads from El Wad to the Temple Mount's Iron Gate. There is some very nice stone work to see there, as well as a fine view of the Western Wall. **Madrasa Jawhariyya** is on this street. Built in 1440, it was once a college, while the building next door, **Ribat Kurd**, was a hospice built in 1293. Across the street were two more colleges, **Madrasa Arghuniyya** (1358) and **Madrasa Muzhiriyya** (1480). And further still is the **Small Wall**. Also known as the Hidden Wall, it's marked by a sign near the Iron Gate. It's now part of a Muslim house, but it's also part of the very same Western Wall revered by Jews.

Shuk el Qattanin was the Market of Cotton Merchants, and the vaulted passageway was built in the 1200s to provide income for the poor. **Hammam el-Ayn** and **Hammam esh-Shifa**, two Turkish style baths, are also on this street.

On El Wad itself is **Beit Sharon**, home of the Israeli controversial politician and fighter Ariel Sharon. He bought this spot in the middle of the Muslim Quarter, as he did many things, to make a statement about the rights of Jews to live anywhere in Israel.

ARMENIAN QUARTER

In the southwest quadrant of the Old City between Jaffa and Zion gates, this quarter manages to maintain its own schools, library, residential section, unique flavor and language. Aramaic, the old biblical language, is still spoken on the street and in the churches. Armenia was the first nation to adopt Christianity in the fourth century, but their kingdom was dissolved later that century, resulting in centuries of exile and persecution, climaxing in the Turkish massacre of 1.5 million in 1915. The exiled community here identifies strongly with their language, culture, and church.

Armenian Compound, *Armenian Patriarchate Road, Tel. 02-628-2331*, lodges around 1,000 Armenians and is closed to tourists, though visits can sometimes be arranged if you call. It used to be a pilgrims' hospice but turned residential to accomodate the refugees after 1915. Fgo in Jaffa Gate and turn right, skirting the Tower of David.

Saint James Cathedral, *Armenian Patriarchate, just past Saint James Street*, is open for services daily 3-3:30pm. Originally built in the 400s CE, the cathedral honors both Saint James the Greater and the Lesser. Saint James the Greater was the first martyred Apostle. He was beheaded, supposedly on this site, by Herod Agrippas in 44 CE and then delivered to Mary on the wings of angels. Saint James the Lesser lies entombed in the northern chapel. He was the first bishop of Jerusalem but was chased out by Jews who disapproved of his teachings. The cathedral was destroyed by Persians in the seventh century, rebuilt by Armenians in the 11th century, and the Crusaders enlarged it 100 years later. The Armenian touch can be seen in all the beautiful tiles throughout the ornate cathedral, with loads of hanging lamps and censors.

The Mardigian Museum, *further along Armenian Patriarchate, Tel. 02628-2331*, is open to all Monday-Saturday 9:30am-4:30pm for NIS 5 (or NIS 3 for students) – follow the Armenian Museum signs or enter from Saint James Cathedral. This museum with nice courtyard and arched colonnades, previously a theological seminary built in 1843, tells the story of Armenia from early Christianity in 46 CE to the Turkish massacre of 1.5 million Armenians in 1915.

The **Convent of the Olive Tree** is down the narrow street near the museum and through the gateway in the wall. Built around 1300 and beautifully, classically Armenian, the best time to visit is 8-9am, though someone from the convent will usually be willing to let you in until noon (admission is free). It's believed that this was the site of the house of high priest Annas, father-in-law to Caiaphas (John 18:13). Some also think that this is where Jesus was imprisoned instead of where the Via Dolorosa stations indicate. And in the 15th century the belief circulated that the olive tree in the courtyard was the very same to which Jesus was tied before being flogged. The stone in the northeast corner is also of theological significance, thought to be the stone Luke (19:40) said would have cried out had not the disciples praised God.

The **Syrian Orthodox Convent** and **Saint Mark's Chapel**, *Ararat*, is the site, according to Syrian church belief, of Saint Mark's house. The Virgin Mary is believed to have been baptized here and that the Last Supper took place here as well – this in contrast to most other Christians who see the Cenacle on Mount Zion as the true locale. Open in the afternoon (ring the bell), the door is marked by a lovely mosaic, and there's an interesting painting, on leather canvas, of the Virgin and Child attributed to Saint Luke. To get there from Armenian Patriarchate Road, turn left on Saint James and again on Ararat, and there you are.

MOUNT ZION

"Zion" first referred to the fortress on the eastern hill of Jerusalem belonging to the Jebusites (one of the tribes occupying Canaan prior to the Israelites moving in) before David took it over. The southwest hill was where David's city was thought to stand, and since Byzantine times has been known as Mount Zion. You can exit the Old City through Zion Gate to get there or take bus 1 or 38 from Western Jerusalem.

The **Cenacle** (Greek for *supper*) or **Coenaculum** (Latin for *dining hall*) is where the **Last Supper** is generally thought to have occurred (except by the Syrian Orthodox, see above). The Room of the Last Supper through the green door is from a Crusader building, and inside there's an interesting scene depicting a pelican (a Christian symbol for repentance) feeding two young ones blood from his heart.

Below is **King David's tomb**. Tradition has it that it was one of the first synagogue spots. There's a tomb there now in a Crusader niche, with plentiful decorations. It's used sometimes as a synagogue, with a blue tiled niche facing Mecca so Muslims can pray here as well, while the Christians pray upstairs. There is no evidence that David was really buried here, it's too far from his city, but it's a lovely spot and highly revered. Open daily 8am-5pm, admission is free.

MOUNT ZION'S MANY RULERS

This is a favorite place for Christians and Jews to fight about. There was a village of Jews here during First Temple times. Then there was a community of early Christians living here, and during Byzantine rule a church was built here. The Persians destroyed the Byzantine church, and then the Crusaders came, killing Muslims as they went, and they built a huge complex here.

So Jews claimed it as theirs, Christians did the same, and in the 15th century the Turks came in and made it a mosque (the mihrab can still be seen on the southern wall). The bullet holes attest to its popularity among the many religions, but now all religions can pray here, and there's a nice view from the roof, as well. It was an important view for Jews before '67 as it was a place from which they could see the Temple Mount (Israel's president used to climb up here to pray during 1948-1967). From up here you can also see the Kidron Valley leading down toward the Dead Sea, the Hill of Ill Repute, and the Hill of Evil Council, the latter named after Caiphus.

Diaspora Yeshiva, *below the Cenacle, Tel. 02-671-6841,* is where many Americans study Torah. Outside across the courtyard and across from David's Tomb is the **Chamber of the Holocaust**, *Tel. 02-671-5105,* open Sunday-Thursday 8am-6pm, Friday 8am-2pm, costing NIS 7, and commemorating the victims of WWII. Not as elaborate as Yad Vashem, it's still an effective display.

The **Museum of King David**, *next door,* exhibits modern art that's meant to evoke his life and spirit. And the **Palombo Musuem**, *across the street to the left, Tel. 02-673-6640,* exhibits works of the same sculptor who did the Knesset gate and pieces in Yad Vashem.

Dormitsion Church, *off the right fork of the road leading to the Cenacle, Tel. 02-671-9927,* is the big, beautiful bascilica commemorating where Mary "fell asleep" (died). Open daily 8am-noon and 2-6pm, admission free, the church stands on the site of the late fourth century Byzantine Haiga Sion, a huge building which was destroyed in 996 and had been described as the 'mother of all churches' because it was believed to be the place where Jesus washed the disciples feet, where the Last Supper took place, where Peter denied Jesus, where Judas betrayed him, and where the disciples were filled with the Holy Spirit and enabled to speak in many tongues. The church here now is relatively new, built in the early 1900's by the Benedictines on land 'given' them by the King of Austria.

The church sustained quite a lot of damage during the fighting in 1948 and 1967, and parts of the bascilica have never been repaired. Mosaics on the wall and floor of the crypt show Mary in a coffin, gaudy with gold, there's a figure of her stretched out in a restful death position, and the floor is inlaid with figures of the zodiac. Downstairs is an interesting mosaic of Jesus surrounded by Biblical women. The complex has a cafe selling cakes and drinks (including beer).

The **Church of Saint Peter in Gallicantu** (Saint Peter of the Cockcrow) stands on the eastern slope of Mount Zion as you descend toward the Sultan's Pool. Open Monday-Saturday 8-11:45am and 2-5pm and with free admission, it's built on foundations from Herodian and early Christian times, though the building there now was consecrated in 1931. The church is known as the site of Peter's threefold denial of Christ, and the grotto below is supposedly the prison where Caiaphas held Jesus prisoner (though not according to the Church of the Holy Sepulchre). There's a fine view from the church balcony, looking over the City of David, the Arab village of Silwan, and the three valleys below.

THE CITY OF DAVID

Southeast of Temple Mount between the Tyropeoen and Kidron valleys is where Jerusalem started back in the 20th century BCE. Excavations began in 1850, but only recently have answers begun to make sense. Archaeologists agree that the steep hill of **Ophel** (*hump*) is in fact the site of the Jebusite city conquered by King David.

It seems the early walls enclosed an area of some eight acres. It was a strategic location, taking into account the major considerations of war and water. The top of a hill is traditionally easier to defend, and nearby was the water source of Gihon Spring (meaning Spring that Gushes). In peaceful times the townspeople came and went through Water Gate, but for seige conditions, there was a shaft to import water without leaving the safety of the city walls. These features played a role in David's strategy for taking the city, as he sent his soldier Joab down the walls of the shaft.

In 1867 the biblical account (2 Sarmuel 5:8) was confirmed by the long shaft found by archeologist Warren. In 701 BCE King Hezekiah, fearing an attack from the Assyrians, adapted the system to prevent David's trick from being turned against him. He built a tunnel to bring water from Gihon Spring into the city and into a resevoir (the pool of Shiloah or Siloam), hiding the spring entrance from prying Assyrian eyes. In 1880 after the tunnel was excavated, an inscription (the Siloam Inscription) was found celebrating the completion of the tunnel by Hezekiah's engineers.

To see the **excavations**, go out Dung Gate, turn left, and walk down the hill to the entrance. There's a signposted path leading round the excavations, pointing out the Jebusite citadel and Jerusalem's Upper City where the wealthy lived before Babylon put an end to their high style. The site is open daily 9am-5pm and it's free.

There's a small **museum**, *100 meters down from the City of David entrance, Tel. 02-628-8141*, with photos of the excavation in progress, and **Warren's Shaft** down the spiral staircase. Open Sunday-Thursday 9am-5pm and Friday 9am-1pm and costing NIS 3.5, bring a flashlight to see the walls that Joab scaled.

Downhill from the shaft, **Hezekiah's Tunnel** is open for soggy exploration, but you'd be advised to do so with a guide. The water reaches a few feet high, the trip takes a good half hour before you emerge wet and mucky out the other end, and a flashlight (not to mention shoes that won't be ruined by a little water) are recommended. Enter at the Gihon source on Shiloah Way (off Jericho Road going toward Kidron Valley from Mount of Olives) and take the tunnel to the Pool of Shiloah (*Silwan* in Arabic, or *Siloam* in Hebrew). It's open all day free of charge, but not necessarily free of hassle, and Arab buses run up and down the valley.

KIDRON VALLEY

Kidron Valley (*Valley of the Dark One*) lies between Temple Mount and the Mount of Olives. In the time of the Israelite kings (1020-922 BCE) Kidron formed the eastern city boundary of Jerusalem. It must have had a running river in biblical times, since Aza told the Levites to clean out the desecrating idols and throw them in Kidron Valley, but it doesn't have a source and can only collect rainwater from the surrounding slopes.

DAY OF JUDGMENT STORIES

According to Jewish legend, people will be assembled together on the Mount of Olives, across from the Temple Mount and the Judgement Seat. Two bridges will appear across the valley, one of iron and one of paper, and all humanity will have to cross one of them, depending on how they have been judged. The iron bridge will collapse under the weight of the guilty, and those sent across it will die, while the paper bridge will easily bear up under the light consciences of those sent upon it, and they will live eternally.

According to Muslim beliefs, Mohammed will sit in Judgement on a pillar by Golden Gate, and everyone will have to pass over arches. Those weighted down by heavy consciences will sink, while those light with goodness will pass over the hair-thin arch to heaven.

The valley winds through Silwan village, out through the Judean wilderness, and down to the Dead Sea. It was used as a burial site for common people, and kings Asa and Josiah burned heathen idols here. The **Valley of Jehoshaphat** (meaning *God judges*) is the part of Kidron Valley between the Mount of Olives and the Temple Mount. Jews, Christians, and Muslims all believe its the place where the 'nations' will be judged on Judgment Day. Thanks to the belief that God would waken the dead to be brought for judgement, Kidron Valley has been a favored burial site, and the tombs to the side of the road are among the best first and second century tomb monuments around. Previously a road that was only suitable for walking, construction is now under way to pave a road to haul in the tours.

Heading south from Ophel on Shiloah Way, the **Tomb of Jehoshaphat** is first. This is a first century tomb on the right, with an interesting frieze above the entrance.

Just in front of Jehoshaphat's is **Absolom's Tomb**, supposedly belonging to the traitorous son of David (II Samuel 15-18), though the fact that it was built in the first century BCE makes this rather unlikely. It's impressive all the same, with its Ionic columns, burial chambers hewn from rock, and cone-like top. It's pock-marked with stone acne thanks to another tradition which calls for parents when they pass the monument with their children to revile the bad son and throw rocks at his tomb.

A dirt path to the left leads to another monument, the **Tomb of B'nei Hesir**. The burial chambers for the Hesir family of priests dates from the late 100s BCE. It's intricately decorated and inscribed, and is impressively carved out of the cliff. According to Christian tradition, James the Just was buried here after his martyrdom.

The **Tomb of Zechariah** nearby is carved entirely out of the rock, with Ionic columns and pyramid roof. Traditon has it that this first century BCE tomb is the burial site of the prophet Zechariah (II Chronicles 24:21) who advocated rebuilding the Temple to the Jews newly returned from Babylon.

HINNOM VALLEY

Hinnom Valley (properly **Gei-Ben-Hinnom**, *Valley of Hinnom's Son*, or sometimes Gei-Hinnom, *Valley of Hinnom*) stretches from below Mount Zion to Kidron Valley. *Gehenna*, the Greek and Latin word for Hell, derives from Hinnom, as does the Muslim *Gahannam*, one of their hells.

Perhaps one reason for all this hellish reference is the child sacrifice that used to go on here as part of the Topheth and Molock cult. Though Topheth's form is unknown, the word has been interpreted to mean "place of fire" or "hearth," and it, too, was a name for hell in the Middle

ABSALOM'S STORY

The story goes that Absalom, who was King David's third son, was renowned for his beauty and graces, and held the love of David and his people. Amnon was David's first-born, and he fell in love with his sister, Tamar. He schemed and lied to get time alone with Tamar, and then raped her. David was angry, but did nothing to punish Amnon, while Tamar went off to live a secluded life in Absalom's home. Two years later, Absalom invited all his brothers to a big sheep-sheering feast, and then he had Amnon killed. Absalom fled to his mother's home in Geshur to escape his father's wrath.

A few years later, after David had cooled down, Absalom came back to Jerusalem, but it took more years yet before he won back his father's favour. When he was firmly back in court life Absalom got himself a small force of men and began to stir things up among his people, instigating resentment against David, and was said to have "stolen the hearts of the people of Israel." After four years of this he went to Hebron with a force of 200, and announced: 'As soon as ye hear the sound of the trumpet, then ye shall say "Absalom reigneth in Hebron."' People from all around joined Absalom, and the rebellion was on. They fought, and Absalom's troops were soundly trounced. When Absalom rode his mule under a large oak tree his hair got tangled in the branches and he was stuck. David's general Joab saw him there and, contrary to David's express orders, took the opportunity to kill Absalom, thrusting three darts into Absalom's heart. They tossed his body in a pit, and David was inconsolable when he heard.

Absalom had planned ahead, however, and while still alive had ordered a memorial stone to be set up for him in the king's dale, saying "I have no son to keep my name in remembrance," and he ordered the pillar to be called Absalom's place (2 Samuel 18:18).

Ages. Ahaz (King of Judah in 736-725 BCE) reputedly sacrificed here and burnt his children in the fire (2 Chronicles 28:3, 2 Kings 16:3) though the rite comes from pre-Israelite Ammonite days. After King Josiah (639-609 BCE) ordered the cultic sites be destroyed, the memory of the sacrifices remained linked to the valley of Hinnom and its name took on the strong associations with Hell, associations that began with Jeremiah, who predicted that the valley of Hinnom would one day be called the 'valley of slaughter.'

The Greek Orthodox **Monastery of Saint Onuphrius (Aceldama)** and the so-called **Field of Blood** or **Potter's Field (Hakeldamach)** are on the southern slope of the valley of Hinnom. According to the New

Testament (Acts 1:18) after Judas betrayed Jesus, his 30 pieces of silver were used by the head priests to buy a field to which Judas went "and falling headlong, he burst assunder in the midst, and his bowels gushed out." The monastery is named after an Egyptian hermit, known for wearing a long beard and nothing else.

MOUNT OF OLIVES

Up above is the **Mount of Olives**, a 2,655 foot hill beyond Kidron Vally that's important in Jewish and Christian theology (the Byzantines built 14 churches up there). Named after the many olive trees that thrived here at one time (a few representative trees can still be seen) this is also where the Last Judgement is supposed to take place. According to Jews, the Messiah is to appear on the western slope, and according to Zechariah (14:4) this is where the Lord's feet will stand on the apocalytic day of the Lord. At that time, presumably, everyone is going to have to travel from their graves get here to be judged, and if you're buried right here, there's that much less to travel.

The valley is replete with cemeteries full of Jewish graves, but Mount of Olives is the oldest and largest Jewish burial site and holds maybe 75,000 graves. In addition, this is said to be the site of an old Israelite shrine, since 2 Samuel tells how King David went up there to mourn Absalom's death. Jesus and his disciples often hung out in the Garden of Gethsemane at the foot of its western slope, and Jesus is said to have ascended into Heaven from the middle peak of Ascension Hill, so the hill is also holy to Christians. There's an Arab village of At Tur (Mount of Olives in Arabic) on the summit, and Arab bus 75 goes there from the bus station on Suleiman. To see the sights, head up in the morning when the churches are open and the sun is still low, then walk down via the churches along the way, or come later in the afternoon when the sights have reopened and the afternoon light imparts a special touch.

North of the terrific vantage point of Seven Arches Hotel are the **Church of the Eleona** and the **Church of the Paternoster**, both behind the same gate, and both founded by Queen Helena in the fourth century. The Church of the Eleona (*elaion* means olives in Greek) was built in the fourth century, destroyed by Persians in 614, and restored in 1927. It's to mark where Jesus revealed his "inscrutable mysteries" concerning the destruction of Jerusalem and the Second Coming to his disciples. The Church of the Paternoster, built in 1875 by French Princess Aurelie de la Tour d'Auvergene, marks where Jesus taught the Lord's Prayer (it's written in 77 languages on the tiled wall). Both are open Monday-Saturday 8:30-11:45am and 3-4:45pm, and entrance is free.

Church of Ascension, *farther north next to Augusta Victoria Hospital,* *Tel.* *02-28-7704,* is open Monday-Saturday for free, but a visit to the tower costs NIS 6). The 45 meter high tower commands amazing views, and the church has nice paintings and mosaics. The **Russian Chapel of the Ascension** boasts the tallest belfry with the best views, but they rarely open their doors to the public.

There is also a **Mosque of the Ascension,** since Islam recognized Jesus as a prophet worthy of veneration. There was a church built here in the fourth century, but the Crusaders renovated it, and when Saladin came in, he authorized some followers to take it over. The stone floor features what's meant to be the footprint Jesus left as he ascended, though bits of it have been chipped away by Byzantine pilgrims seeking holy souvenirs. Ring the bell if the door's closed, and pay NIS 2 to see the sacred footprint within.

Down from the hotel there's a gate on the left leading to two tunnels identified as the **Tombs of the Prophets** Malachi, Haggai, and Zechariah, unlikely given the graves actually date to the fourth century. The tombs consist of 36 niches hewn from the rock; you can visit them Sunday-Friday from 8am-3pm. The orange sign designates the **Common Grave** of those who died in Jewish Quarter fighting in 1948, and next to them is the **National Cemetery.** Further along the path and you come to the **Jewish Graveyard,** the largist Jewish cemetery in the world, dating back to biblical times. Its popularity hinges on the belief that the Mount of Olives is where the Resurrection will take place when the Messiah comes, bringing the Day of Judgement.

Down and to the right is the **Sanctuary of Dominus Flevit** (meaning *The Lord Wept*), built in 1955 to commemorate where medieval pilgrims claimed Jesus wept for Jerusalem. When the present church was built in 1954, a fifth century monastery was discovered and excavated, as well as a large cemetery from 1500 BCE. The cemetery has been covered back up, but some of the tombs are still visible. It's open daily 8am-noon and 2:30-5pm in winter, till 6pm in summer.

Proceeding down the hill you come to the **Russian Church of Mary Magdalene,** *Tel.* *02-628-2897,* open Tuesday and Thursday 10-11:30am, but call ahead to make sure, and admission is free. The seven onion-domed golden cupolas provide a gleaming authentic Russian landmark on the hill. Built by Czar Alexander III in 1885, he had it constructed in the 16th century Russian baroque style and he dedicated it to his mother, the Empress Maria Alexandrovna. The body of a Russian Grand Duchess, Elizaveta Fyodorovna (sister of the last Czarina) who died in the Russian Revolution, was smuggled here via Beijing and is burried in the crypt. The church is now a convent and has a terrific choir, as well as some very fine paintings by Vaisly Vereshchagin and Aleksandr Ivanov. It also claims that part of the Garden of Gethsamane is on its grounds.

The Mount of Olives is also where Mary is said to be buried. The **Tomb of the Virgin Mary**, open Monday-Saturday 6:30am-noon and 2-5pm, admission free, marks the spot, and is revered by Christians and Muslims. This was a burial site during the first and second centuries, a Byzantine church stood over Mary's alleged tomb in the fourth century, and then a Crusader church was rebuilt here in 1130, a big church in the shape of a cross. The church flooded regulary, and now there are steps up to avoid the problem. The Crusader queen Melissanda was buried here, as was Joseph. Now an eastern church, the sounds and incense are meant to appeal to the senses. There is also a Muslim *mihrab* facing Mecca for Arab women with fertility or other women's problems to pray.

Gethsemane (or *Getsemani* – Aramaic, the language Jesus spoke, for *oil press*) is the garden at the foot of Mount of Olives where Christ's Agony and subsequent capture took place, and the garden now supports some of the oldest olive trees on the mount. Inside the garden gate is the **Church of all Nations** (also called **The Bascilica of the Agony**), facing west toward the Old City. The church is open daily 8:30am-noon and 2:30-6pm (till 5pm in winter), while the grotto down below closes year-round at 5pm, admission free. The spot here has been regarded as holy since the fourth century, but the church here wasn't built till after WWI in 1924, financed by twelve countries. Inside, mosaics illustrate the last days of Jesus' life, and the rocky apses are said to be where Jesus prayed three times. **Betrayal Grotto** is where it's believed Judas betrayed Jesus and where Judas was arrested. The floor of the grotto was decorated with mosaics in early Byzantine days, and the tombs were built here later.

Saint Stephen's Church is on the south side of the main road. A 'modern Byzantine' church constructed in 1968, this is where the first Christian martyr is said to have been stoned to death. Ring the bell to come in as there are no set visiting hours and no admission fee, and once in you can see the site where Stephen was slain, remains from the old Roman road, and an anonymous tomb cut into the rock.

MOUNT SCOPUS

To the south is the **Mount of Umbrage**, also known as the Mountain of Perdition, and to the north is **Mount Scopus**, the start of the same chain of hills that includes the Mount of Olives. From up top there are marvelous views of the city and the Judean Desert, as well as the luxury of the Hyatt Regency Hotel. Given its stragetic lookout and location, it's not surprising it's played important roles in centuries of Jerusalem wars. In 70 CE Roman legions under Titus camped here, the Crusaders set up camp in 1099, the British followed suit in 1917, and Arab troops attacked from here in 1948. In addition to war camps, Mount Scopus is a place of learning, hosting universities and hospitals. To get here without doing a lot of up-hill hiking, take Arab bus 75 or Egged bus 4, 4a, 9, 23, or 28. **Hebrew University**'s Mount Scopus campus was founded here in 1925. The university was relocated to Giv'at Ram after 1948, but the Mount Scopus campus was renovated after the Six Day War of 1967. There are free English guided tours around the modern architecture of the renowned campus Sunday-Thursday at 11am, about an hour. They leave from the Bronfman Vistors' Center in the administration building. Even if you don't take the tour, you can visit the **Hecht Synagogue**, one of the major sites on the tour.

Northwest of Hebrew University is **Hadassah University Hospital** (not to be confused with the Hadassah Hebrew University Medical Center with the Chagall windows in the southeast). The **British WWI Cemetery** east of the hospital holds soldiers from the British Commonwealth forces. Also on Mount Scopus to the south is the American-affiliated **Jerusalem Center for Near East Studies** of Brigham Young University.

EAST JERUSALEM

The **American Colony Hotel**, *Nablus*, is worth visiting if you're in the neighborhood (see *East Jerusalem Hotels* for the full description of this sumptuous pasha palace). The **Tomb of the Kings**, *Nablus*, is just near American Colony. Open Monday-Saturday 8am-12:30pm and 2-5pm, it costs NIS 4 and takes two minutes to see. It's not really worth a special trip.

Tourjeman Post, *4 Cheil HaHandasa, Tel. 02-628-1278*, tells the history of Jerusalem during the dicy years of 1948-1967. Currently closed for renovations (call to see if they've reopened to the public), they're generally open Sunday-Thursday 9am-4pm, Friday 9am-1pm. This museum is in an old Tukrkish house and costs NIS 8 for adults, NIS 6 for students, and NIS 5 for children. Its theme is 'a divided city reunited' and it presents a somewhat rose-colored view of the time when the city was divided by barbed wire between Israel and Jordan. To get there, continue south on Nablus till you get to the US Consulate and take the fork northwest on Shmuel Hanavi. Tourjeman Post is just off there.

Garden Tomb is a lovely green leafy garden with paths to all the relevant Christian sites. Very friendly English speaking staff profer literature in many languages, and admittance is free. At the far corner of the garden is a platform from which you can see Skull Hill (*Golgatha* or *Cavalry* from Mark 15:22, both of which mean "Place of the Skull"), the site some believe to be where Christ was crucified. Some also see the craggy hill as resembling a human skull, adding another layer of potential significance. The Tomb, discovered in 1867, is thought to be the one in which Jesus was placed. Though tombs aplenty have been unearthed in Jerusalem, this one seems to match a number of New Testament descriptions (John 19:41-42-, Matt 27:60, Luke 24:1-4): in a garden, hewn from stone, and near Golgotha. The tomb and sights are interesting for devout Christians, and beautiful and peaceful for heretics. Leafy bowers, singing birds, and flowers surround Skull Hill, the Tomb, and its legend which reads "He is not here for he has risen."

King Solomon's Quarry, *across from the Garden Tomb and northeast of Damascus Gate*, is open Saturday-Thursday 9am-4pm, Friday 9am-2pm, and entrance costs NIS 6 for adults and NIS 3 for children. It's also called Zedekiah's Cave, after the sixth century BCE King who was blinded before being led off to Babylonian exile by Nebuchadnezzar after first witnessing the murder of his own sons. Legend has it King Zedekiah used this cave to try to escape to Jericho before Nebuchadnezzar took him captive. According to the Muslims, this was where Korah and his followers were swallowed up by the earth (Numbers 16:32). And it was named King Solomon's Quarry by the Freemasons since Solomon is said to have been one of the first Freemasons, and they believe he hewed stones from here for the First Temple. It is agreed that stones from this quarry were used for buildings in Jerusalem during First Temple times, in Hasmonean times, during Herod's rule, and for the Jaffa Gate clock tower. And, the YMCA got permission to quarry stones from here for their chapel. Whatever you choose to call it, it's deep underground and worth a visit.

The Rockefeller Museum, *Sultan Suleiman, Tel. 02-628-2251*, is open Sunday-Thursday 10am-5pm and Friday-Saturday 10am-2pm, and costs NIS 20 an adult and NIS 12 for students and seniors. Set near the Old City in East Jerusalem, the American Colony convinced Rockefeller to build a museum here to showcase archeological findings. There are exhibits from all ages of human habitation, starting with Paleolithic and Neolithic times, and going on up through the Bronze and Hellenistic, Roman and Persian, Crusader and Islamic periods. They've got a statue of Ramses III, detail findings at Beit Shean, and the history of crusifixion, including the Crucified Man from Giv'at Ha-mivtar – the world's only archeological evidence of crucifixion. It's a pleasant and interesting place to stroll through history and pass an hour or so, and the stucco dancing girls between the North and South wings shouldn't be missed. Come early or late in the day to avoid the crowds.

WEST JERUSALEM (NEW CITY)

Also called the **New City**, West Jerusalem has its own goodly number of sights. There are also all the pleasures of a modern city, including swank cafés, pedestrian walks, and intricate bus routes.

Downtown/Zion Square Area

The **Russian Compound**, *at the foot of Jaffa Street*, was bought by the Russian Church in the mid 1800s (pre-revolution) for their Holyland pilgrims. In their complex the church built a hospital, hospice and a library, while those who couldn't afford the hospice pitched tents. In the British Mandate days (1917-1948) police were stationed here – it's a police station still – and a prison was here as well. The prison is now a museum, the **Hall of Heroism**, *Tel. 02-623-3166*, commemorating Israel's underground movement in the early fight for independence against the British. It's open Sunday-Thursday 8am-4pm and costs NIS 6, or NIS 3 for students.

Parts of Hebrew University moved here after the Mount Scopus campus was given up in '48, and the Supreme Court used to be here as well. The last effort of Mayor Teddy Kolleck, the plaza and with its many palm trees was to be named after him, but was named after the influential Safra family instead.

One of the grand buildings at the foot of Jaffa near the Old City is **Saint Louis Hospital**, a hospital for the terminally ill. During the war for independence, this was no-man's land, site of many incidents. One involved a patient at the hospital who leaned out his window and dropped his false teeth. It took a week of UN intervention for the man to get them back.

Down the hill is **Notre Dame**, not a hospital any longer, but a hospice for pilgrims. This magnificent structure was built by the Roman Catholic Assumpionist Fathers in 1887 for the French Pilgrims, and it came under heavy fire during the War of Independence in 1948, so much so that the south wing facing the Old City became uninhabitable from the bombing and was used as an Israeli bunker instead. In 1970 the Assumpionists sold the building to the Jewish National Fund who turned it into a students' residence for Hebrew University. The Vatican eventually bought the property and from 1973-1978 refurbished it for use as a Catholic hospice.

The Great Synagogue, *King George, Tel. 02-624-7112*, is across from the Sheraton and open Sunday-Friday 9am-1pm. It's an enormous though unremarkable synagogue. You should come in modest attire. Next door, in Heichal Shlomo, is the **Wolfson Museum**, *58 King George*, open Sunday-Thursday 9am-1pm, and admission costs NIS 4. The museum displays Judaica and scenes illustrating Jewish history. Heichal Shlomo, meaning

Solomon's Mansion, is the seat of the Chief Rabbinate of Israel, and the scales on both sides of the entrance stand for justice. **Museum of Italian Jewish Art and Synagogue**, *27 Hillel, Tel. 02-624-1610*, is open Sunday-Thursday 9am-1pm and Wednesday 4-7pm as well, with admission for NIS 4. The 18th century synagogue, brought here from Italy, is the only one outside of Italy where the ancient Italian liturgy is performed.

The Skirball Museum, *Hebrew Union College, 13 King David, Tel. 02-620-3333*, is open Sunday-Thursday 10am-4pm and Saturday 10am-2pm. Admission is free but the explanatory brochure costs NIS 5. There are two floors of finds from archeological excavations, including the "House of David" Stele (the first reference outside of the Bible to mention King David and his dynasty), lots of pottery and funerary offerings, and pictures showing the process of discovery at the ongoing excavation of the ancient cities of Laish/Dan, Gezer, and Aroer. Of special interest to linguists are storage jars from Gezer displaying the earliest alphabet (Proto-Canaanite) known in Israel, dating from the 16th century BCE.

Another fine, small, free museum is the **Anna Ticho House**, *7 Harav Kook, Tel. 02-624-5068*, open Sunday, Monday, Wednesday, Thursday 10am-5pm, Tuesday 10am-10pm, Friday 10am-2pm. Her drawings are interesting, Dr. Ticho's Menorah collection is wonderful, and the cafe is reason enough to stop by. There is a small library there, peaceful and comfortable and lined with books on Jerusalem, art, and literature, and a gift shop as well. The Ticho House was one of the first to be constructed outside the Old City Walls. Built in the late 1800s by an Arab dignitary, and Shapira (a nortorious antiquities forger) was one of his first occupants. Dr. Avraham Albert Ticho left his native Moravia in 1912 to open a eye clinic in Jerusalem; his cousin Anna joined and married him that same year. The Tichos bought this house in 1924 and converted the lower portion to an eye clinic, while Anna applied her talents to the Jerusalem landscapes.

Beit Harav Kook, *9 Harav Kook, Tel. 02-623-2560*, is near Zion Square and open Sunday-Thursday 9am-2pm, Friday 9am-noon. It's a tribute to the life, works, and pedagogical achievements of Rabbi Abraham Yitzak Hacohen Kook, first chief Rabbi of Eretz Yisrael. Built in 1923 and recently restored and opened to the public, there are weekly classes and seminars available as well as tours of the library and exhibits.

Mahane Yehuda, *off Agrippas*, is a street market full of noise and bustle, orthodox Jews and tourists, and tempting smells and great food. It's a wonderful, lively, aromatic scene, and Thursday afternoon is best to see the pre-Shabbat rush. Bountifully-hipped matrons shove about for fruit, vegetables, cheese, pickles, and delectable bakery items in this market whose name means Camp of Judah. Falafel joints dot the corner of HaEgoz and Agrippas, selling pitas for NIS 7 (see *Where to Eat* section for more gustatory options).

Avraham Haba Museum, *43 Hanevi'im, Tel. 02-644-4444*, is temporarily closed and will reopen in April, 1998. Their usual hours are Sunday-Thursday 9am-5pm and they have a large collection of micrography, with the Bible, sacred Jewish texts, and biographies of Jewish leaders. **Artists House**, *12 Shmuel Hanagid, Tel. 02-625-3653*, is open Sunday-Thursday 10am-1pm and 4-9pm, Friday 10am-1pm, Saturday 11am-2pm.

Mea She'arim

This neighborhood of the very orthodox is just north of downtown near Ethiopia Street. Its name means *One Hundred Gates*, and is a reference to Genesis 26:12 and Isaac receiving one-hundred fold from his labors. It's interesting to walk around and see a community that has kept intact many of the traditions and life styles that existed in the Eastern Europe of pre-WWII days. What may be fascinating and unique to visitors, however, is everyday life to the residents in this district, so you need to be careful about stepping on their cultural or religious toes, avoid overboard gawking, and dress modestly (which in this community means no shorts for men, no shorts, minis, or bare shoulders for women; public affection between the sexes is also frowned on). As in Mahane Yehuda, the shops and markets really hum Thursday afternoons as people prepare for Shabbat.

Visitors during Shabbat (after sundown Friday to sundown Saturday) should respect the holiday; they should be on foot, and should not include picture-taking (photography of people won't be very popular at any time unless you ask first).

The **Ministry of Education Building**, *Shivtei Y'Israel*, is between HaNevi'im and Mea She'arim streets. It's is grand building in 16th century Italian renaissance style, built in the 1880s to be the Italian Hospital.

Nearby is the **Ethiopian Church**, *Ethiopia Street*, magnificently domed but rarely visited. Built between 1896 and 1904 with an entrance gate carved like the Lion of Judah, the church is open daily 7am-6pm in summer and 8am-5pm in winter, and admission is free. The lions recall Ethiopa's Queen of Sheba and the lion emblem Solomon gave her when she visited. Across from the church is the **Eliezer Ben Yehuda** house, where he lived and worked on reviving the Hebrew language (much to the disapproval of the very orthodox, who felt Hebrew should be saved for prayer).

Nahl'ot and **Zikhronot** are other religious neighborhoods south of Mahane Yehuda, these ones filled with mostly Sephardic Jews from Yemen, Morocco, Turkey, and Iran. It's another interesting place in which to wander and explore the winding narrow alleys and little shops.

Giv'at Ram

Giv'at Ram is served by buses 9, 17, and 24.

Start your visit to this district with a trip to the **Israel Museum**, *Giv'at Ram, Tel. 02-670-8811,* wonderfully large and full of Israel's treasures. It's a place to visit with time and energy to spare. Most days (all but Tuesday) the museum opens at 10am; Saturday, Wednesday, and Thursday the museum closes at 5pm, Friday at 2pm, and Saturday at 4pm; Tuesday it's open 4-10pm. The entrance fee is NIS 30 an adult, NIS 20 for student or senior, and NIS 15 for youth. Save your ticket, because re-admission on another day costs only NIS 10 when you show your stub. And there are free guided tours (1.5 hours) at 3pm (not including Tuesday or Friday).

Their permanent exhibits show the stuff you want to see when you visit sites around the country and read that their best finds are now located at the Israel Museum. You could go here and only here and still get a sense of the history and richness of the country. There are always changing temporary exhibits as well. The **Youth Wing** is very well done; it's interesting for adults but a must for kids. The **Shrine of the Book** where the Dead Sea Scrolls are kept is also fascinating, and there's a free 45 minute tour Sunday, Monday, Wednesday, Thursday at 1:30pm, Tuesday at 3pm and Friday at 12:45pm. The white dome is sculpted to look like the lid of the jars in which the scrolls were found. The scrolls and clothing remnants on view were preserved by the dry desert air so well the text on the parchments and the status-indicating colored stripes on the cloth can still be seen.

The main building houses the most comprehensive collection of Judaica, with Ashkenazi and Sephardi cultures represented. The remnants of the Harb Synagogue, brought over from Germany, are wonderful, as is the 1701 Vittorio Veneto Synagogue, donated in its entirety, from Italy. In the Archeology wing, get a look at the anthropoid sarcophogai, and the prehistory section as well. And the mosaic from Beit She'an is exceptional. The buildings are arranged around landscaped courtyards, and the **Billy Rose Sculpture Garden** is one of the outdoor exhibits.

Bible Lands Museum, *25 Granot, Tel. 02-561-1066,* is across the street from the Israel Museum, accessible by bus 9, 17, 24, 99, and is open Sunday-Tuesday, Thursday 9:30am-5:30pm, Wednesday 9:30-9:30pm, Friday 10am-2pm, and Saturday 11am-3pm. It has a collection of ancient art portraying scenes and civilizations from the Bible, with Egyptian sculpture, ivories, and ancient seals.

The Knesset, *Eliezer Kaplan, Tel. 02-675-3333,* is located across and up from the Israel Museum. Israel's law-making assembly, it has a free tour that leaves Sunday and Thursday at 8:30am and 2:30pm or when a large enough group has gathered, lasts 15 minutes, and isn't worth the bother. You don't need the tour to see Chagall hall and its truly beautiful tapestries. They were designed by Chagall in 1964 and hand-woven in France. The 12 floor mosaics were also designed by Chagall. The open sessions however, even though they are in untranslated Hebrew, are more interesting. The sessions are Monday and Tuesday from 4pm and Wednesday at 11am. They last two hours and you must bring your passport to get in.

The Supreme Court, *behind the Knesset, Tel.* 02-675-9666, connected by the Rose Garden walk, is open for visits Sunday-Thursday 8:30am-2:30pm. It's worth a visit, both for the magnificence of the structure (with Israeli marble, copper from Solomon's mines, and Jerusalem Stone) and the interesting content of the free one hour tour that leaves Sunday-Thursday at noon. They explain the beautiful and symbolic architecture, and discuss the Israeli constitution (the one still in the process of being drafted), how a supreme court decides laws without one, and the controversial role of today's court.

Across from the Government Center is the Giv'at Ram **Hebrew University Science Department.** The Visitors' Center, *Sherman Building, Tel.* 02-588-2819, offers tours Sunday-Thursday at 10am.

There too is the new **Bloomfield Science Museum,** *Tel.* 02-561-8128, open Monday, Wednesday, Thursday 10am-6pm, Tuesday 10am-8pm, Friday 10am-2pm, and Saturday 10am-3pm. Admission is NIS 20 for adults, NIS 17 for students, and NIS 14 for children. It's a hands-on, interactive museum, popular with children and adults alike. Also on this campus is the **National Library** with the beautiful **Ardon Window,** of second-largest-stained-glass-window-in-the-world fame. The window gloriously depicts Kabbalistic symbols in mystically dark, rich colors. The library is open Sunday-Thursday 9am-7pm, Friday 9am-1pm, and admission is free.

Ein Kerem & Environs
Yad Vashem, *Tel.* 02-675-1611, is open Sunday-Thursday 9am-5pm, Friday 9am-2pm, and is free. Easily accessible by buses 13, 17, 18, 20, 23, 24, and 27, this extraordinarily moving musuem was established in 1953 in memory of the victims of the Holocaust, named "a memorial and a name" from chapter 56 in Isaiah. The **Children's Memorial,** done in 1987, has five flames reflected in countless mirrors. In the dark, names are called out while the flames flicker. The **Garden of Righteous Gentiles** (over 7,000 trees so far) was featured in Schindler's List and honors the many gentiles who helped with kindness and bravery. In the Hall of Members Cemetary burns the **Eternal Flame.** Ash brought from Europe was buried here. The pillars symbolize the chimneys and incinerators of the concentration camps. The **Historical Museum** is the main section.

There is so much to see here, you could easily spend hours. Outside are "Last March" and "Resistance to Warsaw Ghetto," sculptures by Naftalee Bezem representing Jews, from the horror of the holocaust to rebirth, full of intriguing symbols like the fish that stand for fertitlity and the cactus (sabra) for the resilient Israelis. Inside tells the sad story of European Jewery from the restrictions and humiliations of the 30s to WWII's horrors, with documentation, pictures, and films.

Save some time for the **Art Museum** as well. They have a wonderful exhibit on "The Last Ghetto, Life in the Lodz Ghetto" that is interesting and moving. If you can help it, go on your own rather than on a tour to Yad Vashem. It's such a personal experience, time pressures and deadlines don't fit the mood. Also, some of the tour guides tend to shatter private horror and reflection with their intrusive lectures.

The **Military Cemetery**, *Mount Herzl in Ein Kerem*, has **Herzl's tomb**, as well as the graves of **Golda Meir** and **Yitzhak Rabin**. The Rabin grave is heavily visited. Heads of state come here to pay respect and plant a cedar. There's a big Independence Day ceremony here, but unless you feel deeply about the founder of Zionism there isn't much to see here. The **Herzl Museum**, *Tel. 02-651-1108*, open Sunday-Thursday 9am-5pm, Friday 9am-1pm, admission NIS 4.5 and students NIS 3, tells the story of the man who pioneered Zionism up until he died in 1904. **Jerusalem Forest**, *west of Mount Herzl*, a fine spot for a picnic and a cool breeze. Bus 17 can get you there, and bus 19 takes you to Hadassah Medical Center, just 15 minutes walk away.

Ein Kerem (*fountain of vines*) used to be an Arab village and it's said to be where John the Baptist was born. It's a strikingly pretty place, with hills and views and little winding streets. It's now got lots of pottery galleries as well. Along with the churches and hostel, there's a nice garden restaurant (see *Where to Eat* section) as well.

Saint John Ba Harim, *Tel. 02-641-3639*, also known as the **Church of Saint John**, commemorates the spot he was born with a stunning clock tower. Open daily 6am-noon and 2-6pm (2-5pm in winter), there are fine paintings within and ceramic prayer plaques in many different languages outside. There are excavations from early Arab times, and the Grotto of the Nativity below, where you can see a pheasant mosaic from the Byzantine chapel through a grate. The views from the hill are beautiful, and there are pottery galleries nearby.

Across the valley, **Church of the Visitation**, *up Ma'ayan, Tel. 02-641-7291*, also called **Saint Mary's Catholic Holy Church**, has beautiful arches, and a painting of Mary with gold halo and gilt edge. The church celebrates Mary's visit to Elizabeth and has the rock the infant Saint John hid behind when the Romans were looking for babies to kill. The tower is tall, the site peaceful and serene, and there's cool water running in

Mary's Spring. Open 8-11:45am and 2:30-6pm (2:30-5pm in winter), there's cactus and palm fronds in the garden and another swell view over the terraced hills. There's also a hostel nearby (see *Where to Stay*). The pink tower is part of the **Russian Monastery**, *Tel.* 02-625-2565, and you can visit by appointment.

South of the church complex is the synagogue of **Hadassah Medical Center**, *Tel.* 02-677-6271, not to be confused with the Hadassah Hospital on Mount Scopus. Here are the famed **Chagall Windows**, showing the 12 tribes in stained-glass depiction based on Genesis 49 and Deuteronomy 33. Chagall gave the windows to the hospital in 1962. In '67 four windows were damaged in the war and Chagall was cabled. He replied "You worry about the war, I'll worry about my windows." True to his word, two years later he replaced the damaged panes, though three windows still bear bullet holes from the battle. It's open Sunday-Thursday 8am-1:15pm and 2-3:45pm, Friday 8am-12:30pm, and admission costs NIS 12 per adult and NIS 8 for students. There are free tours in English Sunday-Thursday every half hour from 8:30am-12:30pm and 2:30pm, and Friday every hour 9:30-11:30am.

Holyland Hotel's **Model of the Second Temple**, *Bayit Vagan, Tel.* 02-643-7777, is a two-foot-high big nothing, west of Hadassah. Open 8am-10pm daily, it costs NIS 15 for adults, NIS 12 for children and students, and NIS 60 for a family ticket. Bus 21 will drop you a short walk away, but it'll take you longer to get here than it will to see the sight.

Giv'at Hatahmoshet/Ramat Eshkol

Ammunition Hill, *Sderot Eshkol, Tel.* 02-582-8442, Fax 02-582-9132, is near University Boulevard to the north of city center, and is open Sunday-Thursday 8am-6pm, Friday 8am-2pm. On the crest of the hill is an outdoor museum including plaques listing fallen soldiers, pillboxes, trenches, fields of the Harel Tank Brigade, and an Observation Overlook. The Underground Museum was once the main Jordanian command bunker and weapons depot on the 1948 Jerusalem partition line. They also show videos on the Battle for Jerusalem, Six Days in Jerusalem, If I Forget Thee, and audio presentations of In the Eyes of the Enemy and Battle Reports. Surrounding the museum are public gardens (trees and dirt), picnic tables and public toilets. Buses 4, 9, 28, and 29 go there.

To the west are the **Sanhedrin Tombs**, also called the **Judges' Tombs**. Open Sunday-Thursday 9am to sunset, buses 9, 26, 27 take you there and admission is free. The Sanhedrin was ancient Israel's 71 member supreme court, and in this pleasant park is where they are said to be buried.

Southwest of the Tombs is the new **Biblical Zoo**, *BarHan off HaSanhedrin, Tel.* 02-643-0111. Open in summer Sunday-Thursday 9am-7:30pm, and in winter Sunday-Thursday 9am-5pm, and year-round Friday

9am-3pm, Saturday 10am-5pm, and admission is NIS 25 for adults, NIS 18 for children. The old Biblical Zoo was a disappointment, but this new one is a delight.

SOUTHERN DISTRICTS

The **Yemin Moshe** area outside Dung Gate was the first settlement to be built up outside of the protection of the city walls in the 1850s. Walls meant security in those times, and building outside of them didn't catch on at first. **Mishkenot Sha'ananim** (Tranquil Settlement), Yemin Moshe, was one of these early attempts. Sir Moshe (Moses) Montefury started building there (he even brought the windmill, but it didn't work, and it's now a small **museum**, open Sunday-Thursday 9am-4pm, Friday 9am-1pm, and free).

By 1948 the area had fallen into neglect, and in 1967 Teddy Kolleck sold the property to those rich enough to renovate the insides without changing the old exteriors. Mishkenot Sha'ananim is now a guest house of 10 apartments, used by the government to house visiting artists and writers (though no longer for free), and there's an exclusive French restaurant of the same name as well. Across the street on King David is **Liberty Bell Park (Gan HaPa'amon)** which features a copy of the Liberty Bell in Philedelphia. There are several art galleries lining the expensively quaint alleys of Yemin Moshe.

Herod's Family Tomb is just south of the King David Hotel. Thanks to grave robbers, little was here when archeologists came upon the scene, and Herod himself isn't here but was buried near Bethlehem instead. Below in the valley is **Sultan's Pool**, nameed after Suleiman the Magnificent. Not only did he build the Old City walls in the 16th century, he added a dam and fountain to this Second Temple resevoir. These days it's an amphitheater and gets used for open-air concerts.

REHAVIA

This beautiful residential triangle between **Derekh Aza** (Gaza) and **Ramban** (southwest of Independence Park) was developed by German Jews fleeing the Nazi regime in the 1930s. Not much of the original high German cultural flavor remains, but the preserved old stone buildings and well-tended gardens make for a pleasant amble away from faster paced, bus-clogged regions.

Jason's Tomb on Alfassi is in the middle of the district. It was built around 100 BCE as the burial site for three generations of a substantial Jewish family in Hasmonean days. Charcoal drawings of ships on the porch wall indicate the Jasons' wealth was financed by ocean trade, but the pyramid on top was a later add-on. Findings of cooking pots and food shed light on notions of an after life, and the dice included in the collection of essentials may speak to their perception of the importance of gambling at the time and in the great beyond.

Further east on the Balfour and Smolenskin corner is the **Prime Minister's house**. And next door on Balfour is **Schocken Library**, designed by Erich Mendelssohn in the late 1930s (his own house was in the windmill on Ramban near Kikkar Tzarfat).

KOMEMIYUT (TALBIYE)

This district is accessible by bus 15.

Between the district of Rehavia and the Liberty Bell Garden lies the small and equally elegant neighborhood of Komemiyut (Talbiye). This was a wealthy Arab community before the inhabitants were dispossessed in 1948. Their graceful villas are now popular with Hebrew University profs and other successful professionals.

The official residence of the **Israeli President**, *HaNassi*, is near the **Jerusalem Theater**,*southeast on Chopin.*

To the west, is the **Mayer Institute for Islamic Art**, *2 HaPalmah, Tel. 02-566-1291.* They have a worthwhile collection of Islamic paintings, jewelry, and artifacts, it's open Sunday-Monday, Wednesday-Thursday 10am-5pm, Tuesday 4-8pm, and Friday-Saturday 10am-2pm, and the cost is NIS 10 for adults, NIS 8 for students, and NIS 5 for children (and free on Saturday).

The office of the **AACI**, *6 Mane, Tel. 02-561-7151*, down Balfour past the circle to Disreali, Mane is opposite 13 Disraeli. Inside the beautiful stone building and its lovely garden is a wealth of material and information meant to ease the process of living in Israel for Americans and Canadians taking the plunge. Even if you're just visiting, you may want a piece of information, be interested in a social group, concert, tour or lecture, or just welcome the North American accent.

THE GERMAN COLONY

South of Komemiyut along Emek Refaim (take King David south till it turns into Bethlehem and keep going past the train station, fork right and you're there) is one of the 19th century communities built by the German Templars. The streets are peaceful and lovely, the gardens lush, and the old Arab and German style stones emenate serene wealth.

TALPIOT

Beit Agnon, *161 Joseph Klausner, Talpiot, Tel. 02-671-6498*, can be reached with bus 7. Open Sunday-Thursday 9am-1pm, there are tours and an English film presenting Nobel Laureate S. Y. Agnon, his library and home. It's near **Kibbutz Ramat Rachel**, *Tel. 02-670-2555*, a spot that saw a lot of bloody fighting in 1948. Now a tourist attraction, its name (meaning Height of Rachel) refers to Jacob's wife who's buried in Bethlehem. They have guided tours showing kibbutz life and a museum with 1948 War exhibits that's open daily 8am-noon, and bus 7 will take you there. For information on the guest house, see the *Where to Stay* section.

The **Haas Promenade** has view of the mounts and view of the city, while nearby on the east side of Kidron Valley is the Hill of Evil Counsel. The vistas are nice but it's not a big deal. Tour guides treat it mostly as a photo opportunity, though joggers show up for the sunset run. There is also a self-service restaurant there, with seating inside and out, and reasonable prices. Bus 6 or 6A will get you there and back.

TOURS

Egged's Circle Line, *bus station office at 224 Jaffa, or downtown office at 44a Jaffa, Tel. 02-625-4198 or Tel. 02-625-3454*, offers the Circle Line bus #99 to 33 of Jerusalem's main tourist sites. A day pass is NIS 18.5, a two-day pass is NIS 77, including three tourist site tickets. You can look at these places through the windows of your air-conditioning bus, or get off and resume with the next bus two hours later. The bus departs from King David Street every two hours Sunday-Thursday 10am-4pm, Friday 10am-12pm, and the last trip doesn't include Yad Vashem.

Is it worthwhile? If you have to leave Israel the next day and want to get a glimpse of all these spots so you can tell the folks back home that yes, you saw them, go get your ticket. Otherwise you will probably be disappointed. Even if you start with the first bus, you can only disembark and see four places for your money (not counting entrance fees), and the public transport system is just as good for NIS 4 per trip.

Free Walking Tours, every Saturday from 10am-noon, leave from 32 Jaffa. They are informative and enjoyable, and a good way to see some of the Old City, especially if you get in Moosha's group.

Jewish Quarter Tours, *Tel. 02-627-2360*, leave from the Women's Water Fountain in the Jewish Quarter daily (except Wednesday) at 3pm, Saturdays at 5pm, but call first to see if it's on and the exact time (it depends on the season). Jeffrey Seidel charges NIS 15, though it can be waived if you can't afford the fee, and modest dress is required.

Zion Walking Tours, *Jaffa Gate office to the right of David Street, Tel. 02-628-7866 or Tel. 05-030-5552*, has three hour tours ($9 for adults, $7 for students) leaveing at 9am, 11am, and 2pm, and include a rampart walk. They also do a 3.5 hour Mount of Olives tour Monday at 9am, Wednesday at 2pm for $20 (students $16) and a 3.5 hour Southern Wall and Herodian tour Monday at 9am and Wednesday at 2pm for the same price.

SEMINARS, LECTURES, & DIGS

• **Hebrew Union College**, *13 King David, Tel. 02-620-3333, posts a bulletin board out front listing lectures and concerts.*

• **Jeffrey Seidel's Jewish Student Information Center**, *1/15 Hameshoririm, Jewish Quarter, Old City, Tel. 02-627-2360, Fax 02-628-8338, run weekly Torah readings and organize Sabbath Programs, lead Jewish Quarter, Moslem Quarter, and Tunnel Tours, and offer special holiday programs as well. They can also be reached on e-mail at ohel.avrohom@yankel.sprint.com.*

• **Aish HaTorah**, *Beit Ha-Sho'eva Road, Jewish Quarter, is a mostly American yeshiva. Women should apply to the adminstative offices off Shvut Road.*

• **Albright Institute of Archeological Research**, *Nablus Road, has irregular hours but has information on archeological digs.*

• **The Rockefeller Museum Antiquity Department**, *Tel. 02-560-2607, can help set you up on a dig. Or call Tel. 06-658-5367 to find out about joining the* **Beit She'an** *dig.*

• **Archaeological Digs, LTD.**, *Tel. 627-3515, arranges digs in Beit-Gourin every Friday, charging $22 per adult, $17 per child, NIS 16 entrance and transportation not included. For a ride, guide and entrance, it costs $55 an adult, $50 a child.*

• **Archaeological Institute of America**, *656 Beacon Street, Boston, MA 02215, Tel. 617-353-9361, Fax 617-353-6550, email: aia@bu.edu, lists over 300 dig sites throughout the world in their Archaeological Fieldwork Opportunities Bulletin, available for $11 from Kendall Hunt Publishing, Tel. 800/228-0810.*

Archaeological Digs Ltd., *Tel. 02-627-3515*, offers a number of tours, all with a short seminar/slide show introduction, for $13. Meet at 34 Habad above the Cardo at 9:30am. They arrange digs in Beit-Gourim (see below), and do full ($160) and half day ($90) walking tours of the city.

Jaffa Gate unaffiliated entreprenours (also know as pests) will try to hook you for a tour of the city. They may start at $20 or higher , drop easily to NIS 50, and can be bargained way down. But you take your chances on quality, and the city offers tours for free.

Rent-A-Guide, *Tel. 02-676-8111*, offers guided tours for small groups, taking in trips such as Jerusalem, Bethlehem and a kibbutz for $70, or Massada and the Dead Sea for $85.

Egged Tours, *224 Jaffa, Tel. 02-625-4198, Fax 02-624-2150*, is open 7am-7pm. They have tours all over Israel and Jerusalem, starting at $22-

$24 for half a day in Jerusalem to $320 for three days in Eilat. It's the largest tour agency in Israel, but not necessarily the best, and certainly not the most personal or the friendly.

United, *King David Street just near the King David Hotel, Tel. 02-625-2187, fax 02-625-5013*, with pick ups in East Jerusalem at Notre Dame, American Colony or anywhere in West Jerusalem. They have tours from $20 for half a day in Jerusalem to $275 for 3 days in Eilat. The staff is friendly and the tour guides knowledgeable, if you don't mind the nature of a big bus tour.

Galilee Tours, *Hillel opposite El Al, Tel. 02-625-8866*, is Israel's Grey Line representative. They offer tours around Israel and to Jordan.

Many hostels arrange inexpensive tours, providing transport without a guide. **Swedish Hostel**, *29 David Street, Tel. 02-589-4124/02-627-7855*, is one example, but most hostels provide similar services and prices. The **Old City** tour (NIS 20) starts at Jaffa Gate at 9am and is five hours. For **Masada** (NIS 65) you are picked up at your hostel at 3am to allow you to climb the snake path in time for the sunrise. It also takes in visits to the Dead Sea, Ein Gedi Reserve, Qumran, and Jericho. The **Bethlehem** trip (NIS 25) takes three hours, and the **Galilee** (NIS 100) is a full day.

SPNI (Society for Protection of Nature), *13 Helene Ha'Malka, 02-625-2357*, leads excellently guided tours to all over the countryside, most of them including hiking and nature exploration. See Chapter 14, Nightlife & Sports, for more detail.

Neot HaKikar, *6 Shlomzion HaMalka, Tel. 02-623-6262*, specializes in guided tours in the Sinai.

ABC-BTC, *1 Hasoreg, Tel. 02-623-3990, Fax 02-25-7827*, is off Jaffa near Shlomzion. Open Sunday-Thursday 9am-7pm, Friday 9am-1pm, their initials stand for Better Travel Consultants, and they offer tours and tickets for less, and advice for free. They specialize in bus trips to Cairo and Petra/Jordash trips.

Budget Travel ISSTA, *31 HaNevi'im, Tel. 02-625-7257*, sells ISIC cards for NIS 35 (bring proof of student status and some ID), and book student discounts on flights, car rentals, etc.

EXCURSIONS & DAY TRIPS

According to the U.S. Embassy, travel to Hebron and the Gaza Strip are considered dangerous, though it's a good idea to call the Embassy and check the status when you're planning your trip.

The Arab village of **Abu Ghosh** is 13 kilometers west of Jerusalem, accessible by bus 185 or 186 leaving hourly from the central station and costing NIS 3.9 (sherut taxis to Tel Aviv will drop you two kilometers from the from the town). This place is believed to the the original site where the

Ark of the Covenant was kept before King David moved it to Jerusalem, and for this it's considered holy by Jews and Christians. The town was the last of a series of caravan stops to Jerusalem in the 18th century, and Sheik Abu Ghosh made some good money off his pilgrim toll.

On top of a hill is where people believe the Ark sat, and in its stead is now **Notre Dame de l'Arche d'Alliance** (Our Lady of the Ark of the Covenant). Open daily 8:30-11:30am and 2:30-6pm, the church was built in the 1920s over the Byzantine mosaic fragments of an otherwise demolished previous church. Below the hill is a lovely garden and in that garden is the preserved Crusader **Church of the Resurrection**. Open Monday-Wednesday and Friday-Saturday 8:30-11am and 2:30-5:30pm, and free, the church was built in 1142. Beneath the church excavations have revealed remains from Neolithic days. Find the minaret of the mosque next door and the church entrance is on your right. For a bite to eat in Abu Ghosh, the **Caravan Inn** on the road to town has hummus and fine views.

Avshalom, 19 kilometers southwest of Jerusalem, has a spectacular stalagmite and stalactite cave, worth seeing depsite the hordes who think the same. Open Saturday-Thursday 8:30am-3:30pm, Friday 8:30am-12:30pm admission costs NIS 13 for adults, NIS 7 for children. The ticket includes a slide show and guided tour every day but Friday. Friday is special. Though no tours are arranged, it's the only day when you're allowed to take pictures, since unlimited flash photography would damage the mineral formations. Bus 184 or 413 will take you as far as the village of Nes Harim, but that leaves you seven more kilometers to go. You can hike or find a taxi, or better yet rent a car or join an Egged tour from Jerusalem.

Neot Kedumim, *Route 443 off Route 1, near Lod and Ben Gurion Airport, Tel. 08-977-0777, Fax 08-977-0775, or in the US, 914-254-5031, Fax 914-254-4458*, is the **Biblical Landscape Reserve**. Open Sunday-Thursday 8:30am-sunset and Friday 8:30am-1pm (last entrance is two hours before closing), admission is NIS 16 per adult and NIS 11 per senior/student. On their 625 acres you'll find recreated the landscapes of the Ancient Israel, including hundreds of varietals mentioned in the Bible and Talmud. "Discover Your Roots" is their motto, and you can do so by exploring the two to three kilometer trails on your own with a map and guide pamphlet, or by joining one of their two-hour guided tours in English, leaving Tuesdays at 9:30am in winter and 3:30pm in summer of Fridays at 9:30am. Wear good walking shoes and a hat, and bring some water. There are outdoor shaded picnic areas and an indoor kosher dairy dinning room. They also host special events like Bar mitzvah celebrations, Biblical meals, and archaeological excavations. The reserve is located .

SPECIAL RELIGIOUS ACTIVITIES

A much touted, crowded affair is **Christmas in Bethlehem**. There are Anglican, Christ Church, Lutheran, and Roman Catholic services all over town, but everyone wants to go to the Grotto of the Nativity in the Franciscan Parish Church of Saint Catherine. However, not everyone can. You need a special free entrance ticket from the Franciscan Pilgrims Office at the **Christian Information Center**, *Jaffa Gate, Jerusalem, Tel. 02-627-2697, Fax 02-627-2692, or write to POB 14308 Jerusalem.* At present, tickets are possible only for certified Roman Catholics. They can be obtained by written request or in person, but the fussbudget Franciscan priest in charge of such matters has added an intimidating load of requirements and obstacles.

The written requests should be sent from September to November, and must include a letter from your Roman Catholic priest corroborating your Catholic identity, and must have a legible signature and the Parish seal or forget it. If you show up in person at the office, the requirements are the same, but he will stop accepting requests at some undefined point in December unless you had previously sent in a written request. Nothing will move him from this, so don't try.

There are plenty of other services to be seen, however, as well as the televised version in Manger Square. If that doesn't appeal, you might want to reconsider Bethlehem. People mostly stand around in Manger Square for many hours drinking bad coffee, listening to endless choirs, waiting for midnight. And then? Nothing. Midnight Mass from the Church of the Nativity is broadcast onto a big screen for the viewing pleasure of those who can't get in.

Transportation: There are buses running from Talpiot Station in Jerusalem to and from Bethlehem from 8am-3am, NIS 9.80 each way. And the Lutheran Church, *Tel. 02-627-6111, Fax 02-627-6222*, will arrange transport for NIS 28. Special buses leave from outside Damascus Gate, as do regular (and much cheaper) Arab buses.

14. NIGHTLIFE & SPORTS

ETHNIC MUSIC & FOLKLORE

The **Khan Club**, *David Remez Square, Tel. 02-671-8283, Fax 02-673-3095*, is near the railway station. The nightclub folklore show starts at 9pm and costs $15 or NIS 55, with all the free wine (semi-dry white or rosé) and soda you care to guzzle. You should call to reserve, and in the winter call again before heading over to see if there were enough sign-ups for the show to go on. The theater is a stone cave, dim with oriental carpets, and kind of great. The show, unfortunately, is a tourist group thing, with a "Here's Johnny," lounge act tone. Called a nightclub, there's nothing striptease about it. The show is all folkloric dance and song, a cross between *Fiddler on the Roof* and *Beach Blanket Babylon*—cheesey but not campy—with a singer/comedian type who's a cross between Tom Jones and Soupy Sales. Bus 6, 7, 8, and 30 will drop you at the railway station.

YMCA, *Tel. 02-623-3210 for reservations, Tel. 02-624-7281 for information*, has **Arab** and **Jewish Folklore** evenings on Mondays, Thursdays, and Saturdays.

The **Jerusalem Hotel**, *Nablus Road, Tel. 02-628-3282*, features Jazz Night on winter Thursdays and Lebanese Buffet Dinner with Afghani music on Saturdays at 8pm. The ambiance is cozy and Arabic and interesting, and the special evenings are well-attended. Call in advance, however, to make sure it's on and to reserve.

CLASSICAL MUSIC

The **Jerusalem Symphony**, *Tel. 02-561-1498 after 4pm*, performs in the Jerusalem Theater, *David Marcus and Chopin Streets*.

Gerard Bakhar Center, *11 Bezalel, Tel. 02-625-1139*, has concerts of classical, jazz, and Israeli folk music.

Dormitsion Church, *Tel. 02-671-9927*, sometimes has classical organ concerts. **Saint Andrew's** sponsers a Vocal Concert Series, *Tel. 02-673-*

2401, at 8pm, with four concerts for NIS 130. **Saint George's Catheral**, *20 Nablus, Tel.* *02-627-7232*, on the corner of Salah Eddin about eight minutes from Damascus Gate, sometimes has free concerts. **Hebrew Union College**, *13 King David, Tel.* *02-620-3333*, posts a bulletin board out front listing lectures and concerts. And the **Israel Museum**, *Tel.* *02-563-6231*, sometimes has concerts, lectures, and dance as well.

PUBS

Heleni HaMalka and Horkenos streets (near the Russian Compound, just off Jaffa) hold loads of neat old stone houses turned trendily into bars for the yuppie crowd.

Glastnost, *15 Heleni Hamalka, Tel.* *02-625-6954*, has a palm-tree filled patio, meals (NIS 16-28) and beer (NIS 8-15), and the music ranges from jazz to rock to funk (mostly tapes with the occasional live group). Open 7pm to the wee hours, there's hard liquor too, but it'll cost you as much as a meal.

Sergey, *Heleni Hamalka, Tel.* *02-625-8511*, next door to Glastnost, hosts the intelligensia, dishing up beer (NIS 12), mixed drinks (NIS 22) and Italian food to young intellectuals with money.

Over on the other side of Jaffa are some more options:

Tavern Pub, *16 Rivilin, Tel.* *02-624-4541*, is open daily from 2pm-3am. This small, dark, friendly spot has been in business for 33 years, serving mugs of beer and shots of booze for not very much.

The Rock, *11 Yoel Salomon, Tel.* *02-625-9170*, is a cafe and bar that caters to the scruffy-haired low-budget travelers who make good use of the daily happy hour deal from 5-9pm that gets you one free beer with each that you buy. With relatively cheap food (mallaweh is NIS 9, blinzes are NIS 15-20), this can be a pleasant place to hang out, but the music can get over loud and sometimes it's just too precious.

And of course there's **Fink's**, *2 HaHistadrut, corner of King George, Tel.* *02-623-4523*, deservedly written up by Newsweek as "One of the best bars in the world," and not to be missed for a drink served by Moulli, one of the best bartenders (and owners) in the world, accompanied by a cup of goulash (NIS 19) and an interesting mix of politicos, journalists, and regualar locals. See *Where to Eat* for the full picture.

DISCOS

Arizona Pub and Disco, *37 Jaffa near Zion Square*, has happy hour nightly from 7:50-8:10pm. Drink all the gassy weak beer you want and can for NIS 7, and from 8:10-9pm, buy one drink and get one free. After that, dance the night away till 4am. Western in theme and young in clientele, there's no cover, just a one-drink minimum.

The Underground, *8 Yoel Salomon, Tel. 02-625-1918*, is around the corner. Slightly more popular (for now) and definitely more cave-like, the happy hour and drink minimum deals are the same, and so is the sweaty, gyrating crowd, and so is the pounding disco beat.

Talpiot, *to the south off Hebron Road*, has some bigger dance clubs. The **Opera**, **Pythagoras**, and **Decadence** swing into action on Fridays and Saturdays from 9pm-5am, and charge covers from NIS 20-45 (plus the taxi fare home).

Sultan's Pool (Brekhat Ha-Sultan) amphitheater, *down below Yemin Moshe*, has summer shows featuring British and American rock stars. It's a great setting for a rock concert if you like that sort of thing, and tickets start at around NIS 70.

FOLK DANCING

The **International Cultural Center for Youth**, *12a Emek Refa'im, Tel. 02-566-4144*, has folk dancing Sundays at 7:30pm for NIS 12 (bus 4 and 18 will go there). **The House for Hebrew Youth**, *105 HaRav Herzog, Tel. 02-678-8642*, or *Beit Ha'No'ar* in Hebrew, has folk dance classes Thursdays at 8pm. Bus 19 takes you there.

And the **Liberty Bell Gardens** hosts a post-Shabbat outdoors dance jubilee, teaching folk and modern jazz to whomever shows up.

THEATER

The **Jerusalem Cinematheque**, *Hebron Road, Tel. 02-672-4131*, in the Hinnom Valley has two screens showing a number of films nightly at 9:30pm (plus 10pm and midnight on Fridays and 4pm on Saturdays) for NIS 16. Southwest of the Old City, bus 5 and 21 go there. In early July they host the **Israeli Film Festival**, with international and local showings listed in the Jerusalem Post or the theater. **Kakao Cafe**, open daily 11:30am-1am, has good albeit pricy food for a pre or post show meal.

The **Palestinian National Theater**, *Nuzuh, near the American Colony Hotel, Tel. 02-628-0957*, puts on plays and musicals, usually political in content and Arabic in language, though English synopses are provided. Al Hakawati in Arabic, from Nablus the theater is on the first right after Salah ad-Din; plays cost NIS 15-20 and tourists are welcome, but call first to make sure a show is on.

SPORTS & RECREATION

You can go on a **hiking trip** to the Judean Desert. **SPNI** (**Society for Protection of Nature**), *13 Helene Ha'Malka, 02-625-2357*, leads expertly guided tours all over the countryside, most of them including hiking and nature exploration. They also do some trips in Jerusalem, and all are well worth the time and money. The Wednesday trip to the Judean Hills (and Bar Kokhba's cave, and more) leaves from their office at 8am (get there 15 minutes in advance) and costs $46 (bring your own flashlight, lunch, and water).

The guides are very knowlegdable, not just about the history, but the desert plants and geology as well, and it makes for a wonderful combination of legend, lore, hiking – not strenuous but neither is it for the complete couch potato. Their Monday (9am) Wadi Kelt Oasis and Saint George Monastery tour ($45) is very popular; it's been cancelled for the time due to unrest in the Wadi Kelt area, but will be resumed just as soon as political conditions warrant. Visit their offices or call to reserve, or go through ABC-BTC (see below) who are authorized to book SPNI tours.

Bring hiking boots (sneakers are allowed if that's all you have, but they don't protect against sprains) or nature sandals (depending on what hike you're going on). Water (three liter minimum in summer) and a hat are necessary, and lunch for a day hike.

The **Jerusalem Skating Center**, *19 Hillel*, is up above the Croissanteriee. Open Sunday-Thursday 10am-11pm, Friday 10am-2pm, Saturday sundown-11:30pm, skate rental and access to the silicon "ice" will cost you NIS 20.

Swimming pools: Beit Zayit, *Tel. 02-533-2239*, is the last stop on bus 151 and is open daily 10am-5pm, costing NIS 30 (children NIS 24) and NIS 35 on Friday-Saturday (children 24); **Jerusalem Swimming Pool**, *Emek Refa'am, Tel. 02-563-2092*, by bus 4 or 18, is open daily 6am-8:45pm and costs NIS 35, but you need Shabbat tickets in advance.

15. SHOPPING

You have your urban department stores, your regular small stores, airport duty-free shops, and shuks (street markets, bazaars), all with their own protocol and etiquette. The **department stores** are big and modern, and follow the same norms established 'round the world. Credit cards are accepted, they are usually open from morning to night with no mid-day break, and bargaining is absolutely not the done thing.

Smaller stores, especially those selling souvenirs, are often flexible on their pricing. If you're shopping for antiques or Judaica, you should definitely haggle over price. In the **shuks**, bartering is the game, to be entered into with good humor and a sense of humor. You shouldn't buy if the price isn't what you think it's worth, but nor should you enter into the bartering fray if you're not really interested in the item in the first place. In fact, there is a Jewish law stating you must not go into a shop and ask the proprietor how much an item costs if you know you really have no intention of buying, thus saving him from getting his hopes up unnecessarily.

Antiques, by law, are man-made objects from before 1700 CE; they may not be taken out of Israel without written approval from the Director of the Antiquities Authority, and are subject to an export fee of 10% of the purchase price. For more info you can contact the **Antiquities Authority**, *Rockefeller Museum, on Sultan Sueliman, Tel. 02-628-2251, Fax 02-560-2628.*

SHOPPING IN JERUSALEM

Old City Shouk is the primary shopping center. Full of alley ways, shops, stalls, and vendors, you need to enter with a level head and a zest for bargaining. Early in the day is better, before everyone's tempers get ratty.

Palestinian Pottery, *14 Nablus, Tel. 02-628-2826*, across from the American Consulate, is open Monday-Saturday 8am-4pm. Run by the Balian family and established in 1922, this is a factory, showcase, and shop of fine, hand-painted pottery. It's not only a swell place to look around and shop, if it's not busy, Mr. Balian can tell you some interesting tales. His Armenian parents were recruited in 1919 to use their craft renovating the Mosque of Omar. Three years later the Balian family started up their own business, and they've been throwing hand-made pots on wheels and painting them ever since. You can buy plates and bowls for NIS 10-200 and vases for NIS 15-300, depending on size and design, but they don't take credit cards and they don't ship.

Palestinian Needlework Shop, *79 Nablus opposite the Ambassador Hotel, Tel. 02-582-8834, Fax 02-582-5823*, is open Monday-Saturday 8am-7pm and sells handcrafted traditional cross-stitch embroidery on locally woven fabrics. A non-profit project of the Minnonites, it aims to supplement the incomes of local (mostly Ramallah and Surif) Palestinian women. Items range from $2 bookmarks to $50 pillow cases and $55 shawls.

Tarshish, *18 King David, corner of Hess, Tel. 02-625-8039*, is a reputable place to shop for antiques, Judaica (beautiful mezuzim), and Yemenite jewelry (nicer than average). Open Sunday-Thursday 10am-1pm and 4-7pm, the owner is honest, and it's a great place to shop for coins. Credit cards accepted.

Galleria David, *near the bottom of King David*, has good art.

Avi Ben's Wine Store, *22 Rivlin, Tel. 02-625-9703*, has a fine selection of Israeli products as well as an espresso counter serving good, strong coffee for NIS 4.5 and glasses of wine for NIS 7-13.

16. THE DEAD SEA

The **Dead Sea**, also called **Yam ha-Melah** (Hebrew for *Salt Sea*) and Buhr Lut (Arabic for *Sea of Lot*), boasts a shoreline that is the lowest point on Earth. The sea, divided into two basins by the peninsula of Lisan ('tongue' in Arabic), is part of the five million year old Great Syrian-African Rift Valley, and with the Judean Mountains to the west and the Moab Mountains to the east, Israel on one bank and Jordan on the other, it's a special place.

The Sea has been cited in works from the Bible to Beckett's *Waiting For Godot*, where Estragon said "I remember the maps of the Holy Land. Coloured they were. Very pretty. The Dead Sea was pale blue. The very look of it made me thirsty. That's where we'll go, I used to say, that's where we'll go for our honeymoon. We'll swim. We'll be happy." Many still want to go there and be happy, with greater success than Estragon.

The area is as rich in remarkable natural and historic diversity as the sea is in minerals. With **Masada**, **Ein Gedi**, and **Qumran** of Dead Sea Scrolls fame, there are stark desert vistas with craggy canyons, hot springs, cool oases with water falls, nature reserves and bird sanctuaries, salt formations, and of course the sea, where you can sit and float far more easily than swim.

One word of caution: the salt-dense sea packs a real wallop to an abrasion or cut. Even a recent shave can sting mightily in the Dead Sea.

THE NORTHERN BASIN

This stretch of Dead Sea coast is alive with some of the most important historical sites and lushest oasis reserves in Israel. **Qumran**, site of the Dead Sea Scrolls is in the north, **Ein Feshka** and **Ein Gedi** beaches are good for a dip in the brine, **Metzoke Drogot** is an entry into the Judean Desert, **Ein Gedi Reserve** refreshes with waterfalls and wildlife, and **Masada**, last stand of the Judeans against the Roman forces, is in the south.

DEAD SEA VITAL STATISTICS

• **Altitude:** 1,300 feet below sea level (on average)
• **Area:** 405 square miles (1,049 kilometers)
• **Length:** 46 miles (74 kilometers) long
• **Width:** about 10 miles (16 kilometers) wide
• **Depth:** ranging from 1,310 feet in the north to less than nine feet in the south
• **Temperature highs** (F°): Dec-Apr 68°-84°, Sept-Nov 81°-97°, and June-Aug 99°-102°
• **Annual rainfall:** about two inches
• **Evaporation Rate:** about 55 inches annually
• **Rate of Level Change:** the lake is sinking around .4 inches a year
• **Saline Content:** every liter is 30% salt, or 2.5 lbs worth, about seven times as much as the ocean
• **Chemical Content:** chloride, bromide, bicarbonate, sulfate, sodium, potassium, calcium, and magnesium
• **Shore Content:** flanked on east and west by ridges of sandstone and dolomite
• **Source:** Jordan River (diverted for irrigation, reducing flow and lowering its level)
• **Outlet:** none
• **Life Support:** only simple organisms can live in its saline waters

QUMRAN

Khirbet Qumran, *Tel. 02-994-2235,* the ruins of Qumran, is what's left of the site where a community was founded by the Essenes around 150 BCE. Though there were Jewish settlements on this site since the 700s BCE, the Essene community put Qumran on the map thanks to some Bedouin shepherds who stumbled on seven of the ancient scrolls (since labeled **The Dead Sea Scrolls**) in a local cave in 1947. Following excavations revealed additional scrolls, and structures supporting the theory that Qumran had been a center for the Essene sect, who had written and stored the scrolls that were found.

The **Essenes** were a splinter religious sect that formed in the same tumultuous times that gave birth to the Zealots, Christianity, and the Great Revolts. They were pacifists and purists; they emphasized the importance of purity and the ritual bath, de-emphasized property and material wealth, and took off to the countryside to set up pure commu-

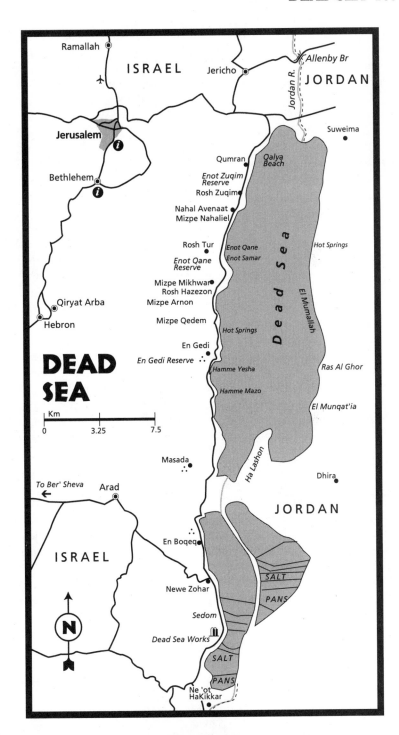

nities and await the Messiah. This Dead Sea Sect was apparently an extremist offshoot of the Essenes. An earthquake in 31 BCE caused the sect to flee the site, but sometime during the rule of Archelaus (Herod's son, who reigned from 4 BCE-6 CE), they returned and rebuilt.

During the Great Jewish Revolt of 68 CE the Romans took Qumran, scattering the Dead Sea Sect. The last known inhabitants were the Romans, who set up a garrison there during the Bar Kokhba Rebellions of 132-135 CE. After that, the place was abandoned and forgotten till the scroll discovery some 1800 years later. After the Six Day War of 1967, Qumran was taken over by the National Parks Authority. Thanks to them, there now is a parking lot, pamphlets with maps, informative signs, snack bar and bathrooms, and an entrance fee.

Slopes pocked with caves rise to the west of the old settlement site. Some of the caves, difficult to access, were used as hiding places for their library when danger threatened. The scrolls were hidden in jars, and the extreme dry climate preserved them for nearly two thousand years. The finds, including copies of the Old Testament, the Apocrypha, and the sect's own works, were written in Hebrew, Aramaic, and Greek on scrolls of leather or papyrus (one was even chiseled on copper) and are now on display at the Shrine of the Book in the Israel Museum in Jerusalem.

To be seen here, along with the now-empty caves, is the excavated settlement, including dining room, scriptorium (presumably where The Scrolls were written), cisterns, tower, and cattle pen. Though the find was extraordinary and the scrolls are fascinating, the actual site is a bit of a let-down. It's a long, hot walk to the caves of fame, and when you get there, they are, well, caves, and no signs indicate which were *the* caves. Open daily 8am-5pm, entrance costs NIS 12 for adults, NIS 6 for youth, and NIS 9 for seniors and students.

ORIENTATION

The National Parks site is west of the Kaliah-Sedom road off the northwestern shore of the Dead Sea, 40 kilometers south of Jerusalem. As you drive along the turn-off, you come to a parking lot busy with private cars and tour buses. To the right is a blessedly air-conditioned building with souvenir shop and snack bar. To the left is the ticket booth that lets onto the excavation site. Marked paths lead to the excavated settlement and off to the caves in the hills.

ARRIVALS & DEPARTURES
By Bus

There are buses from Ein Gedi or Jerusalem. From where the bus lets you off it's about 100 meters up a steep drive to the entrance.

By Tour

Lots of people choose one of many tours operating out of Jerusalem. See *Tours* in the Jerusalem chapter for more details.

WHERE TO STAY

KALIA GUEST HOUSE, *Tel. 02-993-6253,* charges singles NIS 205-250, doubles NIS 250-330. This is the place if you want to stay by Qumran, but most people see this as a day trip from Jerusalem or further south on the Dead Sea.

WHERE TO EAT

There's a **self-serve cafeteria,** *Tel. 02-994-2533,* next to the souvenir shop that stays open until 4pm and will do if you're hungry and don't want to wait for other choices, with sandwiches for NIS 15 and main dishes starting at NIS30.

SPORTS & RECREATION

Three kilometers south of Qumran is **Ein Feshka,** *Tel. 02-994-2355,* also called **Einot Zukim,** a very pleasant place to recuperate from the heat. Go floating in the Dead Sea on the beach (open daily 8am-5pm, NIS 20 for adults, NIS 10 for children) or splash in the pools from the fresh water springs in the Nature Reserve oasis across the road. There's a lifeguard on

METZOKEI DRAGOT

*Just an hour's drive from Jerusalem in the heart of the Judean Desert is **Metzokei Dragot International Center for Desert Tourism**, Tel. 02-994-4777, Fax 02-994-4333. The turn-off from the Dead Sea Coast road is roughly halfway between the Ein Feshka and Ein Gedi oases, up into the rocks and wadis of the Judean Hills. You can go for just a day hike (guided or not) or stay for a while.*

The accommodations are not luxurious, but this is a place from which to explore the desert, not a luxury spa. There are 45 air conditioned rooms with private toilet and shower for $49-$59 a single and $70-$84 a double, breakfast and free access to the mineral beach (worth NIS 25-29) included. They lead tours in the Judean Desert and Dead Sea area, with desert safari vehicles, hiking, mountain climbing, rappelling, and camel safari as options. They also have regular desert tours every Tuesday and Saturday from Jerusalem (call to arrange). The Judean Desert can be quite beautiful, and a tour with some desert company is worthwhile if you have the time (see Jerusalem Tours for more options).

the beach, as well as showers, changing rooms, bathrooms, and drinking water. It's a prime Dead Sea mud wallow spot, and folks stroll caked and crusty before attempting to rinse off. Any buses plying the Dead Sea coastal highway can let you off there.

Go north seven kilometers from Qumran to **Attraction Water Park**, *Kalya Beach, Tel. 02-994-2393*, for a fun way to cool off. Open daily March-October 9am-4:45pm, it costs NIS 55 for adults, is free for children under one meter, and is a good option if the kids are beginning to wilt. Any buses heading north along the Dead Sea can drop you there.

And **Lot's Wife**, *Tel. 07-659-4760, Fax 07-658-4137*, runs a **Dead Sea Cruise**. They leave Tuesday and Thursday at 2:30pm, Saturday at 11:30am and 2:30pm, providing guided tours of Ein Gedi on the Dead Sea, and lunch by prior arrangement. They charge NIS 35 for adults and NIS 25 for children.

EIN GEDI

Ein Gedi (*fountain of the goat*) refers both to the Dead Sea beach and the oasis in the nature reserve, to the east and west of the road, respectively. While a dip in the Dead Sea is a unique and not-to-be-missed experience, Ein Gedi may not be where you choose to try it (your bathing plans might better include Ein Feshka or Ein Bokek), but a visit to the nature reserve, steeped in history and cool spring water, is bound to be rewarding.

ORIENTATION

On the eastern edge of the Judean Desert, Ein Gedi is bordered by the HaHaetakim Cliffs to the west, the Dead Sea to the east, mount Yishai Ridge to the north, and Nahal Hever to the south. On the west coast of the Dead Sea, Ein Gedi is 34 kilometers south of Ein Feshka, 15 kilometers north of Masada, and 25 kilometers northeast of Arad.

Entrance to all the sites are easily accessible from the main road, spreading out over a 2.5 kilometers span. From north to south, their order is: the nature reserve, youth hostel, and SPNI field school; then comes the beach, campgrounds, mini-market, restaurant, gas station, and first aid station; and lastly are the thermal baths, resort, and spa.

ARRIVALS & DEPARTURES

By Bus

If Ein Gedi is to be a day trip involving a few sites and getting back before the last bus departs, plan carefully. Buses 486 and 487 go to and from Jerusalem for NIS 26, leaving as early as 7:45am. The last bus back is at 6pm, 1:30pm on Fridays (the 444 goes all the way to Eilat for NIS 45 at 8, 11, 3, and 6). Buses 384 and 385 ply the Arad (NIS 21.80) /Be'er Sheva (NIS 29) route, leaving Ein Gedi at 8, 11:15, 12:30, 3:30, and 5:45. Bus 486 goes to Masada and Ein Bokek at 11, 12:15, and 2:15) for NIS 3.90. To be sure, check with Egged before setting off.

When arriving, be aware that there are three bus stops. From the north, the first is for the nature reserve, youth hostel, and SPNI field school; the next is the beach, campgrounds, mini-market, restaurant, gas station, and first aid station; and the third is for the thermal baths, resort, and spa.

WHERE TO STAY

EIN GEDI "BEIT SARAH" YOUTH HOSTEL, *Tel. 07-658-4165, Fax 07-658-4445, has dorm beds for NIS 35 (NIS 69 for non-members), including a big breakfast. There are also private rooms for NIS 140 per person (less 4 shekels for members).*

Just around the corner from the nature reserve, this is a lovely place. With 208 beds, they offer a variety of lodging options. Dinners cost NIS 35, and they give discounts to the reserve (NIS 2 off) and 20% discounts off the Ein Gedi Spa as well. The bunks are sturdy and most are made of wood, the rooms are pleasant and clean, with air conditioning and wardrobes, and the bathrooms are clean and big. The office is open 7am-7pm, and the cafe is open 6pm to whenever. The terrace is surrounded by trees and very pleasant, overlooking green lawns, flowers, big beautiful palms, and the Dead Sea.

SPNI FIELD SCHOOL, *Tel. 07-658-4288, has dorm rooms with 6 beds for NIS 645 for the room. Doubles are NIS 245, breakfast included.*

The field school is a 10 minute walk uphill from the hostel (buses 384 and 385 go all the way if you ask). All the rooms have air conditioning and private baths. The accommodations are almost always full of school groups and tours, so arrange ahead if you want to stay there. They also have trail maps and a small museum (entrance NIS 6 for visitors, free for SPNI guests) featuring snakes and a 15 minute video on the desert flora and fauna.

EIN GEDI BEACH allows **camping** for free under the green and yellow awnings. Bring whatever you need; all they provide is the shelter, some bathrooms, and an open-air shower. The kiosk, however, does sell charcoal, flashlights, beer, and sandwiches.

EIN GEDI CAMPING, *Tel. 07-658-4342, Fax 07-658-4455, charges NIS 25 per adult, NIS 13 per child, for camping. Or you can stay in the caravans, for $77 a single, $92 a double, and $15 per each additional person.*

They're located further south, just to the right of the gas station. You bring the tent and sleeping bags, they provide the site, and bathrooms.

They have lockers, too, costing NIS 6 per opening. They also offer 23 air conditioned rooms and 42 somewhat claustrophobic air conditioned caravans for up to six people, with kitchenettes and bathrooms. For this, you also get 30% discounts off the thermal mineral Ein Gedi Spa, with its private beach, TV room, and solarium. There's a gas station and first aid station there as well.

EIN GEDI RESORT AND SPA, *Tel. 07-659-4222, Fax 07-658-4328, charges $122-$143 a single and $174-$204 a double, half board included.*

South of Ein Gedi Camping, the Resort has 120 air conditioned rooms, all with TV, radio, phone, and coffee/tea counter. This is the top of the line at Ein Gedi. Here there are palm trees and flowers, swimming pools (indoor and out), natural sulfur pools, mineral mud baths, private Dead Sea beach, tennis courts, and regular shuttle service to the spa.

WHERE TO EAT

The pickings are slim. There's the **KIOSK NAHAL DAVID**, *just outside the nature reserve ticket booth*, with sandwiches, mineral water, and ice cream.

MILKY RESTAURANT, *Ein Gedi free beach*, open 8am-6pm, is air-conditioned, self-serviced, and reasonably priced. The **KIOSK EIN GEDI** outside sells beer and sandwiches to go.

From 6pm on, the **YOUTH HOSTEL CAFE** serves light dinner fare.

For a more comfortable and pricier setting, try the **EIN GEDI RESORT SELF-SERVICE RESTAURANT**.

SEEING THE SIGHTS

Ein Gedi beach is one of the most popular on the Dead Sea; perhaps because of the nature reserve across the street, it's the only name many people know. The 'beach' is free, and you get your money's worth. The bathing area is one little strip of shore, very rocky, and a trip to the water entails a perilous bare-foot journey across sharp stones. Green and yellow awnings provide shade, and you can camp under them free of charge, though it's not the coziest of places. The kiosk sells charcoal along with expensive Dead Sea beauty products, and the bus schedules to Eilat, Jerusalem, and Be'er Sheva are posted there too.

There's a self-serve restaurant that's quite reasonably priced (open 8:30am-5pm), bathrooms and changing rooms, and it's better than nothing but not as nice as the others.

A couple kilometers down the road, the upscale **Ein Gedi Resort and Spa** (owned by the Ein Gedi kibbutz) is a popular destination for many of the organized tours from Jerusalem. A 10 minute walk north takes you to great globs of **Dead Sea mud**, yours for the slathering, and some freshwater springs as well.

Ein Gedi Nature Reserve

Ein Gedi Nature Reserve, *Tel.* 07-658-4285, was an oasis of abundant fertility even in Old Testament times, and the vineyards of Ein Gedi are celebrated in the Song of Solomon (1:14). The oasis also figured in the history of the time; when young David ran from King Saul's wrath, he hid in a cave in "the wilderness of Ein Gedi" (I Samuel 24:1-4). Around 100 BCE, Ein Gedi had a large Jewish community, and it became the administrative center for Idumaea, the province forcibly converted to Judaism by John Hyrcanus from which Herod's family came. Perhaps for this reason (or for no reason), Herod the Great later conquered Ein Gedi during his rule (37-4 BCE).

Ein Gedi was plundered during the Great Revolt of 68 CE, and figured again as a refuge during the Bar-Kokhba Rebellion of 132 CE when Simon Bar Kokhba and his men hid in a cave some six kilometers southwest. The settlement here flourished from the fourth-sixth centuries, and was highly valued for its production of balsam, but Ein Gedi began to decline in the Byzantine period, and by the 19th century it was home to just a few Bedouin families living in reed huts by the mouth of Ein Gedi Spring. In 1949 the Israel Defense Force opened a route from the south (Sodom) and Kibbutz Ein Gedi was established.

The reserve, officially declared in 1972, is comprised of 6,750 acres including **Nahal David**, **Nahal Arugot**, and the slopes between. The oasis is fed by four springs: David, Shulamit, Ein Gedi, and Ein Arugot, supplying an abundance of fresh water yearly for the verdant vegetation and healthy wildlife community that thrive there. It's a pleasant jaunt for anyone wanting a green change of pace from the Judean Desert, but it's an especially rewarding site for botanists; the oasis is rare in that Tropical, Desert, Mediterranean, and Steppian plants manage to grow side by side.

The reserve is also home to a goodly collection of ibex, whose mating season in September-October is amazing to watch, as is the April scene of female ibex descending to the lowland springs and streams with their young. Hyrax live there, as do hyenas, fox, and four leopards. Ein Gedi is also a bird refuge—Tristam's starling, the Arabian babbler (the bird), and Griffon vultures are just three of the many species who reside there. During migration season, thousands more fly over; it's a wonderful time to visit.

In addition to the natural wealth, there are archaeological finds here as well, including a synagogue and bathhouse from Talmudic times and a flour (or sugar) mill from the Islamic period, a Roman fortress ruin, an Israeli fortress ruin, and a Chalcolithic temple from 5,000 years ago. There are hiking trails to these sites, and to waterfalls and pools, and loads of caves, ranging from one and a half to six hours, and fairly well marked— the ticket office will give you a useful map when you enter. The short trip takes you to Shulamit Falls, and is one of the most popular destinations for the hot and dusty.

Daily hours are from 8am-3pm in winter and 8am-4pm is summer, closing one hour earlier in Nahal Augot. Entrance costs NIS 15 for adults, NIS 8 for seniors/youth, and Visa & Mastercard are accepted. There's a souvenir shop that also sells water bottles in case you forgot to bring one, and a snack bar sells fast foods.

SHOPPING

Ein Gedi Nature Reserve has a shop selling hiking goods like thermal shoulder slings for mineral water bottles (with the adorable Nature Reserve antelope logo), hats, shorts, and more.

The **Kiosk Ein Gedi** by the beach and the shop at the **Ein Gedi Spa** sell Dead Sea mud and other Dead Sea beauty and health products.

SPORTS & RECREATION

Hiking in the nature reserve and bathing in the Dead Sea are the activities of choice. For desert exploration, see Metzokei Dragot.

EXCURSIONS & DAY TRIPS

See Qumran and Masada.

PRACTICAL INFORMATION

There is a **gas station** and **first aid station** by the Ein Gedi Camping Site, south of the nature reserve and free beach.

MASADA

Probably one of the most visited sites in Israel, the rock fortress of **Masada** looms as large in history and in tour itineraries as it does in the Judean Desert hills.

It's a place that actually lives up to its hype; it is awe-inspiring to see the rocky outpost jutting up in the heat above the Dead Sea, with the muted shades of the Judean hills and canyons behind, especially if you can arrange to be there when it isn't aswarm with bus loads of group tours.

The site is officially open 5:20am-6pm, but the times seem flexible. Entrance without cable car tickets costs NIS 14 per adult and NIS 10.5 for students. A cable car ticket one-way is NIS 29 (NIS 18.5 for students) and NIS 40 for return (NIS 22.5 for students).

ORIENTATION

Majestically rising 1,440 feet above the Dead Sea shore, Masada is an isolated mountain plateau among the hills of the **Judean Desert**. It's located near the southern tip of the northern basin of the Dead Sea, off the Arad road, about 15 kilometers south of Ein Gedi and 15 kilometers north of Ein Bokek. From the parking lot you proceed west along the path to the ticket booth and gate, and there you have to choose the Snake Path climb or buy the tickets for the cable car ascent. Either way, once you are atop the rock the excavated remains await you.

You arrive facing southeast (the Snake Path gate is just a little south of the cable car terminal). To your left are a few scattered sites (the Byzantine Cave Dwelling, the Eastern Wall, the Royal Family Residence). If you follow the Eastern Wall 400 meters or so you come to the Water Cistern and nearby Southern Citadel lookout. Southwest from the Snake Path Gate about 200 meters is a cluster of the Southern Villa, the Swimming Pool, Building #11, and the Western Palace.

To the right of the Snake Path and cable car gates you'll find another cluster of sites, with Storehouses, a Villa, the Administration Building, Water Gate, Bath House, and further on, the Northern Palace. And southwest of that, is the Northern Palace Lookout, Synagogue, and Tower, and Roman Ramp.

ARRIVALS & DEPARTURES

By Bus

The 486, 487, and 444 go to and from Jerusalem (the 444 goes south as far as Eilat), and from Be'er Sheva take the 384 or 385. The 421 comes from Tel Aviv once daily at 8:30am.

By Car

Drive up (or down) the Dead Sea coast road and turn west on the road to Arad, following the Masada signs. There's an ample parking lot at the foot of the mountain.

GETTING AROUND TOWN

You have two choices: walking up the Snake Path or riding the cable car. It takes around 40 minutes of fairly steady walking, give or take a rest stop, to reach the top, and 25 minutes going down, and roughly three minutes by cable car.

The **cable car** runs 8am-4pm in winter, 8am-5pm in summer, shutting two hours earlier on Fridays. It leaves every half hour or when 40 people are ready to ride, and takes three minutes.

The **Snake Path**, the only way up the mountain before the Romans built their ramp, is rock-strewn and uneven, so climbing in flip flops can result in stubbed toes. If you're going to do the hike, take plenty of water, and save yourself future pain by doing some leg stretches after your climb and/or descent.

Some people choose to hike up in the wee hours of the night to see the sunrise from the top, then cable car down when it's hot. This is a worthwhile plan, and not only because it avoids the heat of the day. The Masada ruins look eerie in the pre-dawn light, and you get to appreciate more of the magic of Masada before loud tour guides and masses of tourists break the spell. If you do this, take a flashlight, wear sneakers or hiking boots, take adequate water, and wear layers that will keep you warm in the cold desert night but can peel down for the heat.

Others, who want the Snake Path experience but don't want to die of heat stroke in the process take the cable car up and casually saunter down.

WHERE TO STAY

TAYLOR YOUTH HOSTEL, *eastern foothills of Masada, Tel. 07-658-4349, Fax 07-658-4650, is to the left of where the bus drops you. They charge $17 per dorm bed, $36 a single, $52 for doubles, and $67 for a triple, less $1.50 for members, breakfast included.*

Overlooking the mountains of Moab and the Dead Sea, this hostel is a pleasant respite from the heat of the sun, the glare of the rocks, and the noise of the countless tour guides. There's a welcome cluster of green trees offering shade and color around an outdoor roofed patio with tables. There are 104 beds, and the dorm rooms are all air-conditioned, with private baths, and six-eight beds. Dinners are available for $8, and there's a kitchen facility as well. Lockers can be rented for NIS 5.

They allow campers to stay for free on the concrete pavilion outside, but there are no facilities for them. No camping is allowed atop Masada.

WHERE TO EAT

Well, there's **TAYLOR HOSTEL DINING ROOM,** *Tel. 07-658-4349,* with dinners for $8, but you need to put your order in by 6pm. There's also a **snack bar** near the lower cable car landing, and a **restaurant** closer to the parking lot. It's not a place that's really geared toward fine dining; just treat yourself to something nice when you get back to Jerusalem.

SEEING THE SIGHTS

The Masada Story

Masada is best known as the site of the **Zealots'** last gasp against the Romans in 73 CE, but there have been people taking shelter there since men lived in caves in Neolithic times (5,000-3,000 BCE). According to the historian Josephus, a fort was first built on the Judean plateau by high priest Jonathan Maccabaeus around 150 BCE. This fortification was enlarged by Johanan Hyrakanus I (134-104 BCE), the high priest and de facto king. In 40 CE, **Herod** escaped with his family from besieged Jerusalem (during his battles with the Parthians and Hasmonaeans) and fled to the old fortress at Masada, where he left the women, food, and a garrison of 800 men, and went on to Petra to get help.

Herod then went to Rome, was appointed king of the Jews, and returned to liberate his relatives. Later, in 36-30 BCE, Herod constructed a new fortress on the site, making it the biggest in his country. According to Josephus Flavius, Masada was intended as a defense against Cleopatra, queen of Egypt, who was strongly suggesting to Mark Antony that Herod be deposed. After Herod's death Masada became a Roman garrison site, but it was taken by the Jews in 66 CE near the start of the Great Revolt. Two years later, following the destruction of the Temple in Jerusalem, the surviving Zealots fled the tatters of Jerusalem and took up residence in the desert fortress. They lasted three years while Rome's Tenth Legion inched forward with catapults and determination.

The Roman legion under **Flavius Silva** couldn't starve them out because they had so much food, so they began to build a ramp of stone, wood, and sand up the western side of the mountain, and advanced with their battering rams. Eventually the Zealots' leader **Elazar ben Yair** had to see that despite their hopes, the Romans were not going to dismiss their band as an insignificant community, and that in fact they weren't going to stop till Masada (and the last remnants of the Great Revolt) was theirs.

He called a meeting (according to accounts of two women and five children who hid and survived) and said "let our wives die before they are abused, and our children before they have tasted of slavery, and after we have slain them, let us bestow that glorious benefit upon one another mutually." In 73 CE, as recorded by Flavius Josephus, the Romans attained the heights of Masada and found the bodies of the Zealots strewn about.

Though we know of Masada from Josephus, the Talmud omits the story, which highlights its equivocal place in Jewish history. For some, Masada is the greatest symbol of resolution and national defense, but others (such as the rabbis compiling the Talmud) viewed the Zealots with resentment for their ill-fated rebellions.

The Excavation Site

The Excavation (begun in 1963 by archaeologists headed by **Yigael Yadin**) have revealed pre-Herodian remains, including Iron Age pottery shards from the 10th-7th centuries BCE and coins from the reign of

Alexander Janneus (103-76 BCE), as well as structures from the Byzantine period like a small church that was built near Herod's western palace. Most of the finds, however, come from Herod's palaces and the Zealots' quarters. Depending on your interest in this sort of thing, you could do a cursory once over or spend hours seeing all. If you are only going to check out a few spots, the most rewarding by far is the Northern Palace frescos. The painted black lines you see on some structures are there to divide the reconstructed add-ons from the original ruins.

To the North
   Herod's Northern Palace is an amazing structure, built into the rock on three levels and connected by stone stairs. This was the king's private villa, and the attention to detail indicates the luxury in which he lived. The upper terrace contains the living rooms and a semi-circular balcony. The middle terrace is formed by a colonnaded pavilion. Even if you walked up the Snake Path, it's still worth expending the extra energy to climb down to the lower terrace.

   There are still frescos there, brilliantly colorful, protected against the elements (and tourists) by clear sheets of glass that hardly mar their beauty. This courtyard is bordered by a double row of fluted columns, and as further indication of Herod's sumptuous lifestyle, his bathroom floor was heated (though Masada isn't a place one associates with a lack of heat). While excavating, archaeologists found skeletons of a man, woman, and child, Zealots who met their fate surrounded by their belongings of a prayer shall, arrows, and armor.

   On the western side, the **Water Gate**, with its walls of stone and waiting benches, offers a tremendous view over the hills to the north. Down the wall a bit the **Northern Palace Lookout** had fantastic views of Ein Gedi, as well as the slopes leading to the Palace itself. Further south is the **Synagogue**, one of the oldest ever found dating from the time of the Temple. Pillars held up the roof, and still remaining is the base of the wall that divided the large hall. Scrolls were found here, including several books of the Torah now on display at the Israel Museum in Jerusalem, along with silver coins and a prayer shawl.

   On the eastern side is the **Bathhouse**, Herod's own, featuring pillars, three tiled rooms ranging from hot to cold with colorful mosaic floors, and a dressing room with wall frescos. South of that the **Snake Path Lookout** near the cable car terminus has a fine view down the path and across to the Dead Sea.

   In the middle of the complex, the **Administration Building** was once one of Herod's courtyards. The Zealots built one of their ritual baths here, with rainwater collected in the southern pool. When it reached the right height, it drained through a slit into another pool which was used for the ritual immersions. The Zealots used the smaller pool to the west to wash before embarking on the ritual bath. In keeping with the water motif, it now houses **rest rooms**, and fresh water taps help slake summer thirst. The **Storehouses** on the eastern side kept hundreds of jars holding years' worth of supplies. The **Villa**, with its courtyard, pillars and large rooms, was partitioned up by the Zealots to accommodate their families. From the **Quarry** nearby came some of the stone used to construct Masada.

Along the Eastern Wall

The **Snake Path Gate**, typical of other Masada gates, has a stone floor with benches, a guardroom, and white plaster walls made to look like marble. The **Eastern Wall**, constructed by Herod's men, shows the original layout that included inner and outer walls connected by partitions and a few towers.

About 100 meters southeast of the Gate, the **Byzantine Dwelling Cave** was built by monks in an existing crater that was probably a quarry for plaster. Further south, the **Royal Family Residence** was once a luxurious villa built by Herod. With an inner courtyard, it had large rooms separated by pillars and decorated by frescos. The Zealots converted the grand design to suit their needs, and partitioned it into smaller residences. Walking east again, the **Southeast Wall** has a tower and small room. Inside there's a little niche with what might be a Roman inscription. About 200 meters along, the **Southern Wall** has a lookout tower and a bakery (the latter probably added by the Zealots).

The ritual baths played an important role in Zealot life. These have a dressing room with clothing 'shelves.' The southern gate led to water cisterns and caves outside the wall. At the southern tip, the **Southern Citadel** helped fortify Masada at a weak spot.

The Southwestern Cluster

Heading due north some 200 meters from the Citadel you'll reach the **Southern Villa**. It was designed by Herod but not completed, and the Zealots made it into more living quarters. One of the rooms has been set up to look like how the Zealots left it, with hearth and kitchen pots. To the east of that is the **Columbarium** that once contained cremation urns, and north is **Building #11**, with its evocative name. This was one of Herod's villas, converted by the Zealots into a water reservoir. West of that is the **Swimming Pool**, another part of the good life Herod wanted included in his desert fortress. Given the weather, it certainly makes sense.

North 100 meters is the **Western Palace**, extending over an area of nearly 43,100 square feet. It had residential and domestic wings, storage and administrative rooms, a kitchen, and underground cisterns. The throne room was magnificent, and mosaics that remain are some of the oldest in Israel. West by the wall is **Tanner's Tower**, probably where the Zealots treated their hides, using the basins in the walls to store the necessary liquids. And a little north, the **Western Stairs and Gate**, built by the Byzantines, is where you would enter coming from the Arad road. To the north of this is the **Tower**. Originally made of sandstone, the Byzantine monks built the wall around it.

The **Byzantine Church**, southeast 100 meters from the Tower, was built in the 400s CE and had a hall, three rooms, a tiled roof, glass windows, and a mosaic floor. Northeast of the Church, the **Officers' Family Quarters** is split into nine apartments, each with two small rooms and a large courtyard. From here, you're just south of the Administrative Building and its public toilets and just west of the Snake Path Gate and Cable Car Terminal heading back down the mountain.

NIGHTLIFE & ENTERTAINMENT

Masada does a **sound and light show**, *Tel. 07-995-8144*, Tuesday and Thursday nights at 9pm from April-October. Tickets cost NIS 30 (NIS 25 for children). On the Arad side of the mountain, the 50 minute show is done in Hebrew, but you can rent earphones (NIS 13) with simultaneous translations in English, French, German, Russian, or Spanish.

No public buses go there, so you either drive yourself, or take one of the round-trip deals (make arrangements from Tourist Information or your hotel) from Arad and Dead Sea spots for NIS 35.

THE SOUTHERN BASIN

Ein Bokek is the main site on the southern segment of the Dead Sea. A resort town, Ein Bokek is frequented mostly by those with money and skin conditions, though some do come just for the fun and the holiday. The community is formed almost exclusively by large boxy resort hotels offering recuperative spa services to primarily German tourists.

ORIENTATION

There's the Dead Sea east of the main road, the desert cliffs to the west, and hotels all around in Ein Bokek. Fifteen kilometers south of Masada and three kilometers north of Hammei Zohar, the Ein Bokek Tourist office is in the white mall complex just north of the bus stop and south of Hotel Lot. The other shopping center is west, near the Hod Hotel.

ARRIVALS & DEPARTURES

The 444 goes north to Jerusalem (1.5 hours, NIS 31) and Masada (15 minutes). If you don't plan to overnight here, be aware the last one leaves at 4:30pm. The same 444 also goes south to Eilat.

GETTING AROUND TOWN

Ein Bokek is a pretty compact resort spot, and there's not much that's hard to get to. For destinations farther than a mild stroll, the hotels generally provide shuttles.

WHERE TO STAY

The hotels in Ein Bokek are all medium high to high priced; there are no budget accommodations here. All take credit cards, all provide breakfast, and most cater to clients seeking relief from skin ailments.

LOT HOTEL, *Tel. 07-658-4321, Fax 07-658-4623, charges $130-$180 for singles and $140-$190 for doubles.*

The Lot has 190 rooms, half of which face the sea (the views are stunning) and the rest looking over the Moab mountains. All the rooms have cable TV and phone, and are nice enough though not special. Though all are air-conditioned, the rooms on the Masada side are slightly cooler in summertime.

The hotel has a private beach, and an elevator which leads directly to the sea or the swimming pool. And for a little more sun, there's a solarium on the roof. People come here for weeks of treatment when the clinic is open (March-September).

CARLTON GALEI ZOHAR, *Tel. 07-658-4311, Fax 07-658-4503, charges $118-$152 for a single and $148-$190 a double.*

There are two buildings on the hill; the old one is on the right and the new addition on the left combine to offer 250 rooms overlooking the sea, with cable TV, radio, air conditioning, and direct-dial phone. The new wing rooms are nice and large with fridges, while the older rooms, a little cheaper, are a bit smaller with no fridges. The hotel has a synagogue, as well as swimming pools, children's activities, and evening entertainment. The clientele here are mostly for psoriasis treatment, but there's more of a mix of ages.

PARK INN HOTEL, *Tel. 07-659-1666, Fax 07-658-4162, is up on the hill, charging $98-$120 per single, $122-$166 a double.*

Their 102 rooms are all equipped with cable TV, radio, air conditioning, phone, and 220V current, are attractive, and have small balconies. The hotel has a pool with snack bar, tennis court, handball court, solarium, and game rooms. They have a private beach, with free shuttles between hotel and sulfur springs solarium Sunday-Thursday from 7am-

5:30pm, Friday-Saturday till 3:15pm. The solarium, their beach on the Dead Sea, has nude sun bathing, with separate sections for men and women, and they've an additional solarium on the roof, plus a very lovely garden. They also provide therapeutic skin treatments at their Hammei Zohar Spa.

RADISSON MORIAH GARDENS DEAD SEA HOTEL, *Tel. 07-658-4351, Fax 07-658-4383, also up on the hill, charges $170-$190 for singles, $205-$230 for doubles.*

This hotel features 196 rooms in their modern monstrosity between the sea and the cliffs. All the rooms have air conditioning, cable TV, direct-dial phone, views of either the Sea or the Moab ridges, are large, and nicer than most. The hotel facilities include a pool with snack bar, a beauty-health center, indoor Dead Sea pool, Jacuzzi and sauna. There's a special toddlers' pool, floodlit tennis court, and a rooftop solarium. And at night there's the disco, and the staff is helpful and friendly.

HOD HOTEL, *Tel. 07-658-4644, Fax 07-658-4606, costs $146-$177 a single, $177-$216 for doubles.*

The Hod has 203 air conditioned rooms, all with cable TV, radio, and direct-dial phone. Right on the beach, with ice cream parlor and snack bar, they also have a sun deck swimming pool and kids' pool, indoor Dead Sea pool, health club with work-out equipment, pool table and ping-pong, and the glitzy Minus 400 Disco. They sponsor a range of activities for kids and adults, including folk dancing, fashion shows, lectures on subjects from astrology to health & beauty, and bingo or casino evenings. Next door they have a medical clinic. Seventy percent of their guests come from Germany, and most of them are senior citizens. It's a pleasant place with small but comfortable rooms, but what's outstanding about this hotel is the friendly staff, family atmosphere, and attention to personal detail.

TSELL HARIM BEACH RESORT, *Tel. 07-658-4121, Fax 07-658-4666, charges $85-$143 a single and $105-$165 a double.*

The Tsell Harim has 160 rooms, all air conditioned with cable TV, radio and phone. They are private but not really fancy little bungalows with bedroom, bath, and sitting room, and the suites have sun terraces. The resort has its own private stretch of beach, as well as solarium, outdoor pool, toddlers' pool, tennis court, fitness facilities, and massage, and a disco open till late at night. Eighty percent of their guests come for psoriasis care, and the staff doesn't trip over itself in helpfulness.

NIRVANA HOTEL, *further south, Tel. 07-658-4626, Fax 07-658-4345, more isolated and more expensive, has 200 rooms costing $198-$221 a single and $252-$283 a double.*

The rooms all have air conditioning, phone, cable TV, radio, and mini bar. The hotel has a synagogue, private beach, swimming pool, health club, playground for children, and disco for adults.

MORIAH'S PLAZA DEAD SEA, *three kilometers to the south, Hammei Zohar, Tel. 07-659-1591, Fax 07-658-4238, charges $100-$220 a single and $250-$290 a double.* A separate entity from the Gardens Hotel, there are 220 rooms, all with air conditioning, radio, cable TV, and phone. The hotel has all the amenities: a synagogue, private beach, health club, disco, swimming pool, tennis court, and sports facility.

MOTI, *Tel./Fax 07-652-0143*, rents out rooms, $100 per family per night. You can find him in the Onil Tourist Center, which he also runs.

WHERE TO EAT

The food options in Ein Bokek are all middle to high end, and most are in the rip-off category. If you're here, you are a captive market. Aside from hotel restaurants (and they all have at least one), the cafes are centered in the white complex near the sea between the bus stop and Lot Hotel, or in the Petra Shopping Center near the Hod Hotel, where the prices are a bit lower.

In the mini-mall by the Sea

KAPULSKY CAFE is a self-serve affair, offering pizza for NIS 23, pasta at NIS 29, and desserts from NIS 8-18.

There's a **SELF-HELP CAFETERIA** that's just a rip-off.

The **LOVE & PEACE RESTAURANT** has a pleasant seating area with trellises and paper flowers. There are salads from NIS 22, sandwiches for NIS 18, pastas NIS 20-30, and entrees at NIS 35-65. Given the competition, it's not a bad choice.

In the Petra Shopping Center

There is ice cream at the **FORUM** for NIS 5 a scoop.

BARBIQUE CENTER, *Tel. 07-652-0143*, is open noon-midnight offering Israeli barbecue fare.

Nightlife & Entertainment

The main form of nightlife here the disco. Most of the hotels have them, though the action really depends on the season and the clientele of the moment.

Cleopatra Pub, recently opened, provides the cheapest beer around at NIS 2 a glass, in a Bedouin type atmosphere.

SHOPPING

There's a **minimart kiosk** in the mini-mall open 9am-9pm, but it has pretty slim pickings. They do have yogurt, cheese, pita, canned goods, and chocolate for a fairly miserly picnic.

The Petra Shopping Center (near Hod Hotel) looks a bit like a flying saucer and has shops and some restaurants.

Ahava Health Products are the favored souvenirs from the Dead Sea, starting at $6 for a bag of mud, and going up from there.

SPORTS & RECREATION

Outside the private hotel beaches, there's one free **public beach**. This is the best public beach on the Dead Sea.

Hamme Zohar beaches (one free and one with an entrance fee) are nearby, three kilometers to the south. **Hamme Zohar Thermal Baths** has a private beach and an open-air sulfur pool. Admission is $9. Off the beach, **Kupat Holim Hot Springs** offers more clinical treatments, with a hot pool, sulfur or air bubble bath, and massage from $12.

Motoric Camel, open 7am-7pm, offers tractors to rent. It's $40 for a self-driven two hour trip, driver's license required.

Health Spas

The spas around the Dead Sea focus the curative powers of the minerals and climate on skin diseases such as psoriasis, neurodermitis, and vitiligo; muscle and joint diseases, especially polyarthritis; respiratory diseases such as sinusitis and emphysema; and physical rehabilitation and psychosomatic ailments.

Galei Zohar Spa, *Tel. 07-658-4422, Fax 07-658-4503*, open Saturday-Thursday 8am-6pm, Friday 8am-3pm, offers Universal gym room, heated pool, Jacuzzi, sauna, mud treatments, and massage.

Hamei Zohar Spa, *Tel. 07-658-4161, Fax 07-658-4159*, offers clinic treatment at NIS 25, medical exam at NIS 110, rheumatologist exam at NIS 170, sulfur pool at NIS 37, sulfur bath or sulfur pearl bath at NIS 69, pelodium at NIS 105, mud package at NIS 94, and sulfur jacuzzi at NIS 56.

EXCURSIONS & DAY TRIPS

Newé Zohar lies 1.5 kilometers south of Hammei Zohar on Route 31. A regional center and local residential quarter, Newé Zohar has a hostel, camping, a store and cafeteria, police, a first aid clinic, and a gas station. Also at Newé Zohar is **Bet HaYotzer Museum**, which deals with Dead Sea research and history. To the west of Newé Zohar is **Nahal Zohar** and **Mezad Zohar**, canyons with ruins of ancient Israelite and Roman strongholds. You can drive there, or view them from the Arad road.

Further afield are a number of sites in the **Sodom** (Sedom) region. 12 kilometers south of Newé Zohar and 78 kilometers southeast of Be'er Sheva, this is the Sodom of Biblical renown, infamous for its profligate ways and God's subsequent fire and brimstone wrath. The story goes that

God permitted Lot and his wife to escape before the town and its inhabitants were destroyed, but with the proviso that Lot not look back at his wife. He did look, however, and his wife was turned into a pillar of salt before his eyes. Regardless of how one interprets the tale, this area certainly abounds with salt.

Sodom Mountain, about nine kilometers south of Newé Zohar, is an 11 kilometers mountain range running parallel to the coast, made almost entirely (98%) of salt. The **caves**, formed by water dissolving the salt, are quite beautiful, but the danger of avalanches is very real. East of Mount Sodom is the old camp that used to house employees of the Dead Sea Works, and near the camp is a salt rock formation that has been dubbed **"Lot's Wife."**

A few years ago, some Israeli tourism promoters suggested turning Sodom into a casino/night club/strip joint spot, but the Chief Rabbinate firmly nixed the idea, saying that there was nothing to prevent God from destroying the city a second time.

Further south along the coastal Route 90 at the southern tip of the Dead Sea lies the **Dead Sea Works**, a large industrial complex that takes full advantage of the elements to extract the salt, as well as potash, chlorine, and bromide for profitable export.

Nearby are **Nahal Perazim** and the **Flour Cave**, where water currents have carved weird figures and shapes in the soft limestone canyon. Upstream is the Flour Cave, which got its name due to the powdery fine chalk that lines it.

Kikkar Sodom (*Sodom Plains*) are full of salt marshes and lush vegetation, and the fresh springs are popular watering holes for thirsty

HEALTH TREATMENTS
& SUPPOSED BENEFITS OF THE DEAD SEA

- *Bromine:* relaxes the nervous system
- *Magnesium:* tones and refreshes the skin
- *Oxygen-rich air:* lifts spirits and breathing
- *Low altitude:* filters harmful ultra-violet rays while you tan
- *Balneotherapy:* immersion treatment
- *Thalassotherapy:* sea treatment
- *Pelotherapy:* mud treatment
- *Heliotherapy:* sun treatment
- *Climatotherapy:* sun, mud, and sea treatment

local wildlife. It's around 30 kilometers from Newé Zohar, and it takes most of a day to drive, look around, and go back.

PRACTICAL INFORMATION

• **Onil Tourist Center**, *Tel./Fax 07-652-0143*, in the mall complex on the sea, is now a privately run tourist information center run by Moti, a nice man who's lived in the region for 16 years. He also runs rents out rooms, $100 per family per night.

17. PALESTINIAN AUTHORITY

The tourist situation in most of the **West Bank** has been changing dramatically as Israel and the Palestinians hammer out treaties and agreements. PLO chief Yasser Arafat and Israeli Foreign Minister Shimon Peres negotiated through the summer of 1995, interrupted from time to time by terrorist attacks aimed at derailing the peace process, to iron out the kinks involved in Israel's returning the West Bank land. They hoped to reach a full accord in September 1995, leaving aside unresolved issues such as control over holy sites, water rights and the status of Hebron (where 450 Jewish settlers live among 80,000 Palestinians).

In August 1995, Israel was committed to pulling out of six of the seven main West Bank towns over a few months, giving the **Palestinian Authority** (PA) control over many of the West Bank's one million Palestinian residents. The Palestinians would control only 18 percent of West Bank territory in the first stage. There would then be three more withdrawals (one every six months) starting after Palestinian elections were held. Israel would release Palestinian prisoners in three stages.

In September 1995, Rabin and Arafat signed the 300 page **Interim Agreement** (also known as **Oslo II**) on the West Bank and Gaza Strip, establishing guidelines on everything from Palestinian elections and Israeli redeployment to security, water, and prisoner release. Much of what was agreed upon has taken place: in January 1996, Palestinian Council elections were held and Yasser Arafat was elected *Ra'ees* (head) of the Authority; the IDF (Israeli Defense Force) evacuated most West

The Palestinian Authority includes both the West Bank and the Gaza Strip, but in this book I cover only the West Bank, owing to its proximity to Jerusalem as an excursion.

Bank cities (with Hebron the notable exception); in April 1996, the Palestinian National Charter was amended to remove the articles that called for the destruction of Israel; and in May 1996 Israel and the PA began permanent status negotiations on the touchy subjects of Jerusalem, settlements, and refugees.

Yitzhak Rabin's Death

But between the signing of the Interim Agreement and the implementations, Yitzhak Rabin was killed. On November 4, 1995, 25-year-old Yigal Amir assassinated Israel's Prime Minister Yitzhak Rabin at a peace rally in Tel Aviv. Over one million Israelis (both Arabs and Jews) paid respects to Rabin at his funeral, and nearly 80 world leaders (including representatives from six Arab states and President Clinton) attended the Jerusalem funeral. Right-wing Amir shot Rabin to derail the peace talks, and though the talks haven't entirely disintegrated, it's come pretty close.

Acting Prime Minister Shimon Peres called for early elections, but by the time the elections were held in May 1996, three Hamas bombs caused 57 deaths plus a political backlash; the moderates who'd turned from Likud to Labor after Rabin was murdered renewed their conservative sympathies and peace process distrust. **Benjamin Netanyahu**, the Likud party candidate, defeated Shimon Peres by a razor-thin majority of 50.4%. Netanyahu vowed to continue the peace process, but he's had anything but a light touch. For more details, see Chapter 5, *A Short History*.

Despite the frustration, poverty, and anger, many Palestinians welcome visitors into their homes with traditional hospitality, offering conversation as intense and thick as the coffee that accompanies it. Visitors to the West Bank, however, would do well to dress modestly in deference to the residents' values and norms.

While loads of tourists visit **Bethlehem** and a smaller number go to **Jericho** as well, many of the sites in the West Bank are on the US Embassy's "Stay Away" list, due to their hostility and violence potential. **Hebron** is one of the touchiest spots in Israel. By all means contact the embassy for an update on the situation before venturing far afield, and *carry your passport at all times*.

In the next few years, however if progress continues, it is likely that more hotels and restaurants will be appearing in the Palestinian Authority areas, since the desire to share in the Holy Land tourism windfall is one of the incentives driving the peace process.

ORIENTATION

Most of the Palestinian Authority cities are clustered near Jerusalem. **Bethlehem** is just south of Jerusalem, 10 kilometers along the Bethlehem road, and south of that is **Hebron**, some 35 kilometers from Jerusalem.

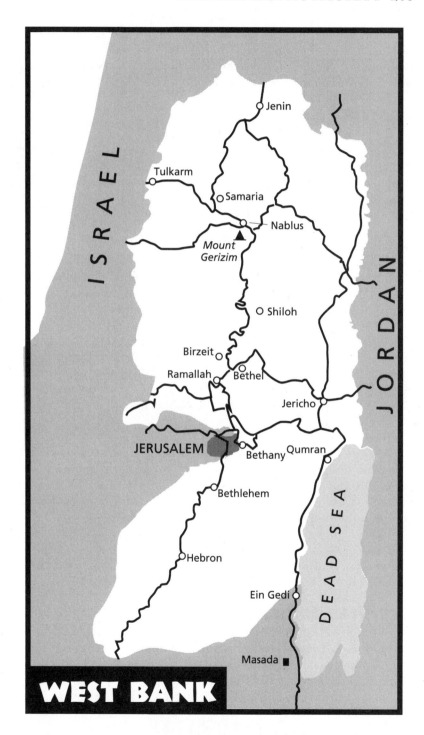

WEST BANK

Ramallah is just a few kilometers to the north, and further north is **Nablus**, a good 48 kilometers from Jerusalem. East of Jerusalem is **Bethany**, and further on is **Jericho**, 39 kilometers east of Jerusalem and near the Allenby Bridge crossing.

ARRIVALS & DEPARTURES

By Car
You can take a rental car into the Palestinian Authority, but Israeli plates will attract some stares and maybe even glares. Renting from an Arab rental agency in East Jerusalem is one way around the problem. For now, all you need is your passport to cross into Palestinian areas, but this may change. Get the most recent embassy update before driving there.

By Bus
When Israel hasn't sealed its borders in reaction to a terrorist event, the Arab buses from the East Jerusalem stations ply the routes to the nearby Palestinian cities. There is one station on **Suleiman** between Damascus and Herod's Gates for southern routes and another on **Nablus** serving northern routes.

When the political situation allows, the 22 goes every 15 minutes or so to **Bethlehem** for NIS 2.5 from the Suleiman Station. The 23 goes to **Hebron** for NIS 7, the 28 goes to **Jericho** for NIS 5, and the 36 goes to **Bethany** for NIS 2. From the Nablus Station, take the 18 to **Ramallah** for NIS 3 and the Tamimi Company 23 to **Nablus** for NIS 6.

By Sherut
Sheruts (share taxis) line up across from the Damascus Gate in Jerusalem, and shout out their destinations to passersby. There are loads to Bethlehem, but you can find sheruts to other places as well. They're a cheap (NIS 2 to Bethlehem, NIS 9 to Nablus), comfortable, and friendly means of transport. And more reliable than the buses.

By Taxi
You can always pay a private cab to take you where you want to go, but don't expect them to be as inexpensive as the sheruts.

GETTING AROUND
A city like Bethlehem is easy to see by foot, but the sights in Jericho are more spread out, so you'll want a taxi (for NIS 60 or so to see the sights, but make the deal before you set out) or rental car to get from place to place, or you can rent a bicycle there (for NIS 2 an hour). The other option is to take an organized tour including Bethlehem and Jericho, and leave the transport to them.

WHERE TO STAY

Bethlehem

Your dollars and shekels will go farthest in Bethlehem, and they want your business.

PARADISE BETHLEHEM, *Manger Square, Tel. 02-674-4542, Fax 02-674-4544, charges $53 a single and $72 a double, breakfast included.*

Is this really paradise? No, but it's not bad–there are 99 rooms, some with bath and some with shower, and all with phone.

THE BETHLEHEM STAR, *Al'Baten, Tel. 02-674-3249, Fax 02-674-1494, costs $35 a single and $55 a double most of the year, breakfast included, but $65 a single and $150 a double during Christmas and Easter.*

The Bethlehem Star has 72 rooms, half with bath and half with shower. The rooms all have heat and phones, with TVs by request.

HANDAL, *Abdul Nasser, Tel./Fax 02-674-4888, charges $25 a single and $40 a double, breakfast included, and the rates go up a few dollars in high season. Name may have changed*

There are 42 rooms here, most with baths, and a few have showers. Rooms also have heat, phones, balconies, and TVs by request.

THE PALACE HOTEL, *Manger Street right by the Church of the Nativity, Tel. 02-674-2798, 02-674-4100, Fax 02-674-1562, has 27 rooms for NIS 80 a single and NIS 100 a double, breakfast included, prices negotiable.*

The Palace has a lovely stone courtyard. The rooms are okay, brown and not exciting; the facade is definitely grander than the interior.

CASA NOVA, *off Manger Square to the left of the Basilica of the Nativity, Tel. 02-674-3981, Fax 02-674-3982, costs $20, breakfast included–with other meal plans are available. Reserve up to a year in advance for Christmas. Telephone number may have changed.*

The Casa Nova has marble and stained glass, but is for pilgrims only.

Jericho

NEW JERICHO PENSION, *Jerusalem Road, Tel. 02-992-2215, is across from the New Jericho mosque. Singles are $13-$15 and doubles are $20.*

Near city center, their rooms feature wooden beds and good mattresses, while the common room has a TV and radio.

HISHAM'S PALACE HOTEL, *Ein as-Sultan Street, Tel. 02-992-2156, charges NIS 40 for singles without bath, and NIS 100 a single with bath, NIS 80 for doubles.*

Hisham's is downtown near city center, and sports a porch. The rooms have balconies and fans, but not the most modern facilities. It's a shabby place.

Ramallah
AL-WIHDEH HOTEL, *26 Main Street, Tel. 995-6452, provides rooms for NIS80-150.*
Near the center of town, all rooms come with private bathroom, TV, and telephone.

Other hotels are now under construction. Check with the **Palestinian Tourist Office** in Bethlehem for the latest scoop and to see if the Jericho YMCA is open. Do the same for Ramallah and Hebron depending on the political climate when you visit.
Beit Sahour, *a village near Jerusalem, Tel. 02-674-3921*, is setting up a B&B program – a call will tell you if it's started yet.

WHERE TO EAT
Bethlehem
Manger Square is chock-a-block with restaurants serving the standard Arabic foods, or head up the winding streets and visit one of the smaller stalls and bakeries.

Jericho
Small restaurants near the center of town serve big plates of falafel, rice, sauce and salad for NIS 10, and good Arabic coffee plus a glass of cold water for NIS 1.5.

SEEING THE SIGHTS
Bethlehem
Its name means House of Bread in Hebrew (*Beit Lehem*) and House of Meat in Arabic (*Beit Lahm*) but it's really a place of churches, though it's inhabited half and half by Muslims and Christians alike. It's easy to visit from Jerusalem on your own if you don't want to do the tour. You get hassled less by souvenir hawkers if you don't pile out of a tour bus, and you get to wander the narrow streets and the market as well.
This is where Rachel died, where shepherd David was found, and, most famous of all, where Jesus was born to Mary in a manger. The *intifada* affected Bethlehem as it did all of the West Bank, but it's come back with a bang; tourism is booming, and Christmas in the square is a thronged event once more.
The main church here is the **Church of the Nativity**, shared by Greek Orthodox, Armenian, and Catholics alike, open daily 6:30am-7pm in summer and 7am-6pm in winter. Sponsored by Constantine in 326 CE at Helena's prompting, restored by Justinian, and spared Persian destruction (thanks perhaps to the mosaic of the Three Kings in Oriental dress),

this is the oldest continuously used church in the world. The entrance is off Manger Square, and there are 12 rules for visitors, including: no headdresses, and no animals. It's a beautiful church, with a faint smell of incense.

The **Grotto of the Nativity** is part of a natural cave, and it's divided among three denominations, with Greek Orthodox dominating. There are Crusader mosaics on the walls, old religious graffiti on the columns, and a star with the Latin inscription *Hic De Virgine Maria Jesus Christus Natus Est* (Here, of the Virgin Mary, Jesus Christ was Born) marking the sacred spot.

Then there's the **Roman Catholic Church of Saint Catherine**, *Tel. 02-674-2425*. It was built in the late 1800's and is nice enough, though it's nowhere near as impressive as the Grotto of the Nativity. The walls have fine wood carvings of the 14 Stations of the Cross, and the first room, the **Chapel of Saint Joseph**, is where Joseph is said to have had his vision prompting them to flee to Egypt in order to escape Herod's violent ways. Below in the **Chapel of the Innocents** is the burial cave of less fortunate children murdered by Herod. The Franciscan Fathers hold a procession daily, and the church is open daily 5:30am-noon and 2-8pm.

Near the Basilica down Milk Grotto Street is **Milk Grotto Church**, *Tel. 02-674-2425*. This cellar is believed to be the cave where Mary, Joseph, and Jesus hid from Herod before taking off to Egypt for a while. The cave rock was once a milky white (hence the name), but it's been darkened by time and smoke. There's another milk connection, however, beyond rock coloring. A few drops of Mary's milk is said to have dropped while she was nursing Jesus, whitewashing the rocks and causing women ever since to come here to pray for fertility. Open daily 8-11am and 2-5pm, you may need to ring the bell for a monk to let you in.

On Star Street about 500 meters north of Manger Square is the **Well of David**, *Tel. 02-674-2477*. Open daily 8am-noon and 2-5pm, the restored cisterns are believed to the very same from which David was offered water while he was fighting the Philistines, whereupon he turned and made an offering to God.

Between Bethlehem and Jerusalem on Nablus Road is **Rachel's Tomb**, *Tel. 02-678-7507*. Open Sunday-Thursday 8am-5pm, Friday 8am-2pm, it's a sacred site for Jews, and synagogues have been built up and torn down here through the ages. Rachel died in Bethlehem giving birth to Benjamin, and despite her sad story the tomb is viewed as the place to come to pray for a child or a healthy pregnancy. It's a 20 minute walk from the Basilica, but the tour buses just pass on by and point at it out the window.

The **market**, *up the hill from Manger Square*, is wonderful and colorful. There are clothes and plastic wash tubs, live chickens and trays of sweets, mounds of fresh produce, stalls of shoes, and another world from Jerusalem.

Bethlehem Museum, *Paul VI, Tel. 02-674-2589,* just a few blocks down from the market has Palestinian crafts and traditional costumes, and is open Monday-Wednesday, Friday, and Saturday 8am-5pm.

Near Bethlehem

Just four kilometers from Jerusalem, **Bethany** is where **Lazarus** (and his sisters Mary and Martha) lived. There's a **Franciscan Church,** *Tel. 02-627-1706,* to mark where Jesus slept, and it has some impressive mosaics depicting the Last Supper and Lazarus rising from the dead. Earlier shrines, one built in the fourth century, have been excavated nearby, and there's part of an abbey built in 1143 by Queen Melisende to the south of the church. It's open 8-11:30am and 2-6pm in summer, 8-11:30am and 2-5pm in winter.

Greek Orthodox Church is built above the **Tomb of Lazarus.** Open daily 8am-7pm, a donation of NIS 2 is expected by the caretakers showing you to the tomb. Farther up the main road is the **Greek Orthodox Convent** with its silver domes, built over the rock Jesus sat on while waiting for Martha from Jericho. To see the rock, ring the bell. Dress modestly.

Shepherd's Field is just past the village of Beit Sahur (see below) to the east of Bethlehem. The **Field of Ruth** is where the biblical Book of Ruth is supposedly set, and Shepherd's Field is where the angel pronounced the birth of Jesus to those out with their flocks (Luke 2:9-11). There's a 6th century **Byzantine basilica,** *Tel. 02-674-3135,* with a **Greek Orthodox monastery,** the **Holy Cave** dating from 350 CE with mosaic crosses in the floor, and a small cave with human bones. Down the road is the **Franciscan Shepherd's Field** with its own monastery from 400 CE and a collection of ancient shepherd cooking pots and coins, open daily 8-11am and 2-5pm.

The ruins of **Herodian** are 10 kilometers southeast of Bethlehem, up in the Judean Hills on a pointy peak. Back when King Herod was waxing fearful about assassination, he had this hideout constructed with watch towers (four) and huge double walls. Within was a sumptuous palace with baths and gardens. Rebels from the Jewish revolts took advantage of Herod's solid construction, and holed up there for a while. Open daily 8am-5pm and costing NIS 12 (NIS 6 for students), you can get there from Bethlehem by taxi (about NIS 30-40 round trip).

Less accessible but more remarkable than Herodian is **Mar Saba Monastery,** carved into a canyon above the Kidron River. This is where Saint Saba took to asceticism in 478 CE, and his spirit lives in the tourism restrictions. Women are forbidden to enter and must make do with an outside view, while men must wear pants and long-sleeved shirts to go inside. Open daily 7-11am and 1:30-5pm, you'll need a private taxi from Bethlehem to get here.

Jericho

The Palestinian Tourism literature says "Since the dawn of history, Jericho has been the bride of the Jordan Valley whose wedding is still going on." Whatever, precisely, this means, it's a beautiful oasis town with lots of green. There are orchards and oranges, graceful palms and Arabs in headdress herding goats.

Tel Jericho (also known as **Tel as-Sultan**) has a piece of the old **city wall** (the one that came tumbling down) dating back to 2,600 BCE. You can see it from the main road, where people stop to snap pictures of it, or trek closer to see the excavated remains of 23 cities built one on top of another. There's also a seven meter **Neolithic tower** going back to 7,000 BCE.

Ein as-Sultan, the spring of Elisha, is Jericho's water source just across from the Tel. Water gushes at 1,000 gallons a minute and irrigates the wadi.

Mount of Temptation, *three kilometers northwest of town*, is where Jesus is said to have fasted for 40 days and nights. There's a Greek Orthodox monastery 350 meters up in the cliff, lots of caves, and the climb takes about half an hour.

Hisham's Palace at Khirbet al-Mafjar is one of few well-preserved examples of eighth century Islamic architecture (some of the finer finds are on display at the Rockefeller Museum in Jerusalem). There's also a small pottery museum on the site. The best find, still on location, is the beautiful and undamaged mosaic.

Saint John's Monastery, four kilometers east of Jericho and nearing the Allenby Bridge, is where Jesus was baptized. One of the most beautiful monasteries, however, is the Greek Orthodox **Monastery of Saint George of Koziba**. It's set in the truly stunning Wadi Kelt, one of the most popular hiking destinations when local tension was less evident. It's a four hour path through Wadi Kelt to Saint George Monastery, the caves below look beautiful, and the view of Saint George Monastery, carved out of canyon rock, is magnificent.

The sheer rock walls of the wadi stretch 35 kilometers between Jericho and Jerusalem, and three springs feed the oasis. It's worth taking a look from the road even if the hike isn't possible (check with the embassy for an assessment of the situation).

Ramallah

Up in the hills, some 900 meters above sea level, **Ramallah** is just 16 kilometers north of Jerusalem. Before 1967 this was a prosperous town, a cool summer holiday spot for wealthy Arabs. Relatively liberal, the people are friendly and construction is booming.

The **market** by the bus station is open Saturday-Thursday till 3pm and Friday till noon. There's also the **Silvana Chocolate Company**, *Tel. 02-995-2467*, just 1.5 kilometers down from Manara Square on Jaffa Street, open for tours and tastes Monday-Saturday 7:30am-4pm.

Beitin (also known as **Bethel**) is five kilometers northeast on the road to Nablus. It's supposed to be where Jacob slept and dreamt of a ladder going up to heaven. Jacob woke up, built an altar, and named the place Beit El (House of God) according to Genesis 28:12-19. There's a Jewish settlement nearby named Beit El, with a *tefillin* factory. This was the site of more settler unrest (a Palestinian was killed) in August '95 in protest against the Palestinian-Israeli accords, and it's not recommended as a safe destination.

Birzeit is the home of **Birzeit University**, the West Bank's largest (with around 2,500 students). Twelve kilometers northwest of Ramallah, the university has been a center of young and vocal protest to Israeli occupation, and was shut down from '88-'92. The old campus is next to the last bus stop, while the new campus is two kilometers out of town.

Nablus

Not counting East Jerusalem, **Nablus** is the largest city in the West Bank, home to a large Muslim community and a small Samaritan community of around 500–two thirds of the world's total Samaritan population. Founded by Titus in 72 CE as Flavia Neapolis, it was built near the old city of Shekhem. After Solomon died in 922, Jeroboam (who had earlier rebelled unsuccessfully against Solomon and fled to Egypt to escape punishment) returned to rule the ten northern tribes in the Kingdom of Israel from the new northern capital of Shekhem from 922-901 BCE.

Shekhem was built up to rival Jerusalem, and while it never quite managed the feat, it housed many kings and was a religious center till the Babylonians swept in around 587 BCE. Since then Crusaders, earthquakes (there was a nasty one in 1927), the British Mandate, the Israeli occupation, and the intifada have consumed Nablus, and it's now trying to get on its feet again.

Nablus has a busy **market**, full of fresh fruit and big pans of sweets.

Jacob's Well, *three kilometers to the east, Tel. 09-837-5123*, is a famous pilgrim site, but there's not much there now. It's supposed to be where Jacob pitched his tents, is now enclosed in a subterranean Greek Orthodox shrine, *and is open daily 8am-noon and 2-5pm.* Nearby is the **Tomb of Joseph** where it is believed Joseph's bones (which had been carried out of Egypt) were buried as per Joshua 24:32. It was a Muslim shrine and now it's a Jewish shrine, but it's still just a tomb, *open daily 6am-10pm and modest dress required.*

Mount Gerizim, *to the southeast,* has some swell views of Shomron Valley. The Samaritans believe it's the place where Abraham bound Isaac in sacrificial preparations and also where the original 10 Commandment tablets are buried. This is where the Samaritans perform their bloody paschal lamb sacrifice before audiences of Jerusalem and Tel Aviv gawkers. It's a hefty hike up the mountain, but taxis can be hired for around NIS 15.

Sabastiya, *11 kilometers northwest,* is the site of the Israelite, Hellenistic, and Roman ruins of **Shomron** (Samaria). Despite all the history that took place here there's not that much to see. There's a Roman theater ruin and the Israelite and Hellenistic acropolis walls, and column bases of the Temple of Augustus. Untended and free (for now), there are service taxis from Nablus to the base of the hill for around NIS 3.

Hebron

In Hebrew, *Hevron* means friend, and the Arabic name for the city (*Al khalil ar-Rahman*) means compassionate friend, all a bit ironic given the thick veil of hostility that shrouds the place. It's been important in Jewish lore ever since Abraham chose Hebron for his family cemetery. All the matriarchs and patriarchs of Judaism (except Rachel, whose tomb is near Bethlehem) are said to be buried here in the **Cave of Makhpela**, a very holy and revered site for Jews and Muslims alike.

It's also claimed that Adam and Eve were buried there, and that was why Abraham chose it. And the biblical references continue with Moses who sent scouts to Canaan, only to have them come back telling tales of the giants of Hebron. Herod built a synagogue to worship there, transformed by the Byzantines into a church, made over by the Muslims into a mosque, and back to a church again by a new wave of Crusaders. The Mamluks added some minarets as they changed it back to a mosque, and the Israelis, who were only allowed to stand outside and pray in 1929, have reinstituted a synagogue. This prayer house battle is indicative of the Hebron temperament, and while Muslims and Jews both pray in the same structure over the same holy cave, the hostilities are such that it's unlikely you'll be getting to see it.

The history of settlements and stubbornness, killings and massacres are as endemic to the place as the worship wars. In 1925 a Russian yeshiva was set up. Angry Arabs responded violently in the 1929 riots. Israel captured it in 1967, and a number of settlements were begun. In February

1994, an American Jew named **Baruch Goldstein** massacred a number of Palestinians as they prayed in the mosque, and it's not gotten much friendlier since then. The embassy security officer said Hebron was still tense and certain strike dates and anniversaries were observed, such as the 23rd, anniversary of the Baruch Goldstein massacre, as well as the 9th and 17th. There's still a lot of bitterness over Baruch Goldstein, and attempts to glorify him and turn him into a martyr have intensified things.

Add to the stew the fact that Israel is turning the West Bank over to the Palestinians, and that the settlers now in Hebron refuse to leave, and you get a sense why they can't all just get along over there. While the governments try to work out a deal, the individuals clash and spar with predictable frequency and intensity. Check with the consulate before attempting a visit here.

SHOPPING

Shops on the way to **Bethlehem** contain ridiculously priced religious shlock, with a little Bethlehem bubbled snow shaker going for $7! In Bethlehem there are tourist souvenirs on the square, with astonishingly garish, bloodied crucifixes of olive wood and mother of pearl for $150.

Tamimi Ceramics, *Tel. 02-992-0358, Fax 02-992-9253*, sells hand-crafted ceramics in Hebron.

SPORTS & RECREATION

SPNI, *13 Helene Ha'Malka, Jerusalem, Tel. 02-624-4605*, offers a popular Wadi Kelt hike.

Bicycles, *in Jericho*, can be rented from a shop just off the central square and east of the municipal buildings for NIS 2 an hour.

EXCURSIONS & DAY TRIPS

The Alternative Tourism Program in **Beit Sahour**, *Tel. 02-674-3921*, is setting up a program to offer a Palestinian experience in lieu of (or along side) the normal sight-seeing trip. Beit Sahour, a small Palestinian village just outside of Jerusalem, would organize things so you could visit and see the town, meet the people, and even volunteer in the community.

They have lectures on topics such as Christian-Islamic Coexistence, Liberation Theology, and the ever popular Taxation. For more info, call Dr. Majed Nassar at the Medical Clinic or Mr. Ghassan Andoni at the Palestinian Center for Rapprochement at the numbers above.

Deir Hanna, up north in the Bet Netofa Valley in Central Galilee and 20 kilometers northwest of the Golani junction, is a small Palestinian village with archaeological remains of its Crusader and Turkish past. In the 17th century, Said al-Omar (Daher al-Omar's brother) used this place as his military base against the Turks, and there are Citadel ruins from this time.

PRACTICAL INFORMATION

- **B'Tselem**, *43 Emek Rafaim, West Jerusalem, Tel. 02-561-7271*, is the Israeli Information Center for Human Rights in the Occupied Territories.
- **Currency**: The **New Israeli Shekel** (NIS) is the most common currency, but US dollars and Jordanian dinars are also generally accepted. There are plenty of money changers around, and there are the banks, as well.
- **Gaza Center for Rights and Law**, *Imam building on Omar al-Mukhtar, Gaza, Tel. 07-686-6287*.
- **Jerusalem Media and Communication Center**, *18 Nashashibi, Sheikh Jarrah, East Jerusalem, Tel. 02-581-9776*.
- **Medical Services**: see Jerusalem.
- **Newspaper**: *The Jerusalem Times*, the independent Palestinian English weekly, is available in the shuk inside the Damascus Gate, and in hotels in East Jerusalem.
- **Palestinian Authority Tourism Office**, *Manger Square, Bethlehem, Tel. 02-674-1581, Fax 02-674-3753*. They're open Monday-Saturday 8am-4pm and provide maps of Bethlehem as well as updated information on the rest of the West Bank.
- **Palestine Human Rights Information Center**, *12 Masa'udi, East Jerusalem, Tel. 02-628-7076*.
- **Police** in **Bethlehem**: *Manger Square, Tel. 02-674-8222;* in **Jericho**, *Tel. 02-992-2521*.
- **Post office** in **Bethlehem**: *next to the tourist office, Tel. 02-674-2668*. It's open Monday-Wednesday, Friday and Saturday 8am-2:30pm, and Thursday 8am-12:30pm, and they have a poste restante section.

18. PRACTICAL INFORMATION

- **AACI—Association of Americans and Canadians**, *6 Mane, Tel. 02-561-7151*, is opposite 13 Disraeli. They are a good English-speaking resource covering a wide range of possibilites. If you want to move (or retire) to Israel, meet the American/Candian community, get a job or attend lectures, concerts, or mixers, AACI has the information (see Rehavia section of *Sights* for more).
- **American Consulate General**, *27 Nablus Road, East Jerusalem, Tel. 02-625-3288*, bus 23 or 27, is open Monday-Friday 8am-4pm. The Executive, Commerical, and Administrative Sections, however, are located at *18 Agron Road*. They don't accept phone inquiries during the hours they are open; call about visas, and routine passport and citizenship questions from 2-4pm. American citizens with emergencies can call *Tel. 02-625-3201*.
- **American Express**, *40 Jaffa*, is open Sunday-Thursday 9am-5pm and Friday 9am-1pm. They charge no comission to change travelers checks, and you can get US cash for a 3% fee.
- **British Consulate**, *19 Nashashibi, near Sheikh Jarrah, East Jerusalem, Tel. 02-582-8281*, is open Monday-Friday 8am-12:30pm.
- **Buses, Arab** have one station on *Suleiman between Damascus and Herod's Gates* for southern routes and another on *Nablus Road* serving northern routes.
- **Bus Station, Egged Central**, *Jaffa Road, Tel. 02-530-4704*, way west of downtown, has intercity buses, intracity buses, and a baggage check at NIS 4 per item per day.
- **Car Rental: Avis**, *22 King George, Tel. 02-624-9001*; **Budget**, *8 King David, Tel. 02-624-8991*; **Hertz**, *18 King David, the Hyatt, Tel. 02-623-1351*; **Thrifty**, *18 King David, Tel. 02-625-0833*.
- **Christian Information Center**, *the square just inside Jaffa Gate, Tel. 02-627-2695, Fax 02-628-6417*, is open Monday-Friday 8:30am-1pm.

They have information on churches, services, and special events like Christmas.

• **Currency Exchange** is possible at hotels and a variety of banks (**Leumi**, *21 Jaffa*, **HaPoalim**, *1 Zion Square and 16 King George*, and **First International**, *10 Hillel*, to name at few) but the best exchange rates without commission is available at American Express (see above).

• **Disabled Services: Yad Sarah Organization**, *43 HaNevi'im, Tel. 02-644-4444*, loans medical equipment for one month (extendable to three months) for free (full deposit required). They're open Sunday-Thursday 9am-7pm, Friday 9am-noon, and are available for emergencies.

• **English Books: The Book Mavin**, *21 Agrippas Tel. Tel. 02-624-5902*, is open Sunday-Thursday 8am-8pm and Friday 8am-2pm. They've a fair selection of used books, buy used books for credit, and offer two for one type specials. **Muffet Books**, off Agrippas just before the Mahane Yehuda Market, Tel. 02-625-9872, sells new and used. They say their address is *2 Kiach*, but the street sign says *Alliance Israe'lite*. **Sefer Ve Sefel**, *2 Yavetz, Tel. 02-624-8237*, in a small walkway off 47 Jaffa, is a pleasant book store whose name means "mug and book". Open Sunday-Thursday 8am-8pm, Friday 8am-2:30pm, there are lots of books (including a large travel section), used and new. **Steimatzky**, *7 Ben Yehuda on the midrahov, Tel. 02-625-5487*, has other branches as well. Open 8:30am-10pm, Friday 8:30am-2:30pm, Saturday 8:30-11pm, they sell new books. **Tmol Shilshom Bookstore Cafe**, *5 Yoel Salomon Street, Tel. 02-623-2758*, has live jazz every Saturday night, a happy hour, milk shakes and cheese shnitzel, and lots of books.

• **Film Developing: Kodak Express**, *25 King George, Tel. 02-625-6557*, does 36 prints for NIS 38. **Photo Ha-Bira**, *91 Jaffa, Tel. 02-623-1915*, at sells rolls for NIS 8, develops at NIS .55 per print and is open Sunday-Thursday 8am-1pm and 4-7pm, Friday 8am-2pm. **Photo Yehezkel**, *47 Jaffa, Tel. 02-625-5590*, sells at NIS 8.9 per roll, develops at NIS .33 per print, and is open Sunday-Thursday 9am-7pm, Friday 9am-2pm.

• **First Aid for Tourists**, *Bikur Holim Hospital, 74 HaNevi'im, Tel. 02-670-1111*, is on the corner of Strauss, which is the east extension of King George, and is available 24 hours a day.

• **Franciscan Pilgrims Office**, *same building as the Christian Information Center, inside Jaffa Gate, Tel. 02-627-2697*, is open Monday-Friday 9am-noon and 3:30-5:30pm, Saturday 9am-noon. They handle reservations for Franciscan sanctuary Masses and sell pilgrimage certificates.

• **Help Lines: Alchoholics Anonymous**, *Tel. 02-563-0524*; **Gay and Lesbian Support Line**, *Tel. 02-624-2853*, is also called **Ozen Kashevet**; **Mental Health Hotline**, *Tel. 02-1201*, is also called **Eran** and is open 8am-11pm but gives an alternate number (in Hebrew) when closed;

Rape Crisis Center, *Tel. 02-625-5558*, is open 24 hours and will help you to police and through procedures.

• **Jewish Student Information Center**, *5 Beit El, Jewish Quarter, Tel. 02-628-2634, Fax 02-02-628-8338*, across from the Hurva Arch is open Sunday-Thursday 9am-7pm, Friday 9am-sundown.

• **Jewish National Fund**, *1 Keren Kayemet, Tel. 02-563-9650, or the Tannenbaum Center, Hadassah Ein Kerem hospital*, is open Sunday-Thursday 8:30am-3pm, Friday 8:30am-noon. You can plant a tree with them for $10.

• **Laundry: Ha-Merkaz Laundry**, *11 Kakal off Usushkin, Tel. 02-566-4246*, is open Sunday-Thursday 8am-1pm and 3-7pm, Friday 8am-1pm, and do 5kg wash and dry for NIS 25; **Michali Laundry**, *36 Azza Street, Rehavia* and **Suzana Laundry**, *46 Emek Refa'im Street, German Colony*, are open Sunday-Thursday 7:30am-11:30pm, Friday 7:30am-3pm, and Saturday 6pm-11:30pm and charge NIS 16 to wash and dry; **Superclean Laundromat**, *16 Palmah, Tel. 02-566-0367*, is open Sunday-Thursday 7am-7pm, Friday 7am-2pm, and does 6kg wash/dry/fold for NIS 30 and 10kg for NIS 40; **Tzipor Ha-Nefesh**, *10 Rivlin Street, Tel. 02-624-9890*, has wash and dry facilities (NIS 15 for 5kg), plus a cafe and email center; **Washmatic**, *35 Emek Refa'im, Tel. 02-563-1878*, is open Sunday-Thursday 8am-7pm, Friday 8am-2pm and has small load wash/dry/fold for NIS 45 and large load for NIS 61.

• **Libraries: American Cultural Center Library**, *19 Keren Hayesod, Tel. 02-625-2376, Fax 02-624-2560*, is open Sunday-Thursday 10am-4pm, Friday 9am-noon, answer phone questions from 8am, and are closed all Israeli and American holidays. The library carries American magazines and newspapers (such as five-day-old Herald Tribunes and two-week-old NY Times), as well as books and videotapes on American themes. **Abramov Library**, *Hebrew Union College, 13 King David, Tel. 02-620-3270*, is a quiet, pleasant, cool library with Newsweek and the Jerusalem Post as well as books and journals on Judaica and archaeology. They're open Sunday-Thursday 8am-4:45pm and have a copy machine, 30 agorot a page.

• **Medical Emergencies**, *Tel. 101*, are handled at the sign of the **Magen David Adom** (Israel's Red Cross) *next to the central bus station or inside Dung gate*. **Blue Cross-Blue Shield**, *Hadassah Ein Kerem and Mount Scopus hospitals, Tel. 02-677-6040*, covers members for pre-paid hospitalization.

• **Pharmacies: Iba Pharmacy**, *7 Ben Yehuda, Tel. 02-625-7785*, is open Sunday-Thursday 8am-7pm, Friday 8am-2pm; **Super-Pharm branches**, *4 HaHistadrut off King George, Tel. 02-624-6244*, and *5 Burla, near Hebrew University, Giv'at Ram, Tel. 02-563-9321*, are open Sunday-

Thursday 9am-9pm and Saturday from sundown-9pm. There are also pharmacies on Jaffa and around the city.

• **Police**, *Russian Compound off Jaffa, Tel. 100* for emergencies. **Tourist Police**, *30 Jaffa Street, Tel. 02-539-1254.*

• **Post Office**, *23 Jaffa, Tel. 02-629-0647*, is the main branch and is open Sunday-Thursday 7am-7pm, Friday 7am-noon, with poste restante, telegram, and fax services.

• **Supermarkets: Coop Supermarket**, *King George at Ben Yehuda*, is open Sunday-Tuesday 7am-8pm, Wednesday-Thursday 7am-10pm, Friday 7am-2pm. **Supermarket**, *7 Mordechai Ben Hillel off 9 King George*, is open Sunday-Thursday 7:30am-7pm, Friday 7:30am-3pm. **Supermarket**, *Agron near King George*, is open Sunday-Tuesday 7am-midnight, Wednesday 7am-1am, Thursday 24 hours, Friday 7am-Shabbat, and Saturday after Shabbat-midnight.

• **Telephone** service from **Bezek**, *1 Koresh, Tel. 02-624-6196*, is behind the post office. They have booths to facilitate international calls; open Sunday-Thursday 8am-10pm, Friday 8am-2pm. **SolanTelecommunications**, *2 Luntz, Tel. 02-625-8908*, off Ben Yehuda and near Cafe Rimon, does the same for less money and they're open 24 hours a day, seven days a week. After midnight their discount rate is even cheaper.

• **Ticket Agencies: Ben Naim**, *Tel. 02-625-4008*; **Bimot**, *8 Shammai, Tel. 02-623-4061*; **Kla'im**, *Tel. 02-625-6869.*

• **Tourist Information**, *17 Jaffa, Tel. 02-628-0382*, is open Sunday-Thursday 8:30am-4:30pm, Friday 8:30am-12:30pm. It's not manned by the warmest of beings, but he'll answer your questions if he can, and there are plenty of brochures and maps. **Computerized information**, *26 King George, corner of Schatz*, is available 24 hours a day. The **Ministry of Tourism**, *26 King George, Tel. 02-675-4910*, are the offices of the bureaucracy, not the place that handles garden variety tourist questions and concerns. For other **tourist questions**, call *Tel. 02-675-4811.*

INDEX

THINGS CHANGE!

Phone numbers, prices, addresses, quality of food, etc, all change. If you come across any new information, we'd appreciate hearing from you. No item is too small! Drop us an e-mail note at Jopenroad@aol.com, or write us at:

Jerusalem Guide
*Open Road Publishing, P.O. Box 284
Cold Spring Harbor, NY 11724*

OPEN ROAD PUBLISHING

U.S.A.

Colorado Guide, $16.95
Hawaii Guide, $17.95
Arizona Guide, $16.95
Texas Guide, $16.95
New Mexico Guide, $14.95
Disneyworld & Orlando Theme Parks, $13.95
Boston Guide, $13.95
Las Vegas Guide, $13.95
San Francisco Guide, $14.95
California Wine Country Guide, $12.95
America's Cheap Sleeps, $16.95
America's Grand Hotels, $14.95
America's Most Charming Towns &
    Villages, $16.95
Florida Golf Guide, $16.95
Golf Courses of the Southwest, $14.95
Washington DC Ethnic Restaurant
    Guide, $9.95

MIDDLE EAST/AFRICA

Israel Guide, $17.95
Jerusalem Guide, $13.95
Egypt Guide, $17.95
Kenya Guide, $18.95

UNIQUE TRAVEL

New Year's Eve 1999!, $16.95
The World's Most Intimate Cruises, $16.95
Celebrity Weddings & Honeymoon
    Getaways, $16.95
CDC's Complete Guide to Healthy
    Travel, $14.95

SMART HANDBOOKS

The Smart Runner's Handbook, $9.95
The Smart Home Buyer's
    Handbook, $16.95

CENTRAL AMERICA & CARIBBEAN

Caribbean Guide, $19.95
Caribbean With Kids, $14.95
Central America Guide, $17.95
Costa Rica Guide, $17.95
Belize Guide, $16.95
Honduras & Bay Islands Guide, $15.95
Guatemala Guide, $17.95
Southern Mexico & Yucatan Guide, $14.95
Bermuda Guide, $14.95
Bahamas Guide, $13.95

EUROPE

London Guide, $14.95
Rome & Southern Italy Guide, $13.95
Paris Guide, $13.95
Moscow Guide, $15.95
Prague Guide, $14.95
France Guide, $16.95
Portugal Guide, $16.95
Ireland Guide, $16.95
Spain Guide, $17.95
Italy Guide, $19.95
Holland Guide, $15.95
Austria Guide, $15.95
Czech & Slovak Republics Guide, $16.95
Greek Islands Guide, $16.95
Turkey Guide, $17.95

ASIA

Japan Guide, $19.95
Tokyo Guide, $13.95
Tahiti & French Polynesia Guide, $17.95
China Guide, $18.95
Hong Kong & Macau Guide, $13.95
Vietnam Guide, $14.95
Thailand Guide, $17.95
Philippines Guide, $16.95